MEMORIES OF MUHAMMAD

MEMORIES *of*
MUHAMMAD

WHY THE PROPHET MATTERS

OMID SAFI

HarperOne
An Imprint of HarperCollins*Publishers*

HarperOne

HarperCollins books may be purchased for educational, business, or sales promotional use. For information please write: Special Markets Department, HarperCollins Publishers, 10 East 53rd Street, New York, NY 10022.

HarperCollins Web site: http://www.harpercollins.com
HarperCollins®, 📖 ®, and HarperOne™ are trademarks of HarperCollins Publishers

FIRST EDITION

Library of Congress Cataloging-in-Publication Data

Safi, Omid
  Memories of Muhammad : why the Prophet matters / by Omid Safi.
  —1st ed.
    p. cm.
  ISBN 978–0–06–123134–6
  1. Muhammad, Prophet, d. 632—Biography. I. Title.
    BP75.S25   2009
    297.6'3—dc22
                          2009030503

09 10 11 12 13   RRD (H)   10 9 8 7 6 5 4 3 2 1

CONTENTS

The "Muhammad Problem"

A LOT OF PEOPLE ARE having a "Muhammad problem" these days.

It's nothing new. People have been attacking Muhammad for 1,300 years, some because of their religious beliefs and others because of their political convictions. He was attacked by his own family during his lifetime for his progressive views, in medieval times he was attacked by authors like Dante and Martin Luther, and more recently we have all read the headlines about the infamous Danish cartoon controversies in which a Danish newspaper, in response to terrorist acts done in the name of Islam, published editorial cartoons depicting the Islamic Prophet in ways considered by many blasphemous and Islamophobic. Before we can deal with how Muslims themselves have come to remember, revere, and contest the memory of Muhammad, we must deal with these many outside attacks, which are important not only for what they reveal about non-Muslims' ability to understand the significance of one of the leading figures in human history, but also because Muslims today are exceedingly concerned, even defensive, about what others say regarding their Prophet. In short, what is said about Muhammad affects all of us, regardless of our faith.

It has become commonplace to acknowledge that we live in an interconnected world. Yet it is not just goods (the clothes on our backs, oil, cars) and people (immigrants, refugees) and ideas (human rights, democracy) that now flow freely across the world; it is also the religious insights, sensitivities, and prejudices of our fellow human beings that we increasingly come face-to-face with. This is particularly relevant to the case of Muhammad, probably the least known and most misunderstood of all the founders of the major world religions. The geopolitical reality of our world means that many Muslim-majority countries (Iraq, Afghanistan, Iran, Saudi Arabia, and Pakistan, as well as Palestine/Israel because of the ongoing trauma there) dominate international news, and this has resulted in a hitherto unseen interest in Islam among many people. The interest is also more personal for many: in the United States alone, some six million Americans have adopted the Islamic faith, about the same number as there are American Jews or American Orthodox Christians. Perhaps a similar number of Americans now have Muslims as members of their families. One particularly poignant reminder was the 2009 speech of President Barack Obama in Turkey, in which he stated: "The United States has been enriched by Muslim Americans. Many other Americans have Muslims in their family, or have lived in a Muslim-majority country—I know, because I am one of them."[1] President Obama's personal narrative, received with thunderous applause by Muslims, is a powerful demonstration of the ways in which the American story and Muslim narratives are irrevocably intertwined now.

In the full human community worldwide, there are some 1.3 billion Muslims. Whether some of us think of ourselves as Americans first or citizens of one shared planet first, it is simply part of being an educated citizen to have accurate knowledge about the faith of Islam. Muhammad stands at the center of this faith, and there is no way of being familiar with Islam without taking a long, hard, and close look at this figure who is so beloved by Muslims and yet often vilified by certain non-Muslims.

Today many of the atrociously offensive and polemical statements against the Prophet Muhammad come from some Christian leaders who seem persuaded that in tearing down the faith of other human beings they are building up the faith of their own flock. The former president of the Southern Baptist Convention, Jerry Vines, who is from Jacksonville, Florida (my own birthplace), described the Prophet Muhammad as a "demon-possessed pedophile." Another Christian critic of the Prophet Muhammad is Franklin Graham, who is the son of the famed revivalist Billy Graham and who was handpicked by President George W. Bush to preside over his January 2001 inauguration. The younger Graham has described Islam as a "very evil and wicked religion."[2] The 2008 Republican nominee for the presidency, John McCain, sought the endorsement of two evangelical Christian leaders, John Hagee and Rod Parsley, and referred to the latter as his "spiritual guide."[3] Hagee, a noted Christian Zionist, has stated that he believes that the threat of Islam surpasses that of Hitler and that Muslims have a Qur'anic mandate to kill Jews and Christians. Parsley has been even more specific, stating that "Islam is an anti-Christ religion" and that "Muhammad received revelations from demon spirits, not from the living God."[4]

These have not been isolated episodes—they have been repeated in the most public of settings. Another prominent Christian leader, Pat Robertson, appeared on *Fox News* on September 18, 2002, to declare that the Prophet Muhammad "was an absolute wild-eyed fanatic. He was a robber and a brigand. . . . I mean, this man [Muhammad] was a killer." Robertson went on to call Islam "a monumental scam," "evil," and "demonic."[5] Another Christian leader, Jerry Falwell, even used the ultimate post-9/11 code word for the embodiment of all evil in reference to the Prophet Muhammad during a *60 Minutes* interview, calling the Prophet a "terrorist."[6] One could go on and on here, but these examples probably suffice to make the point. These Christian leaders are not marginal figures. They utter such statements in the most public and high-profile media outlets. If we were dealing with Muslim figures making similarly offensive comments against Christ or labeling all Jews as evil, there would be an international outrage followed by calls for the immediate removal of these figures. Likewise, one could predict the swift outcry if Falwell or Robertson had labeled Judaism as demonic or satanic. Yet when statements about

Islam or Muhammad are made, the treatment is different. At best, when these Christian leaders call Muhammad a terrorist or the Antichrist, they are seen as exercising their "free speech" rights rather than as being purveyors of hate speech. At worst, there is perhaps a nagging suspicion among some listeners that these statements contain a kernel of truth. In the beginning decade of the twenty-first century, it seems undeniable that at least some Christians (and some champions of Western hegemony) have a Muhammad problem—and thus an Islam problem.

The reason for this problem is not hard to fathom. With the exception of the most bigoted, most Christians today, including the Catholic and Protestant authorities, have rightly come to see that Muslims, Jews, and Christians all worship the same One God and that all believe in the ideas of revelation, redemption, righteous ethics, and accountability. For some Christians, however, the idea of God having reached out to humanity after Christ remains an enigma. Muhammad remains for these Christians—though not all of them—a theological challenge. In lashing out against Muhammad, they seek to affirm the special relationship they believe God has established with humanity through Christ. Yet this vehemence has prevented them from being able to see Muhammad in the light of history and faith and thus understand Islam on its own merits.

WE KEEP TALKING PAST one another when it comes to Muhammad, and this seems to have resulted in a cognitive dissonance. Try this out the next time you are in your local bookstore: walk over to the Islam shelf and have a look at all the volumes about the Prophet Muhammad. Even a cursory look indicates that our public discourse about the Prophet Muhammad seems to suffer from a split personality: on the one hand, we see books by pious Muslims (and sympathetic non-Muslims) proclaiming Muhammad as one of the great teachers of humanity and one of the great divinely sent prophets.[7] On the other hand, we see other titles that promise to provide the reader with "the truth about Muhammad" but in fact are marred by a host of inaccuracies, prejudices, and flat-out lies. These titles present Islam either as a demonic heresy designed to mock Christianity or as an aggressive ideology intent on world domination or destruction. Many of these books are composed by writers who have no expertise in Islam, no familiarity with Islamic history, and no command of the languages necessary to acquire such understanding, such as Arabic and Persian. For that matter, many of them also seem woefully unaware of the problematic aspects of the history of Judaism and Christianity, not to speak of the racism and other ills of Western societies. Yet their lack of qualifications has not prevented these authors from engaging in a great deal of Muhammad-bashing and Islam-bashing.

In a sad display, we are even witnessing the recycling of many hackneyed clichés and insults that a century or two ago were directed against Jews now being directed against Muslims. In particular, in some of the same ways in which Jews were questioned regarding their "loyalties" to Europe as well as to Judaism, many now view Muslims with great suspicion and question their loyalties as citizens. Muslims have become the target of a new version of anti-Semitism. One of the most bitter and ironic aspects of this new anti-Semitism is that at least some of these attacks are being led by largely secular Jews whose ultimate concern is the preservation of the current status of the state of Israel, with all its profoundly problematic policies toward the native Palestinian population there.[8] One small though influential example would be that of the largely discredited neoconservative movement, which provided the ideological support for much of the foreign policy of the George W. Bush regime. Much of the neoconservative ideology involved the simultaneous advocacy of a muscular defense of Israel and the demonization of Islam. It boggles the mind that many of the children and grandchildren of Jews who themselves were the targets of anti-Semitism could now be directly engaged in spreading a variation of the same poison of anti-Semitism against other members of the human family, especially other children of Abraham. One of the conclusions that one can reach is that often the prejudice against Islam is not the actual disease. It is the symptom of a deeper malaise— prejudice and racism.

Yet Muhammad-bashing is not a new phenomenon. The last decades of the twentieth century and the beginning of the twenty-first have seen both the continuation of old polemics against Muhammad and the deployment of new ones. One thousand years ago, the polemics were about violence, sex, and heresy. Today the polemics are still primarily about violence, sex, and heresy. One cannot help but wonder at how unoriginal these polemics have been over the course of the last thousand years. If the subject matter was not so offensive, perhaps one could joke that in one thousand years they could have come up with a new polemic!

In this volume, we deal extensively with the context of Muhammad's life—and yes, his battles. We address his marital life, which Islamophobes and polemicists so frequently characterize as hedonistic and perverted. We also explore the relationship between Islam and other religions, the difficulty that Christians have had in accepting a divine dispensation after Christ, and how Muslims have dealt with earlier divine revelations. These are all important topics that deserve to be treated at length and with accuracy and scholarly rigor. We strive in this volume to stop talking past one another and begin talking with one another.

Getting Beyond Distortions: Ghosts of a Medieval Polemic

In the last few years, there have been many images and depictions of Muhammad in the Western imagination, and many of them have been violent, grotesque, and unflattering. These images can be jarring: no founder of any other religious tradition is represented so consistently negatively—not Confucius, not Lao-tzu, not Moses, not Buddha, and certainly not Christ. Some of the recent negative images of Muhammad are purely recycled images of hate from the bygone era of the Crusades and Christian polemics against Islam. What is particularly intriguing about these negative stereotypes is how unoriginal and unimaginative they are. Many medieval polemics present images of Muhammad as demonic, cursed, or satanic, or even as the Antichrist.[9] Some classics of Western literature, such as Dante's *Inferno*, depict Muhammad as being cut open right down through his torso and cast into the ninth circle of Hell. The gruesome opening lines of this narrative read as follows:

> *No cask ever gapes so wide for loss*
> *of mid- or side-stave as the soul I saw*
> *cleft from the chin right down to where men fart.*
>
> *Between the legs the entrails dangled. I saw*
> *the innards and the loathsome sack*
> *that turns what one has swallowed into shit.* (Inferno, *canto 28,*
> *lines 22–27)*

A pious Muslim would so shudder at the mention of these words that she would have to add the phrase *astaghfirullah* ("I seek forgiveness from God") for merely uttering them. Yet since we have to know what the history of our encounters with one another has been, we move on to the rest of Dante's encounter with Muhammad, from the twenty-eighth canto of Dante's *Inferno*:

> *While I was caught up in the sight of him,*
> *he looked at me and, with his hands, ripped apart*
> *his chest, saying: See how I rend myself,*
> *see how mangled is Mohammed!*
> *Ahead of me proceeds Ali, in tears,*
> *his face split open from his chin to forelock.*
> *And all the others whom you see*

sowed scandal and schism while they lived,
and that is why they here are hacked asunder.
A devil's posted there behind us.[10]

What is particularly intriguing is not just how mean-spirited and offensive these images are, but the fundamental misunderstandings of Islamic teachings that they reflect. Where does the idea of Muhammad being split down the middle come from? It comes from a perversion of two Islamic tropes: in a verse of the Qur'an, God, speaking in the royal "We," comforts Muhammad by saying to him:

Did We not open for you your heart
And did We not remove from you your burden
The burden that weighed heavily on your back
And did We not raise for you your Remembrance (Qur'an 94:1–3)

The expression "opening one's heart," which is used repeatedly in the Qur'anic context, ties together the physical process of exhaling (specifically after the tension of holding one's breath) with the spiritual process of elation, of expansion, of being filled with air and life and spirit. In another verse of the Qur'an (20:25), Moses prays to God to have his heart expanded. Interestingly enough, the chapter in which this verse appears is called *Ta Ha*, traditionally one of the names of the Prophet Muhammad.

The verse quoted here about heart-expansion is enacted, as it were, in the traditional biography of the Prophet's life through an episode of Muhammad's childhood. According to this narrative, an angel descends on Muhammad, reaches into his heart, and removes the source of all impurity by washing Muhammad's heart until it is pure.

If we return to the image in Dante, we see now just how distorted and distorting his polemic against Muhammad actually is. A verse of the Qur'an that has to do with God comforting Muhammad and filling him with spiritual elation and a narrative about Muhammad's heart being purified are recast by the polemical Christian tradition as an image of Muhammad thrown into hellfire while being cut open from the throat to the area below the stomach. Dante turns a verse related to heart-expansion and spiritual elevation into a symbol of eternal punishment. The very Prophet who in Islamic teachings ascends to the zenith of Paradise to have a face-to-face encounter with God (as we shall see in chapter 4), and who chooses to return to humanity to give others the chance to have their own meeting with God, is relegated by Dante to the bowels of Hell. This is what I have referred to as the cognitive dissonance we are experiencing about Muhammad, and it exacerbates the profound modern challenge to have sustained and engaged dialogue across faith lines. Dante is beyond a doubt one of the geniuses of Western literature, but if we are to have a meaningful religious dialogue today across religious lines, we need to do better—much better—than the Italian sage.

The Founding Fathers' (and the Current President's) Positive Image of Islam

Fortunately, the Western representations of Muhammad in particular and of Islam more broadly have never been uniform, and uniformly bad. In particular, an Enlightenment tradition even looked to Islam as a more "rational" religion and offered fairly positive evaluations of Muhammad.[11] For example, during the age of Romanticism, Thomas Carlyle countered the frequent medieval polemic against Muhammad for allegedly being a charlatan: "A false man found a religion? Why, a false man cannot build a brick house!" Carlyle also summarized the impact of Islam in the following positive terms:

> *To the Arab Nation it was as a birth from darkness into light; Arabia first became alive by means of it. A poor shepherd people, roaming unnoticed in its deserts since the creation of the world: a Hero-Prophet was sent down to them with a word they could believe: see, the unnoticed*

becomes world-notable, the small has grown world-great; within one century afterwards, Arabia is at Grenada on this hand, at Delhi on that;—glancing in valor and splendor and the light of genius, Arabia shines through long ages over a great section of the world. . . .

I said, the Great Man was always as lightning out of Heaven; the rest of men waited for him like fuel, and then they too would flame.[12]

Closer to the American tradition, Benjamin Franklin famously stated that the standards of religious freedom in America had to be so broad that, when he was placed as a trustee of Westminster Hall, "even if the Mufti [chief jurist] of Constantinople [from the Muslim Ottoman Empire] were to send a missionary to preach Mohammedanism to us, he would find a pulpit at his service."[13]

This openness to Islam was actually quite commonplace among America's founding fathers. When George Washington was asked in 1784 what kind of workers should be hired to work at Mount Vernon, he responded by stating that the best workers, regardless of their background, should be hired: "If they are good workmen, they may be from Asia, Africa or Europe; they may be Mahometans, Jews, Christians of any sect, or they may be Atheists."[14] Over the course of U.S. history, Muslim Americans have indeed fulfilled this promise of being hardworking and contributing citizens of this society that keeps the memory of George Washington alive. The lasting relationship between Muslims and America was further cemented through the U.S. treaty with Tripoli in 1797:

The government of the United States of America is not in any sense founded on the Christian Religion; as it has in itself no character of enmity against the laws, religion or tranquility of Musselmen [Moslems].

To which President John Adams added: "Now be it known, That I, John Adams, President of the United States of America, having seen

and considered the said Treaty do, by and with the advice and consent of the Senate, accept, ratify, and confirm the same, and every
clause and article thereof." In other words, the relationship between
the United States and Muslims goes back to the very origins of the
American experiment and was formed in part by the inclusive attitude
of many of the founding fathers.

If there is a figure even more quintessentially American than
Benjamin Franklin or George Washington, it would have to be
Thomas Jefferson. In 1765 Jefferson was studying for his bar exam
to qualify as a lawyer. To acquaint himself with what various traditions had to offer about the law, he purchased the most recent and
accurate translation of the Qur'an available, a work by George Sale
called *The Koran: Commonly Called the Alcoran of Mohammed*, which
had been translated from the original Arabic in 1734.[15] Jefferson's
personal copy of the Qur'an eventually became part of the holdings
of the Library of Congress, and it recently gained a great deal of attention when it was used in the swearing-in ceremony of Keith Ellison, the first Muslim American elected to the U.S. Congress. Many
modern-day bigots and alarmists, viewing the choice of the Qur'an
(instead of the more common Bible) as yet another slippery slope
that would lead to the implosion of American identity, called Ellison
unpatriotic and a threat to American values. Ellison was making a
deft point through his use of the Qur'an as the scripture on which
to be sworn into Congress: if Thomas Jefferson owned and studied
the Qur'an, if he saw no contradiction between being American and
being Muslim, why should we?

Jefferson's interest in Islam and "Oriental wisdom" more broadly
was no passing fancy. He began a study of the Arabic language and
grammar and obtained many books on the history of Islam and
Muslim civilizations. He supported the establishment of academic
programs for the study of "the Orient." In his autobiography, he
used language that indicated his desire to see this country become
not merely a Christian country but a home for all. He made this point
emphatically in his discussion of a legal bill:

Where the preamble declares that coercion is a departure from the plan of the holy author of our religion, an amendment was proposed, by inserting the word "Jesus Christ," so that it should read, "a departure from the plan of Jesus Christ, the holy author of our religion." The insertion was rejected by a great majority, in proof that they meant to comprehend, within the mantle of its protection, the Jew and the Gentile, the Christian and Mahometan, the Hindoo, and infidel of every denomination.[16]

Today we would avoid phrases like the "Alcoran of Mohammed" or "Mahometans," instead preferring to use terms like "the Qur'an" and "Muslims." Yet here is what is beyond doubt: on the eve of the founding of the American nation, leading forefathers like Benjamin Franklin and Thomas Jefferson felt compelled to study the Qur'an and the life of Muhammad, and they included Muslims as among those who were entitled to protection and freedom of religion in this country. We have a similar choice today: we can walk in their footsteps and create an open and dynamic society in which we celebrate the plurality of faith, or we can retreat back to the negative attitudes of Dante and the medieval polemicists. These are both parts of the Western—and more specifically, American—encounter with Islam, yet one choice leads us to mutual coexistence and the other to the furthering of hostility and tension.

Perhaps the most powerful declaration of support for Islam from an American political leader was the June 2009 speech of President Obama in Cairo. In this historic speech, Barack Obama began by offering:

I have come here to seek a new beginning between the United States and Muslims around the world; one based upon mutual interest and mutual respect; and one based upon the truth that America and Islam are not exclusive, and need not be in competition. Instead, they overlap, and share common principles—principles of justice and progress; tolerance and the dignity of all human beings.[17]

He went on to quote from the Qur'an ("Be conscious of God and speak always the truth") and offered that he too promised to follow the spiritual and moral guidance of this verse and speak truthfully. He recalled many historic markers between Islam and the United States, including Morocco (a Muslim nation) having been the first to recognize the United States of America, John Adams's comments on the Treaty of Tripoli, and the election of the Muslim American Keith Ellison to Congress. In quite possibly the most emphatic statement of support any American president has ever made on behalf of Islam, he stated: "And I consider it part of my responsibility as president of the United States to fight against negative stereotypes of Islam wherever they appear."[18]

Recognizing the appeal to Muslims of the life of the Prophet, Obama deftly included a reference to the most powerful spiritual narrative in the life of the Prophet, that of the heavenly ascension (which we study in depth in this volume). In speaking of his vision for Jerusalem as a place where Muslims, Jews, and Christians could worship freely and side by side, Obama referred to Jerusalem through the analogy of Muhammad's heavenly ascension: "a place for all of the children of Abraham to mingle peacefully together as in the story of *Isra*, when Moses, Jesus, and Muhammad (peace be upon them) joined in prayer."[19] The power of this kind of reference was not lost on Muslim audiences. Never before had an American president showed such a profound understanding of the symbolism of Prophet Muhammad's ascension or used it in such a poignant way to paint a picture of the coming together of humanity. These were just words—but words that promoted a sense of peace, pluralism, and respectful coexistence.

Polemics Against Muhammad Today

The polemics against Muhammad today may be unoriginal, but they have in fact changed since the days of medieval theological polemics. The modern reality is both more complicated and more urgent.

The medieval polemicists against Muhammad might be forgiven for having lacked reliable scholarly resources or for having had no personal contact with Muslims who might have persuaded them that Muslims are in fact human beings. Today's polemicists cannot claim any such ignorance. On the one hand, one can turn with great confidence to an abundance of books, Internet resources, experts, and documentaries for information about various aspects of Islamic teachings, history, and society. Yet ironically, the same proliferation of media has resulted in a dilution of the standards of scholarship. It can sometimes be hard for the untrained eye to detect which books were written by scholars trained in the field of Islamic studies and which were composed by prejudiced bigots who have found a new victim and an additional target for their hatred. Prejudice and hate are fluid, ever seeking new victims. In days past, Jews and African Americans would have been the target; today it is Muslims and Hispanics, and God knows who will bear the brunt of xenophobia in the future.[20]

Adding to the complications is the issue of how the Internet, the blogosphere, and the twenty-four-hour news cycle thrive on the manufacturing of conflict. The old mantra of journalistic news, "if it bleeds, it leads," today rewards those who speak in the most confrontational, the most polemical, and simply the loudest voices. How different this mentality is from the traditional Islamic teaching that the drum makes a loud sound because it is . . . *hollow*. In contrast, this same Islamic source asserts, the perfume seller need not boast about the quality of his merchandise, since the fragrance of the flowers is its own witness.[21]

One way to see how the globalized conflict-manufacturing machine works today is to explore the two major crises associated with the Prophet Muhammad over the last generation. The first was the controversy that erupted upon publication of *The Satanic Verses* by the British novelist Salman Rushdie, who had written many passages that offended Muslim sensitivities, such as having the prostitutes in a brothel bear the names of the wives of the Prophet. The character of "the Messenger," obviously a parody of Muhammad, was called "Mahound," which was the name that medieval Christian polemicists used for the Prophet. There were worldwide demonstrations by many Muslims against Rushdie, and the most (in)famous condemnation came from Ayatollah Khomeini, who issued a fatwa against Rushdie on Valentine's Day 1989. However, the overwhelming majority of people who demonstrated against the novel had never read the expensive, lengthy, English-language novel.

The situation had changed drastically by September 2005, when the Danish newspaper *Jyllands-Posten* published cartoons depicting the Prophet Muhammad as a terrorist. These cartoons tapped into the all-too-familiar tropes of violence and gender oppression. This time the situation was a bit different: millions of people around the world could see the offensive cartoons on their computer with the click of a button. In a perfect postmodern twist of irony and self-reflexivity, some of the cartoons poked fun at the obscure Danish paper's attempt to generate self-serving controversy. The editors who had commissioned the cartoons claimed that "the cartoonists treated Islam the same way they treat Christianity, Buddhism, Hinduism and other religions."[22] This turned out to be another lie. The hypocrisy of the editors' championing of "freedom of speech" was eventually revealed when they confessed that they had earlier turned down cartoons lampooning Jesus Christ because they deemed them offensive.[23] Furthermore, the editors had traveled to the United States to meet with some of the leading Islamophobic leaders who had been leading the attacks against Muslims.[24] The editors tried time and again to pose these cartoons as a litmus test for Danish Muslims: those who could stomach them were genuinely committed to being a part of Danish society, and those who could not would never be truly Danish. In reality, Islamophobes from the States, allying themselves with right-wing, anti-immigration factions in Denmark, had led a campaign against Muslims in that country for years. One example is the cooperation between the noted American Islamophobe Daniel Pipes and the right-wing Danish journalist Lars Hedegaard in writing "Something Rotten in Denmark?" There is indeed something rotten in Denmark, and in much of Europe—the rising tide of racism and anti-immigrant sentiment that shows up in France, Denmark, the United Kingdom, Germany, the Netherlands, and elsewhere.[25]

In other words, the cartoons were not really about Muhammad: they were about the anxieties of some Danes about the changing demographics and nature of Danish society. The cartoonist used Muslims' sensitivity and devotion toward the Prophet to create a combustible and antagonistic situation that, by default, would end up marking Muslims as permanent outsiders.[26]

The cartoons eventually elicited responses that ranged from the boycott of Danish products (at a cost of about $170 million to the Danish economy) to attacks on Danish embassies in multiple countries (including Islamabad, Pakistan, in June 2008, as well as the torching of the embassy in Lebanon). Over one hundred people, mainly Muslims, died in demonstrations, mostly by being shot at by police in Pakistan, Nigeria, Somalia, Afghanistan, and elsewhere. Aside from the truth about Muhammad and the lives of these members of the community of Muhammad, the other casualty of this sad episode was the ability of many to envisage a pluralistic society in which people of all races and religious backgrounds live together in peace and harmony.

Be that as it may, it should also be mentioned that the response of many Muslims during these protests and demonstrations fell far short of the lofty ideals that Muhammad established. During his lifetime, especially in the first decade of his prophetic career, Muhammad was often mocked, ostracized, exiled, and subject to assassination attempts. The enemies of Muhammad bribed children to cast stones at him, and one particularly obnoxious neighbor dumped rubbish on his head every morning when he passed by her house. Yet time and again, Muhammad forgave those who persecuted him, even famously refusing to take revenge on them when he had the chance to do so after the conquest of Mecca. As to the woman who dumped trash on Muhammad's head every morning, her relationship with the Prophet became transformed. One morning when Muhammad was walking by her house, no trash was dumped on him. Muhammad went inside the house and mercifully asked if all was well. The woman was sick in bed. Upon seeing his compassion and care for her when she had treated him so poorly, she wept and became one of his followers. This is yet another example of compassion, kindness, and forgiveness overcoming hatred and animosity. At the end of the day, it is love and compassion that are qualities of light, attributes of God, and their light illuminates every dark space of the heart.

When again and again his followers asked him to curse his persecutors—as the biblical prophets had done so often—Muhammad refused, stating that he was sent to be the Prophet of Mercy (*Nabi al-Rahma*) and not to curse humanity. Since one of the tasks that the Qur'an sets for Muslims is to engage in ethical self-critique and to critique their own families and communities in the sight of God (Qur'an 4:135), one has to admit that spiritually all is not well today in the community of Muhammad. There is a very small minority of Muhammad's people who, sadly, express their connection to the Prophet primarily through outrage rather than mercy.[27] Throughout this book, we explore the various ways in which different groups of Muslims have found inspiration in Muhammad to seek beauty and wisdom—and also the ways in which some have sought to justify their violence and prejudice by referring to certain episodes in Muhammad's life and teachings.

Sources for the Life of the Prophet

If we hope to arrive at a historically accurate understanding of the life, teaching, and significance of Muhammad, the question of which sources we turn to is of paramount importance. In this volume, I have tried to consult the widest range of sources about Muhammad, while privileging the most historically reliable. To begin with, I have combed the Qur'an. The Qur'an is not seen by Muslims as the words of Muhammad but rather as the divine revelation that conveys the words of God through the Prophet. The Qur'an is not a book "about" Muhammad per se: it is not the Gospel of Muhammad.

There are no miracle narratives in the Qur'an about Muhammad feeding the poor or healing the sick. Rather, the Qur'an itself is deemed to be the miracle in terms of its spiritual power, beauty, and eloquence. Nevertheless, we can turn to the Qur'an to get a better sense of the world in which Muhammad appeared, and the world he worked to refashion.

Our second source is the *hadith*, which are the statements attributed to the Prophet Muhammad. The hadith were first collected orally for decades, but eventually they were written down. There are multiple hadith collections of various degrees of reliability; together they form one of the major sources for understanding the life of Muhammad.

Our third source is the *Sira* literature (the life of Muhammad genre), which attempts to take the brief Qur'anic references and fill them in to create whole narratives. The earliest of these is the Sira of Ibn Ishaq, which was composed some 150 years after the time of the Prophet.

Our fourth source is the vast array of devotional material. Although sometimes these are of dubious historical value in understanding the historical Muhammad, they are invaluable to an understanding of how Muhammad came to be received and imagined in Muslim piety.

A good way to see how all these sources come together, while maintaining some tensions, is to take one issue, such as how the Islamic tradition understood the relationship between Muhammad and the earlier revelations.

Muhammad the Biblical Prophet

One of the more tangible ways to trace the continuity of the Muhammadi and biblical traditions is through the various commemorations of the life narrative of Muhammad (referred to as the *Sira*) in the Islamic tradition. Through the centuries, there have been many versions of his life, and they often seek to tell the stories of Muhammad through the lens of an epic. Like all epics, they are concerned with drama and conflict; these narratives devote a great deal of attention to Muhammad's conflict with the Meccans and the battles fought against them at Badr, Uhud, and Khandaq. The earliest and in some ways most authoritative of these "life of Muhammad" treatises was *Sirat Rasul Allah* ("Life of the Messenger of God"), written by Ibn Ishaq (d. 767), which survives today through the surviving edition put together by Ibn Hisham (d. 833). In other words, the full biography of Muhammad as we possess it today dates back no more than 150 years after the time of the Prophet himself. Today the *Sirat Rasul Allah* is published in multiple languages, even as modern Muslim authors continue to write more contemporary lives of Muhammad narratives. Yet the first such *Sirat Rasul Allah* not only provides a life of Muhammad but also attempts to document God's involvement in human history from creation through the biblical prophets leading up to Muhammad's time. The first half of the book begins with the creation narrative and proceeds to cover the familiar biblical history. The book devotes a chapter to each major prophet: Noah, Abraham, Lot, Job, Joseph, Moses, Ezekiel, Elijah, David, Solomon, Isaiah, Daniel, Ezra, John the Baptist, and Jesus Christ. In addition, a few chapters are devoted to more minor prophets. The second half of the book is the biography of Muhammad. The structure, therefore, is quite similar to that of the Christian Bible, in which the New Testament, the narrative of Jesus and the early community, comes after the Old Testament, which treats the prophets, from creation to those anticipating the arrival of Christ. To put it differently, for the first and most significant biographer of Muhammad, there was no sharp divide between the tale of Muhammad and that of earlier biblical prophets. Muhammad's narrative continued even as it culminated in the story of God's revelation to humanity. In time, the first volume of the book became more marginalized, to the point that in the late twentieth century it had to be pieced back together. This later marginalization is an indication of the willingness of the later Islamic tradition to posit a sharper demarcation between the Muhammadi Revolution and the previous prophetic revelations.[28] Throughout the centuries, Muslims have oscillated between emphasizing the continuity with earlier revelations and positioning the Prophet as superseding all of them. In a way, this tension is not that different from the multiple ways in which Christians articulate their relationship to the existing Jewish tradition.

Through the centuries, volumes very similar to *Sirat Rasul Allah* would be produced that situated Muhammad's prophethood in a broader biblical context. A good example is the work of Kisa'i, who died around 1200. He composed a volume titled *Qisas al-anbiya'* (Tales of the Prophets). This volume begins with the creation (of God's Throne, the Earth and the Heavens) before moving on to the creation of Adam and Eve; humanity's expulsion from Paradise; Noah's ark; Abraham's migration; the children of Abraham, Isaac and Ishmael; Joseph in Egypt; Job's suffering; Moses and Aaron; Joshua, Solomon, David, and Jesus. In other words, the Muslim readers of these texts—who by and large no longer referred directly to the biblical texts—saw these biblical prophetic figures as part of their own universe and read their own spiritual genealogy as including the familiar biblical prophets before culminating in the Prophet. Each chapter builds on the verses in the Qur'an that specifically mention each prophet and elaborates on the brief Qur'anic narratives to create a full narrative.

Volumes like the *Tales of the Prophets* by Kisa'i also became connected to a glorious courtly tradition of illuminated artwork. Artists at courts began to design richly illuminated manuscripts depicting the tales of the prophets. For example, see the two images reproduced here from an illustrated version of the *Qisas al-anbiya'*. The first mentions Abraham's sacrifice of his son Ishmael.

Medieval Muslim miniature, depicting Abraham's sacrifice of Ishmael.
From the Qisas al-anbiya'.

The story of Abraham's sacrifice, so central to the Jewish and Christian traditions, also figures prominently in Islam. The basic outlines of the Qur'anic narrative are quite similar to the biblical account, though the son, old enough to have given his consent, is deemed to be a willing participant in the episode. Muslim sources disagree about which son of Abraham, Isaac or Ishmael, was to be sacrificed. Some follow the lead of the Jewish tradition in identifying the son as Isaac, while the majority of the tradition states that, since Ishmael is older than Isaac, he is the "only son" of Abraham, and thus the one whose sacrifice God asks of Abraham. Both the overlap with the biblical narrative and the differences from it are characteristic of the Islamic tradition's relationship with the earlier revelations.

Another image from the *Qisas al-anbiya'* depicts Adam and Eve in celestial settings.

Muslim miniature depicting Adam and Eve in Paradise.
From the Qisas al-anbiya'.

This image is particularly instructive in that Adam and Eve are depicted as medieval Persians, wearing the garb of that society. It is a vivid reminder that we always remember and imagine the holy ones of the past partially through our own present lenses.

Illustrated manuscripts like this one would remain restricted to courtly contexts because they were quite expensive to produce. Yet the narratives from these tales became part of the vast network of storytellers in Muslim societies and formed the basis of the familiarity the majority of people had with prophetic history. To put it differently, most premodern Muslims learned their sacred history orally through fantastic stories that were circulated heart to heart and often told by masterful storytellers in coffeehouses and similar contexts.

How were such narratives fleshed out from the often brief Qur'anic references? Obviously, the Muslim scholars who followed in this tradition had to rely on a great deal of Jewish and Christian material in composing the narratives about the world before Muhammad. According to scholars, these included Hebrew works such as the Midrash Rabbah and Syriac works like the *Book of the Treasures of Caves*, many of which are no longer extant.[29] It should be remembered that this was a time when much of the ancient Near East was witnessing a gradual and incremental conversion from Christianity and Judaism to Islam. As is often the case, the converts did not abandon their traditions but simply adopted and assimilated whatever did not contradict their new faith. This rich Jewish and Christian material is often referred to in Islamic sources as the *Israi'iliyat* (the Israelite literature), the wisdom of the Children of Israel. Today the *Israi'iliyat* is the focus of a complex discussion among modern Muslims. Some Muslims argue that these strands are yet another proof of the intricate and organic continuity among the Jewish, Christian, and Islamic traditions over the millennia. Long before the Crusades and modern colonialism, these traditions comingled. Others have attempted to argue on the grounds of "purity" that the Islamic tradition can and should be purged of interpretations that do not originate in the Qur'an and the traditions of the Prophet.

The conversation does not always break down into a conventional conservative-liberal split. For example, many Muslim feminists argue against the interpretation of Eve as being derived from a "crooked rib" of Adam on the grounds that the Qur'an itself makes no mention of this. Yet whatever the source of such misogynistic traditions, by the time of Kisa'i (the author of the *Tales of the Prophets*), the notion of Eve being created from the crooked rib of Adam had been woven into the understandings of many Muslims and was even attributed to the Prophet Muhammad himself. These types of often patriarchal creation myths stand in stark contrast to the more egalitarian creation model of men and women in the Qur'an. In the Islamic scripture, both men and women are said to be created from a singular soul (*nafs^in wahidat^in*, in Qur'an 4:1), which, suggestively enough, is grammatically described as being feminine. Furthermore, in the Qur'anic creation account, the "fall" is not attributed to Eve alone: both Adam and Eve are described as having fallen prey to Satan, and both are held accountable and thus expelled from the garden. Modern Muslims' debates about these types of verses are not only about gender norms. They are also part and parcel of how Muslims negotiate and contest their spiritual destiny, which remains both woven into—even entangled in—and distinct from the biblical legacy.

How Do People of Different Faith Traditions Talk with One Another?

The rules for having a productive and insightful conversation across religious and cultural lines are not all that different than the rules for having meaningful interpersonal relationships. One has to be mindful of one's own baggage, avoid projecting one's own problems onto other people, listen carefully to what others are telling us about their own story, and avoid jumping to quick conclusions. Judging others is often an exercise in self-righteousness, and not entirely helpful. Let us review these rules in the context of our venture into the memory of Muhammad.

1. Being Mindful of Our Own Baggage and Motivations

In this volume, we deal with both the issues that Muslims take delight in and those that vex them and have led to a great deal of debate and discussion, even embarrassment. Debate and discussion is a necessary part of an honest dialogue. Yet one cannot enter into a discussion and dialogue with Muslims without being mindful of one's own history and both the strengths and shortcomings of one's own tradition. One of the most common mistakes made in cross-religious conversations is that people end up comparing the loftiest and noblest aspects of their own tradition with the most hideous aspects of others. If we wish to understand the "memory of Muhammad," we need to do more than listen to Muslims' accounts—we also need to come to terms with the reality and history of other traditions.

A historical example illuminates this point quite nicely. A monumental figure in the history of early modern Christianity was Martin Luther, who is forever associated with the Protestant Reformation. Luther, living in the aftermath of the 1453 Otto-man conquest of Constantinople, was mindful and aware—even fearful—of the presence of Muslims ("Turks" to him) and was keenly interested in the study of Islam. Yet he was not interested in understanding Islam per se, or getting to know Muslims as human beings. Instead, he studied Islam in order to confirm his own preconceived notion that it was heretical and also inferior to Christianity. Here are his words from the preface to a 1543 Latin translation of the Qur'an:

> *I have wanted to get a look at a complete text of the Qur'an. I do not doubt that the more other pious and learned persons read these writings, the more the errors and the name of Muhammad will be refuted. For just as the folly, or rather madness, of the Jews is more easily observed once their hidden secrets have been brought out into the open, so once the book of Muhammad has been made public and thoroughly examined in all its parts, all pious persons will more easily comprehend the insanity and wiles of the devil and will be more easily able to refute them.*[30]

In other words, Luther's task in writing this preface was not actu-ally to convey what he had learned about Islamic teachings, but rather to refute the alleged "errors" of the Qur'an as well as the "very name of Muhammad." It is intriguing to note how Luther also connects the refutation of Muslims with that of Jews, an indication of what we have identified as multiple manifestations of anti-Semitism against Judaism and Islam. No wonder that Luther identified both Muslims and Jews (and the pope!) as people of the devil.

2. Acknowledging the Problems of One's Own Tradition ("Removing the Plank from One's Own Eye")

It is easier sometimes to talk about the problem of "those people" or even "you people" than it is to honestly come to terms with the challenges that all of us face.

The accounts that present Muhammad as a violent extremist and a sex addict are as distorted as any reading of the Bible that presents Moses as exclusively having been a fugitive murderer (Exodus 2:11–15), Abraham as a would-be child-killer (Genesis 22:1–19), and Jesus as a young man with an anger management problem who kicks over tables in official settings (Mark 11:15; Matthew 21:12). Most people of faith would say that these depictions represent a distortion of the Abraham they know, the Moses who brought them the Torah, and the Christ who embodies God's love for them.

More sophisticated polemics take verses of the Bible literally and remove them from their context. Imagine a reading of Judaism and Christianity that worked by focusing on these biblical verses alone:

On violence: "Happy shall he be who takes your little ones and dashes them against the rock!" (Psalms 137:9)

On working on the Sabbath: "The whole congregation brought [a man who had been collecting sticks] outside the camp and stoned him to death, just as the Lord had commanded Moses." (Numbers 15:36)

On gender relations: "Wives, be subject to your husbands as you are to the Lord. For the husband is the head of the wife just as Christ is the head of the church." (Ephesians 5:22–23)

On Jesus bringing not peace but a sword:

> *But whoever denies me before others,*
> *I also will deny before my Father in heaven.*
> *Do not think that I have come to bring peace to the earth;*
> *I have not come to bring peace, but a sword.*
> *For I have come to set a man against his father,*
> *and a daughter against her mother,*
> *and a daughter-in-law against her mother-in-law;*
> *and one's foes will be members of one's own household.*
> (Matthew 10:33–36)

How do we respond to these verses? Most committed Jews and most faithful Christians would have a hard time taking these verses as the essence of their faith. Some would be inclined to run to their Bible to make sure these verses are not in fact fabricated. They are not. Others would protest that their faith is informed by a God of love and justice, one Who so loves the world that He gave His only Begotten Son for the sins of humanity, or that the stoning verses of the Bible are an admonition to underscore how seriously we are to take God's commandments.

My reason for bringing up these verses is not to belittle Judaism or Christianity. It is only a person with a small sense of himself who enjoys cutting others down to size. The reason to point to this pattern is that a very similar process works with Islam. A common ploy by Islamophobes is to go to a predictable list of verses in the Qur'an and the words of Muhammad and to argue that these verses—with no context, no interpretation, and no alternative set of verses—represent the essence of Islam for all eternity, no matter what Muslims may say or how they may protest. Didn't Shakespeare remind us that "the devil can cite Scripture for his purpose"? Some of the favorite verses of Islamophobes include:

> *On gender:* "Men are in charge of women, because God has made the one of them to excel the other, and because they spend of their property (for the support of women). So good women are the obedient, guarding in secret that which God has guarded. As for those from whom you fear rebellion, admonish them and banish them to beds apart, and scourge them. Then if they obey you, seek not a way against them. Lo! God is ever High, Exalted, Great." (Qur'an 4:34)

> *On warfare:* "Then, when the sacred months have passed, slay the idolaters wherever you find them, and take them (captive), and besiege them, and prepare for them each ambush. But if they repent and establish worship and pay the charity tax, then leave their way free. Lo! God is Forgiving, Merciful." (Qur'an 9:5, the "Verse of the Sword")

> *On conflict with the Jews as part of the apocalypse:* "God's Apostle said, 'The Hour will not be established until you fight with the Jews, and the stone behind which a Jew will be hiding will say, "O Muslim! There is a Jew hiding behind me, so kill him."'" (*Hadith Bukhari*, vol. 4, book 52, no. 177)[31]

How do we respond to these verses? Most committed Muslims would want to begin by affirming that they are not fabricated (they are not). Then most would protest that these verses do not represent the essence of their faith, that they were contextual revelations that corresponded to a particular moment in time, and that they should not be taken as applicable for all times and places—and certainly not for our time and place.

I bring up these parallel examples of "difficult" verses from the Abrahamic traditions to make a simple point. If we start this intellectual and religious journey predisposed to seeing the evil in the other tradition, then there is little point to reading further. There are many other books that will gladly confirm our preexisting prejudices against other traditions. If, on the other hand, we are willing to participate in a culture of generosity that affirms that *all* of our traditions contain verses, teachings, and practices that are at first glance—and sometimes at second and third glance—profoundly problematic, and that we must come to terms with them, and that all of our traditions also contain profound beauty and wisdom, then there is a journey we can take together. And what a worthwhile journey it is! By studying one faith we can learn more about our own and about the challenges of being religious in today's world more generally.

Perhaps there even remains a hope of not only learning *about* one another but also learning *from* one another. It is one thing to state that Muslims need to be knowledgeable about Judaism and Christianity, but are we ready to take the next step of learning from the law of Moses and the gospel of Jesus? And likewise, aside from learning *about* Muhammad as a prophet and important historical figure, are we ready to learn *from* Muhammad's model of standing up for the poor and the marginalized of society while simultaneously opening our hearts to the Divine through prayer?

3. Projecting Our Own Problems onto Others

Anyone who reads volume after volume by Western authors who accuse Muhammad—and in fact all of Islam—of espousing violence as an essential and cardinal virtue might have to wonder whether there is some measure of what psychologists call "projection" going on here. Could it be that the United States itself, which has become a colonizing and occupying empire, is attempting to deal with its own present violence by projecting it onto a past "other"? Could it be that our own oversexualized American society uses sex to sell everything from flavored water to cars? Could it be that our own society is still challenged in profound ways with the struggle for gender equality? And could it be that all the talk about heresy and deviation has something to do with the anxiety many Americans and Europeans have about increasing levels of "foreign" migration? Could such feelings be entering into the passionate debates about what it means to be a "real" American, or a "real" European, in an age of massive global population shifts? Is the attempt to essentialize and demonize Islam a desperate attempt to construct "American values" in much the same way that some people constructed American values against communism in an earlier era? And could it be that all the talk about Islamic designs to take over the world (or destroy it) actually masks the reality that it is the United States that has thousands of military bases in over one hundred countries? That it is the United States that is the largest producer and stockpiler of nuclear, chemical, and biological weapons in the world? That it is the United States that possesses enough nuclear weapons to ensure that even Twinkie bars and cockroaches (to list the two most famous putative survivors of a nuclear attack) would not survive our mutually assured destruction?[32]

As the United States engages in wars against countries with Muslim-majority populations and remains mired in political conflicts in the Middle East ranging from Iraq and Afghanistan to Iran and Palestine/Israel, some have begun to point to analogies between Iraq and Vietnam. It was with respect to the people of Vietnam that Martin Luther King Jr. stated:

> *Perhaps only his sense of humor and of irony can save him when he hears the most powerful nation of the world speaking of aggression as it drops thousands of bombs on a poor, weak nation more than eight thousand miles away from its shores.*[33]

Could it be that such a sense of humor and a commitment to uphold the sanctity of all human life would prevent us from sinking into the dark abyss of hatred toward any block of humanity? Only after we deal honestly and self-critically with our tendency to project our own shortcomings and failings onto others can we move on to an honest and rewarding study of other religious traditions.

4. Learning About One Another, Learning from One Another

The last decades of the twentieth century and the first decade of the twenty-first have witnessed a great deal of discussion about "globalization." While definitions of globalization vary, generally there is a recognition that today there is an unprecedented movement of goods, peoples, and ideas all around the world. Some facets of globalization have been celebrated, as it undoubtedly makes it possible to learn more about other cultures and civilizations, and it is also easier than ever for people to visit one another in a globalized world, whether in the flesh or "virtually." Other aspects of globalization, however, have brought about real anxieties for many: for some there is the fear of the loss of indigenous local cultures, and others face the real prospect of losing jobs to unseen overseas labor forces. In addition, globalization has had a part to play in the rise of nationalistic violence, the destruction of the planet's environment, and the growing and massive discrepancy between the superpoor and the rich. Through both the celebration and the anxieties, one fact remains: we are much more aware of our interconnectedness with other peoples than we have been at any other point in human history.

Many of those who are committed to a global outlook are likely to celebrate this awareness. One is reminded of the words of Martin Luther King Jr. when he prophesied about all of God's children being caught up in an inescapable network of mutuality, or the words of the Prophet Muhammad when he described humanity as being like members of one body. Those who are more inclined to treasure the innate worth of a particular ethnicity, nationality, or religion over our shared humanity, however, or who deny that shared humanity, are likely to bemoan this more global outlook and to see it as diluting or eroding their own distinctiveness. Yet celebrate it or not, the fact of the matter remains that we have no choice today other than to know about one another. Whether our goal is learning to share the one planet or trying to dominate other parts of the world, we cannot do without intimate knowledge of one another. For that reason alone, it might be said that our age calls for resources that introduce us to one another.

This book is intended to be part of that dialogue. Its ambitions are unambiguously humanistic in its commitment to upholding the worth of multiple cultural, religious, and civilizational units in an age when many would prefer to see us approach one another through paradigms of conflict. We have heard far too much these days about a "clash of civilizations," allegedly between Islam and the West. My own commitment is to a global dialogue along the lines envisioned by the Qur'an, where we are told that God created all of us from a single male and a single female and fashioned us into tribes and nations so that we might come to know each other intimately (Qur'an 49:13). It is to this honest and self-critical dialogue between civilizations that this volume aims to contribute.

Whose Muhammad? Contested Images of the Prophet

As we shall see, most Muslims have refrained from making images of the Prophet, preferring instead to focus on depictions through calligraphic representations and narratives. Their concern has been that, given Muslims' deep affection and reverence toward Muhammad, images of him could lead people to confuse the worship of the God of the Prophet with the worship of the Prophet of God. We shall also see, however, that a miniature tradition, admittedly a courtly legacy, flourished in medieval times, especially in Iran, South Asia, Central Asia, and the Turkish lands. In modern times, some of these areas have continued to produce physical images of the Prophet; they may be most popular in present-day Iran, where it is quite common to find necklaces bearing the likeness of Muhammad and posters of the Prophet being sold on street corners. This is a simple way of documenting the tension and disagreement among Muslims about how to best carry on the memory of Muhammad.

This book is a way of making these contested memories of Muhammad, sometimes narrative and sometimes pictorial, intelligible to multiple audiences, both Muslim and non-Muslim. Beyond a doubt, it is intended to probe the most authentic and historical sources about Muhammad, to situate him historically, and to provide important details about his life, the revelation of the Qur'an, and the fundamental teachings of Islam. It is intended to engage the memory of Muhammad and to explore how Muhammad has been remembered, commemorated, and contested by his followers throughout the centuries. It is also intended to provide an account of how Muhammad has been received in the hearts of his community and how he should be received today and tomorrow.

So whose Muhammad is being conveyed here? The reader has every right to ask this question and to be assured that the Muhammad presented and confronted here is authentic, real, and recognizable. The announcement that any religious figure *should* be remembered surely raises the question of whose understanding is being privileged. There was only one Abraham, one Siddhartha Gautama Buddha, one Moses, one Jesus, and one Muhammad. Yet if these world-altering historical personages were singular, there have been almost as many imaginings of them as there have been faithful folks who have attached themselves to their memory. In a previous age, some tried to express this as the difference between the Jesus of history and the Christ of faith, between the Muhammad of history and the Muhammad of faith. Today we are likely to complicate things a bit by saying that even when we try to tell the history of Muhammad "as it really was," it is difficult if not impossible to get away from a particular understanding of Muhammad.

So it does seem fair to say a word about my own relationship to these memories of Muhammad. Perhaps the best way to do so is to share a crucial moment of my family's life. My family's narrative is very much a part of the great age of globalization, this age of moving back and forth across this planet. I was born in the United States, but raised as a child in Iran during the 1970s and the first half of the 1980s. My parents always say that Iran was a great place to raise a family at that time. In 1985, owing to the horrors of the Iran-Iraq War, we had to leave Iran, and had to do so quickly. I still remember the six of us packing what we could into two suitcases. Most of what we packed were the expected clothing items. The one exception was a beautiful image, an icon of sorts, of the Prophet Muhammad that had always adorned our home in Tehran. It had graced the dining room in our home, and it seemed unthinkable to me to either leave it behind or move into a new home where meals would not be presided over by the image of Muhammad. So I carefully tucked the image away, and I have carried it with me to each home I have lived in over the last few decades.

Iconic image of the Prophet from the author's personal collection.

This image is a lovely depiction of a kind, gentle, yet resolute Prophet, holding on to the Qur'an and looking straight at the viewer with deep and penetrating eyes. He is depicted as a handsome man, with deep Persian eyes and eyebrows, and wearing a green turban. We all imagine the great ones at least partially in our own image; in the case of this Iranian icon, Muhammad is depicted not as an Arab but with distinctly Persian features. Then again, that is probably not any stranger than imaging a first-century Palestinian Jew (Jesus Christ) with the European features of blond hair, white skin, and blue eyes!

Since our return to the United States, the icon has once again been displayed in our house. Our home also features images of Christ and the Buddha, but having an icon through which to imagine the presence of the Prophet has been important for me and my family. Here is an image of that image:

Whenever Iranians came to our home, they would recognize the image as a common one they had seen on posters in Iran. But something strange would happen when we invited to our home Sunni Muslim friends from Pakistan, Afghanistan, or Egypt, who experienced a cognitive dissonance of sorts: how could a pious Muslim not only make an image of the Prophet but also display it proudly in their home? Once a dear friend from Pakistan came to our home for dinner, and we shared a wonderful meal. A great lover of Islamic arts, he admired the many examples of Islamic calligraphy around our home, and we had a lovely time deciphering the Arabic inscriptions. He finally came to pause in front of the image of the Prophet and politely asked who the image was depicting. I was surprised that this learned friend, very knowledgeable about Islam, would not have immediately identified the very common image of Muhammad; I stated that, of course, it was the Prophet. My friend's complexion changed from disbelief to offense, and he proceeded to emphatically state that it could not be, because "Muslims do not depict the Prophet." His insistence was partially out of concern that, in our devotion and love toward the Prophet, Muslims not fall into the trap of worshiping

Muhammad instead of the God of Muhammad. I did my best to inform him that there were millions of such depictions in Iran and elsewhere, and that for many of us it was not a distraction from God but rather a reminder of God to focus on the Messenger of God. And yet I remained unsure of how to respond to his assertion that "Muslims do not depict the Prophet." Wasn't the very item that he was standing in front of proof that at least some do?

Faith is sometimes a very delicate matter that is best handled with care and sensitivity. Now when Muslim friends come over to our home and ask about the image, I try to surmise from what I know about them whether I should reveal the identity or simply state: "It is an image of a holy man who is exceedingly dear to me."

I bring up this example to indicate that different Muslims have always had differing memories of Muhammad. Over the years I have come to see that many of these memories are motivated by differing aesthetics and varying understandings, but that the memories of almost all Muslims are rooted in a devotion to Muhammad. My family's display of the image remains part of our devotion, and the friend's protest was also part of his devotion to make sure that the memory of the Prophet was not sullied by undue innovations.

It might be easier if instead of the image of the Prophet they asked me about my own memory of the Prophet. If someone were to ask me who Muhammad is to me, I would say that my understanding has been shaped simultaneously by the Sufi mystical tradition of Islam and the Shi'i tradition of devotion to the Family of the Prophet. For me, Muhammad is above all else *rahmat^un li-'l-alamin*, a source of mercy to all the worlds, as the Qur'an (21:107) proclaims him, and the *Nabi al-Rahma*, the Prophet of Mercy, as the Muslims have remembered him. For me, Muhammad represents the completion of the possibilities available to us as human beings, not because he is superhuman, but precisely because he embodies the meaning of what it means to be fully human. The fullness of his humanity is particularly important to me in his life as the ideal father, husband, friend, leader, and prophet. He ascended to God and out of compassion returned to lead others so that they too might ascend to God. These are facets of my memories of Muhammad, and aspects that I seek to transmit to my children.

Part of my premise in this volume is that if our aim is to develop an understanding of the significance and centrality of Muhammad for Muslims, then we have to step in and out of his life narratives and look at how Muslims have remembered and interpreted these significant episodes. Our approach, then, oscillates between the "historical Muhammad" and the "Muhammad of grace," to evoke two ideas of Muhammad. I go over the main episodes of Muhammad's life and in each case pause to reflect on how Muslims have seen these events in both historically and spiritually meaningful ways. As one example, let us look at the narrative of Muhammad's birth.

Between Muhammad and the Memory of Muhammad: A Prophet Is Born

The New Testament accounts of Jesus's birth are well known to most, right down to the Wise Men of the East (the number traditionally put at three) who came seeking a newborn king with gifts of gold, myrrh, and frankincense. The Wise Men were said to be following a star visible even in their country (traditionally identified as Persia), signaling the cosmic significance of the birth of Christ (Matthew 2:1–12). In time, these accounts became woven into a larger set of narratives, some from pagan sources, resulting in our familiar Christmas celebration.

The birthday celebrations of Muhammad are also important events for Muslims. Known as "Mawlid," they are important holidays for Muslims who commemorate the opening of this gate of mercy into our world. There are many traditional poems and prayers that Muslims sing on this occasion. At the same time, some more conservative Muslims attack these practices as, at best, heretical innovations and, at worst, ways to worship Muhammad instead of God. In other words, the commemoration of Muhammad's birth is an occasion for Muslims to both celebrate his birth and contest his memory.

The narratives of the birth of Muhammad retain many of the features found in the birth of founders of other religious traditions. One of the most fascinating accounts was written by a fourteenth-century Iraqi historian, Ibn Kathir. This narrative is also filled with a vast set of extraordinary episodes in Heaven and on Earth. Ibn Kathir records that the birth of Muhammad was such a blessed event that it led to the despair of Satan. Ibn Kathir relates that Satan cried out on four occasions: the day when he was cursed by God, the day when he was exiled from Heaven, the day when the Prophet Muhammad was born, and the day when the opening verses of the Qur'an were revealed to Muhammad.[34]

The birth of Muhammad was also filled with signs here on Earth. His mother, Amina, who was in Arabia, saw a light go forth from her womb that lit up castles all the way to Syria and Byzantium.[35] When the baby Muhammad emerged from the womb, he dropped to the ground, took up a handful of dirt, and raised his head toward Heaven. Amina reports that it was as if her whole house was bathed in light, and it looked as if the stars had come so close that she could touch them.

Muhammad's birth is also seen as heralding the end of polytheism and the restoration of faith in the One God: according to Ibn Kathir's narrative, upon the birth of Muhammad the pagan idols looked gloomy, and some fell down from their places.[36] His birth also affected the existing religious communities: over in Iran, the fire of the Zoroastrian temples went out, and the famed domed palace of the Chosroe (the Persian king) shook so much that fourteen of its balconies fell down. According to Ibn Kathir, the Jews of Mecca and Medina had premonitions about the birth of a new prophet indicating that the gift of prophecy would leave the children of Israel for the Arabs. Among the Christians, the Negus of Abyssinia and the monks of Byzantium had visions that "a prophet has come in your land. While he was arriving, his star arose."[37]

To our own contemporary eyes and ears, some of these episodes may appear to be fantastic, awe-inspiring, or incredible. Eruptions of the sacred realm into our physical realm of existence challenge many of the scientific principles that most moderns have internalized. It may come as little surprise that even in the fourteenth century a historian like Ibn Kathir would share some skepticism about some of the most fantastic episodes by adding his own commentary, such as: "This is extremely strange," or, "There is dispute over the veracity of this," or the traditional Muslim favorite, "And God knows best." Clearly, even within the faithful community of Muhammad, there was always a range of approaches as to what could be and could not be believed and about the significances and meanings associated with the events of the Prophet's life. In some ways, far too much attention has been paid to the divergence between traditional pietistic Muslim accounts of the Prophet and the polemical presentations of yesteryear and today. Not enough attention has been paid to the internal Muslim varieties of Muhammad, the multiple memories of Muhammad.

And it is not only Western scholarly sources that have been overly concerned with the Western polemic (and occasional praise of Muhammad). Even Muslims themselves have been preoccupied with what non-Muslims think of them and, in particular, the much-beloved Prophet. One indication of this is that virtually every single Islamic center I have ever visited in North America has a copy of a book entitled *The 100: A Ranking of the Most Influential Persons in History*, written by Michael Hart. The author of this volume is a Jewish astrophysicist who concluded that the Prophet has been the most influential figure in human history.[38] The volume sold some 500,000 copies, yet it would be fair to say that few Muslim readers of the *The 100* had heard of Michael Hart before or knew about his controversial proposition that the way to solve the racial and identity crises in the

United States was to partition the country into three racial zones: one for blacks, one for nonblacks, and one for those who voluntarily choose integration.[39] Why would so many Muslims purchase a book by such a racially divisive figure? It was simply because he had ranked Muhammad as the top figure in human history. When we as Muslims look to others to give us a sense of affirmation, however, we are demonstrating an inferiority complex. So many modern biographies of Muhammad contain a lengthy section filled with every laudatory comment that Western non-Muslims have made about the Prophet. For the last two hundred years the majority of the world's Muslim population has been colonized, and once-proud peoples who rightly saw themselves as matching or surpassing others in the realms of science, literacy, and civilizational might were all too often reduced to borrowers or followers. Thus, the impetus in the works of many Muslim intellectuals in the twentieth century to catalog every positive statement that a European figure has made about Muhammad in history.

There is one last important point: up to now we have mainly talked about the history of derogatory representations of the Prophet in Western sources and the range of Muslim memories. Yet to speak in this way risks perpetuating a dichotomy between those who are "Western" and those who are "Muslim." This dichotomy, like so many dichotomies, is dangerous—and today it is patently false. Islam is already the second-largest religion in Europe and will soon be the second-largest in North America. There are some six million Muslims in America who are, to put it simply, both Western and Muslim. There are tens of millions of Muslims in Europe and a similar number in Russia. And many of the leading Muslim intellectuals whose works are read all over the world in fact hail from Europe and North America. So, having explored the tortured history of Western and Muslim accounts of the Prophet in the past, we should safely put aside this facile dichotomy for today's world.

As we have stated, the issue of Western representations of Islam— in particular of the Prophet Muhammad—is both important and somewhat overemphasized. Modern Muslims' obsession with how Westerners represent the Prophet is inseparable from the issues of global power, hegemony, and colonialism. In this volume, we look simultaneously through two lenses: the narratives of the Qur'an and the oldest biographies of the Prophet Muhammad; and the ways in which the episodes of Muhammad's life have been understood, elaborated, and contested by different Muslims. These differences, which became more acute as the modern era approached, are directly related to the changing fortunes of Muslims—from being a superior civilizational force in the world for about one thousand years to enduring the more recent traumas of colonialism.

In bygone ages, it was Muslims who could confidently look at themselves as ruling over areas larger even than the Roman Empire at its zenith and who could view themselves as having achieved the pinnacle of science and learning from China to Spain. Long ago, Muslims were the cultural transmitters of the East and the West—in an age when terms like "the East" and "the West" were meaningless. Far from the inferiority complex that would arise later, Muslims felt confident about their civilizational prowess and their religiosity. Part of this confidence was reflected in their memory of the Prophet. Muslims cultivated tender poetry in the tradition of devotion to the Prophet in which they addressed Muhammad in the following fashion:

Your beautiful face
The envy of idols.

However much I try to describe you
in loveliness
You exceed that.

I went from horizon to horizon
I sought the love of all the lovelies
I saw much that is beautiful

But
You . . .
are something else.

This devotional tradition has not disappeared. It is still very much alive in the memory, and in the hearts, of many Muslims worldwide. In fact, the poem cited here was one of the favorites of a leading group of South Asian Muslims who cherished a tradition known as Qawwali, popular in South Asia and now beyond, thanks to the efforts of figures like Nusrat Fateh Ali Khan. This particular poem was one of the favorites of a leading Qawwali group known as the Sabri Brothers, who titled their song *Ya Muhammad, Nur-e Mojassam* ("O Muhammad, Embodied Light"). The poem went on to state:

O Muhammad
Embodied Light

My Beloved
My Master

You are:
The image of the perfection of love
The illumination of God's beauty

It is this tradition of keeping alive the memory of the Prophet that we trace in this volume. If we wish to understand the intimacy that most Muslims feel with the Prophet, then it is vital to engage this tradition.

Perhaps the ultimate contrast with the inferiority complex of many modern Muslims can be envisaged through the study of a common mystical statement from premodern Islam. This statement comes from the collection of texts known as *hadith qudsi* (sacred traditions), which reportedly document private conversations between God and

Muhammad. These statements are pivotal to the mystical life of Muslims. According to one such hadith qudsi, God revealed to Muhammad: "Lawlaka, ma khalaqtu. . . ."

Were it not for you
[O Muhammad]
I would not have created
the Heavens and the Earth.

This statement became so beloved to so many Muslims that in the poetic tradition it was enough to refer to it by simply stating the one word *lawlaka* (if not for you), and the audience would infer the full significance. Even some of the scholars who have doubted its authenticity still say that if the statement reflects a pietistic account more than an actual conversation between God and Muhammad, its meaning is still valid! My own approach in this volume is quite simple: As a mere author, I make no claims about the ultimate purpose of God's creation, or about whether God in fact so loved Muhammad that He created the world for the Prophet's sake. What I do claim is that Muslims, historically, have so loved Muhammad that they have expressed their devotion to the Prophet through this statement that he is the ultimate cause of creation. In this understanding, Muhammad is a Logos-like figure, of the variety that we encounter in the first lines of the Gospel of John: "In the beginning was the Word, and the Word was with God . . ." (John 1:1). Some Muslims have asserted a very similar notion—that the first thing God created was the Light of Muhammad. This Light of Muhammad, preceding creation, takes up a similar place for Muslim mystics that the notion of Logos does for many Christian theologians, as does the modern Muslim insistence that "Muhammad was just a man, a mere mortal man." There might have been one historical Muhammad, but there have been many memories of Muhammad. Here we navigate from the historical Muhammad to these multiple memories, which matter because all Muslims at the end of the day relate not to an abstract notion of Muhammad but to particular memories, specific understandings. We cannot understand the different interpretations of Islam without understanding these multiple memories of Muhammad.

How to Address the Prophet Muhammad (S)

Muslims traditionally do not mention the name of the Prophet without adding a blessing after it: *Salla Allah" alayhi wa sallam* ("May God bless him, and send him peace"). Within the text of the Qur'an, it is stated: "Indeed God and the angels send down blessings on the Prophet, so ye who have faith, send down blessings upon the Prophet" (Qur'an 33:56). If God and the angels bless Muhammad, Muslims have deemed it proper to do the same. Even in English, many traditional Muslim sources put the symbol (S) after Muhammad's name, standing in as an abbreviation of the pietistic phrase *Salla Allah" alayhi wa sallam*. Similar honorifics are added after the names of other prophets, usually one such as *'Alayhi salam* ("peace be upon him"). In Persian, Turkish, and South Asian Muslim contexts, often an additional phrase, like *Hazrat*, is added before the names of prophets. The term *Hazrat* means "Presence," and the implication is that in the beings of the prophets one detects the Presence of God. So whereas in English one might casually mention "Muhammad," in Islamic etiquette the proper way of acknowledging the Prophet is more akin to "the one in whom we detect the Presence of God, Muhammad, may the peace and blessings of God be upon him." Such pious language may sound stuffy or overly ornate in English. In Islamic languages, however, to neglect it smacks of a lack of spiritual etiquette.

The last word in this introduction we offer to the famed and much beloved thirteenth-century Muslim poet and sage, Mawlana Jalal al-Din, better known in the West as Rumi. Described as an "offspring of the soul" of Muhammad and as one who specifically resembled the Prophet,[40] Rumi conveys some heartfelt anecdotes about the Prophet.

God knows best, as Muslims say, about the historical veracity of these accounts, yet there is a truth about them that endures for the people of Muhammad.

One narrative recalls that a companion of the Prophet named Anis ibn Malik was entertaining a guest. After the meal was finished, Anis saw that the napkin the guest had used was yellow (from grease). He called on the maid and told her to throw the napkin into the fire-pit. The maid followed Anis's directions. All the guests were bewildered, however, when the napkin failed to catch on fire and make a lot of smoke. After an hour, she took the napkin out of the oven, and it came out clean and white, with no impurities on it. The guests were amazed and said to Anis: "O exalted companion of the Prophet! How come the Napkin didn't burn, and how come it became cleansed?" Anis said: "It's because Mustafa [Muhammad] would wipe his hands and lips on this napkin."

Rumi concludes his tale with this invitation, which seems apropos for our venture into the memories of Muhammad:

O heart who is fearful of the torment of hellfire,
get acquainted with such a hand and such lips.

If the Prophet bestowed such honor upon an inanimate object,
imagine what he would do to the soul of the lovers![41]

CHAPTER ONE

The World Before Muhammad

A FEW SHORT YEARS AFTER the Arabian prophet Muhammad began his public ministry in the year 610 of the Common Era, the rich and powerful aristocracy of Mecca began persecuting the poorest and most vulnerable followers of Muhammad. The Arabian society of the seventh century was a tribal one: one's identity was inseparable from one's clan and tribe, and the measure of one's character was directly related to the nobility of one's tribe. The Meccan aristocracy was concerned not only about the message of faith in the One God and accountability for one's actions that Muhammad was preaching. These rich and powerful merchants were zealously devoted to the polytheist beliefs of their forefathers and the stratified model of their society, which had them in a privileged position at the top. The radical egalitarianism of Muhammad, who preached that the only distinction in the sight of God was based on a person's piety, not lineage, was a challenge not only to their polytheistic outlook but also to their very society. To have harmed Muhammad himself would have been too risky, since he came from the distinguished tribe of Quraysh. So the Meccan powers responded by identifying and persecuting those followers of Muhammad who were slaves and outcasts or who came from undistinguished tribes that would not dare to support them. At one point, Muhammad and his community were actually banished from their homeland of Mecca to a barren valley. It seemed that Muhammad's revolution might be over before it had begun.

Rejected by most of his own tribe, and with no safe haven in Arabia, Muhammad sent about eighty of his followers to Abyssinia to live under the protection of a Christian king, Negus, who was known for his justice and compassion. Living in that Christian land, they neither became Christian nor sought to convert the locals. Rather, they were able to live in peace and tranquillity in Abyssinia, where they were free to worship according to their own faith. In a short while, the Meccan polytheists came to recognize the danger of allowing the young Muslim community a sanctuary anywhere and sought to have the refugees returned to Mecca. Armed with the most eloquent of Arab tongues to impress Negus (and the finest leather goods with which to bribe his advisers), the Meccans asked for the immigrants to be returned to their homeland. This was a seminal moment for the nascent movement of Islam: had the refugees been handed over, the young flame of Islam might have been put out at that moment. The Christian ruler asked the leader of the Muslims why they had abandoned the religion of their forefathers, while not accepting the Christian faith of their host nation. The answer provided by the Muslim refugees' leader, a cousin of Muhammad named Ja'far, was deemed important enough to preserve verbatim:

> *O King, we were a people steeped in ignorance, worshiping idols, eating unsacrificed carrion, committing abominations, and the strong would devour the weak.*
>
> *Thus we were, until God sent us a Messenger out of our midst, one whose lineage we knew, and his veracity and his worthiness of trust and his integrity.*
>
> *He called us unto God, that we should testify to His Oneness and worship Him and renounce what we and our fathers had worshiped in the ways of stones and idols; and he commanded us to speak truly, to fulfill our promises, to respect the ties of kinship and the rights of our neighbors, and to refrain from crimes and from bloodshed.*

So we worship God alone, setting naught beside Him, counting as forbidden what He has forbidden and licit what He has allowed. For these reasons have our people turned against us, and have persecuted us to make us forsake our religion and revert from the worship of God to the worship of idols.

That is why we have come to thy country, having chosen thee above all others; and we have been happy in thy protection, and it is our hope, O King, that here, with thee, we shall not suffer wrong.[1]

This is how Muhammad's followers came to characterize their own world before Muhammad, before God's revelation of the Qur'an to them. They saw their society as one in which the strong oppressed the weak and the "ways of the forefathers" had become more sacrosanct than the ways of God. Instead, they came to follow a prophet whom they had known, one whose trustworthiness was already the stuff of legends, and one who led them to sincere faith in God. Their world, the world before Muhammad, was one that they characterized as "ignorant" (*jahil*) and uncivilized.

In this book, we trace the legacy of the social and spiritual revolution brought forth by Muhammad. The word "revolution" is used too lightly at times, but in the case of Muhammad it seems to fit. This was a part of the world that had been surrounded by two vastly superior civilizations, the Persians and the Byzantines. In less than one hundred years, the civilization that centered on the teachings of Muhammad would rule from India to Spain, an area greater than Rome at its zenith. Even more significant than the quick spread of this empire, however, would be the spiritual tradition at the center of the Muhammadi Revolution. The followers of Muhammad identified their message as the same message that had previously been given to Abraham, to Moses, and to Jesus—a message that was now being given to a people who had never before had their own prophet. So what was so revolutionary to them about this message in this context?

As we shall shortly see, in the world before Muhammad the "ways of the forefathers" had provided a model for behavior that was authoritative. Those ways were custom and religion, tradition and authority, rolled into one. Time and again, however, the followers of Muhammad would turn those social and theological norms on their head, clinging instead to the message of a God that their ancestors had deemed silent and uncommunicative. Muhammad himself was fond of comparing some of his followers to stars that light up the spiritual night. If we are to understand why the message entrusted to Muhammad seemed so luminous to them, first we have to grasp why the "night" of their world seemed so stark in comparison.[2] Before taking a look at the message of Muhammad, we need to take a closer look at this world—the world before Muhammad.

BEFORE MOVING TO A close study of Muhammad's world, it is worth pondering the echoes of this episode today. In our own age, many Muslims find themselves yet again living as immigrants and refugees in other lands that are (at least nominally) Christian. Our own land—the United States—is one that has offered these latest refugees a chance to practice their faith in relative freedom. Many Muslims in the United States, likewise, are descendants of the Africans stolen from the other shore of the same continent that Muslims fled to in the time of the Prophet Muhammad. Like those immigrants to Abyssinia, Muslims in this land are also seeking to establish their vision of a righteous community, one in which they can live side by side with their neighbors as full citizens. Also as happened in that Abyssinian society, there are powerful and tyrannical forces today that seek either to turn away this latest wave of émigrés and return them to some other persecuted shore or to take away their freedom to live and practice their faith in freedom. The memory of these episodes is quite real in the United States: many African American Muslims in the 1970s named their organizations and mosques after Bilal, an ex-slave Abyssinian follower of Muhammad who was among those most viciously tortured by the Meccan aristocracy, and whom we meet again in a later chapter. The experiences of Muhammad's followers in Abyssinia still echo today, and we return to these themes in the conclusion to the book.

But for now, let us begin by situating the Muhammadi Revolution in the context of both pre-Islamic Arabia and the biblical tradition that preceded Muhammad.

Pre-Islamic Arabia: Continuity or Rupture?

Our attempt to grasp the nuance of the cultural matrix of pre-Islamic Arabia is hampered by a dearth of sources, as well as by multiple layers of bias in both Muslim and Western scholarship. Arabia both before and after the rise of Islam possessed a rich literary culture, although in the pre-Islamic period this culture was exclusively oral. In other words, it featured a literary though not a written culture. The Qur'an, like the rest of Arabic literatures, was entrusted to the hearts of those who were noted for their ability to memorize. While the pre-Islamic Arabs did produce a wealth of quite gorgeous poetry, that material is preserved only in editions produced by Muslims a few centuries down the road, making it a bit hard to sort out what belongs to the pre-Islamic period and what was projected by later Muslims onto their own past.

One of our richest sources for gaining a better understanding of the world before Muhammad, ironically, is the Qur'an itself. Regardless of whether a person chooses to accept or reject the Qur'an as a direct revelation from the One God, it remains the case that the Qur'an is unmistakably a seventh-century Arabic document. Indeed, it is the only extant, written seventh-century document in Arabic. In examining the tensions between Muhammad and his community as recorded in the Qur'an, we can learn a great deal about the fabric of Muhammad's society.

The first challenge of studying pre-Islamic Arabia is dealing with the tendency of Western scholars to look at Arabia as a cultural wasteland. In western Asia at that time there were two clear super-powers, the Persian Empire and the Byzantines. Compared to these two civilizations, Arabia is often imagined to have been a backwater region incapable of any glory or beauty. This explains why the dominant Western narrative can account for the subsuming of those superpowers by the Islamic civilization that grew out of this region only by attributing the spread of Islam to brute force.

In addition to the Western tendency to view Arabia as a backwater region that was inferior to and cut off from its superior surrounding civilizations, part of our difficulty in penetrating the pre-Islamic milieu is due to the bias of the Muslim sources. Picking up on the polemic of the Qur'an toward the theological-ethical depravity of pre-Islamic Arabia, Muslims generally depicted the time before Islam in the starkest fashion possible in order to form the strongest contrast with the luminosity of the Qur'anic revelation. Early Muslims, for the most part, were not interested in simply passing on the culture of the pre-Islamic period for the sake of posterity.[3] Furthermore, they were inclined to depict the Qur'anic revelation as marking a clean cultural break with what came before. In reality, history does not have such abrupt ruptures and usually features gradual processes of assimilation, contention, engagement, and adaptation, as well as rejection. In other words, rather than taking the phrases "pre-Islamic" and "Islamic" to refer to clearly demarcated eras, it might be preferable to ask how the Muhammadi Revolution came to engage the strong and lingering legacy of Arab culture, which formed the very context of the revelation.

There are many areas in which the Muslims' critiques of pre-Islamic culture would seem to be well deserved—for example, in the areas of polytheism and misogyny. Yet, as it has been said, no race or creed ever has a monopoly on goodness and beauty, and part of our task is to uncover the richness of the milieu in which the Qur'anic revelation appeared. Another aspect of our approach is to identify themes and elements from the pre-Islamic society that continued to shape the ways in which Islamic discourses and practices expressed themselves. In other words, it is both the continuities and the ruptures that will shape our inquiry here.

To understand something about the continuity between pre-Islamic Arabia and its surrounding cultures, it is vital to know something about the networks of trade and the desert-treading camels that were vital to nomadic Arab life.

Desert, Trade, and Camels

Far from being the primitive cultural wasteland it has often been assumed to be, Arabia was not entirely isolated from surrounding civilizational units. Prior to the rise of Islam, Arabia was already connected to its neighbors linguistically, commercially, culturally, religiously, and politically. These connections continued and were greatly amplified after the rise of Islam. One of the best ways in which we can trace these transcultural continuities in Arabia prior to the rise of Islam is by looking at the Nabataeans.

Almost one thousand years before the rise of Islam, Arabian Nabataeans served as an important cultural conduit between the regions of inter-Arabia and the Hellenic Mediterranean. Prefiguring the hybridity and cosmopolitanism that came to be a key characteristic of the Islamic civilization, the Nabataeans combined aspects of the Arabic, Greek, and Aramaic heritages. They were responsible for introducing much of the region's irrigation systems, resulting in a rich agricultural production of grapes and dates. In addition, they were among the main organizers of the trade in myrrh and frankincense. These products, produced from shrubs and trees in present-day Oman, Yemen, and Somalia, were carried through the Arabian desert all the way to Egypt, Rome, and Palestine. Each country had a use for them, usually in religious and political contexts: Egyptians used myrrh and frankincense in embalming, and the Romans used massive quantities in their funerals. The historian Pliny reports that the Roman emperor

Nero burned the equivalent of one year's worth of Arabian incense at a funeral. According to passages in Leviticus and 1 Chronicles, Jews used frankincense in temple ceremonies and sacrifices.[4] Well known to many is the passage in the New Testament (Matthew 2:11) where the (three) Wise Men from the East, traditionally known as the Magi, come to visit the Virgin Mary and the newborn Jesus:

> *And when they were come into the house, they saw the young child with Mary his mother, and fell down, and worshiped him: and when they had opened their treasures, they presented unto him gifts; gold, and frankincense and myrrh.*

As this narrative conveys, the demand for myrrh and frankincense was obviously well documented in the time of Christ. This demand had led over the centuries to a rich and lucrative trade, and the Arabian towns positioned along the caravan routes became important resting places, trading posts, and sites for business ventures. This was particularly the case for Mecca, which, as we shall see, was simultaneously a center of trade and pilgrimage.

The Arabian Peninsula is often referred to as the Jazirat al-'Arab, meaning "the Arab Island." If ships were required to move from and through this "island," the "ships of the desert" were the famed camels of Arabia. Camels were essential for transportation, pilgrimage, military expeditions, and trade across the desert, and they were crucial in enabling Arabia to avoid being an isolated island.

Camels have very tender feet; the sand-covered paths of the desert were actually much easier on them than stone-paved roads. Chariots and wheeled carriages would have proven futile in the sandy deserts of Arabia. Camels proved to be central to the nomadic lifestyle of many Arab tribes. An old joke about the Arabic language is that every word has four layers of meaning: a basic meaning, a secondary meaning opposite to the basic meaning, something related to camels, and a fourth obscure layer of meaning. Exaggerated as this joke might be, it does convey some sense of the centrality of camels to Arab life. The importance of camels in Arabian life would be reflected in the Arabic language. In fact, scholars have estimated that there may be well over one thousand words in Arabic for camel.

The linguistic importance of camels also showed up in that most crucial of Arabic arts, poetry. Arabic poetry was as likely to center on the faithful companion of long desert voyages as it was to praise an earthly beloved who had departed on a camel caravan. Man's best friend in Arabia was not a yellow Lab but a camel. The affection between travelers and their trusted "ships of the desert" was legendary. In this tender verse, an old traveler praises his camel that has grown old with him:

> *Yet rejoices in her bridle, and runs still as if she were*
> *a roseate cloud, rain-emptied, that flies with the south wind,*
> *or a great-uddered she-ass, pregnant of a white-bellied sire worn*
>   *lean*
> *by the stampeding and kicking and biting of bellow stallions.*[5]

Clan and Tribal Loyalties, Poetry, and Honor

The word "Arab," much like the term "Hebrew," is thought to have originated in the notion of being nomadic. In speaking of nomadic cultures, we should not think of aimless wandering through a desert. In fact, given the sparse nature of the Arabian desert, random wandering would be a sure path to a painful death from thirst so severe that the swelling of one's tongue would result in suffocation. Rather, the goal of a nomadic life was to follow the lead of the elder of the family (the *shaykh*) and lead one's herd from one oasis to another. Nothing was more paramount than following the guidance of those who knew the path, understood the promise that awaited them at the next oasis, and lived with the reality of the danger of losing one's way. Equally important was the notion of sticking together to protect the clan from the inevitable raids (*ghazwa*) that were also a ubiquitous feature of Arabian society. Given the urgency of following the lead of the elders and sticking together in the face of an unknown and lurking enemy, it is not surprising that the ethos of Arabian society prior to the rise of Islam was staunchly conservative. What was referred to as the Custom or the Way (*Sunna*) of the Forefathers was an authoritative paradigm to be followed. The Qur'an mocks the Arabs who dogmatically follow the ways of their forefathers, however, because guidance to the contrary has come to them from God:

> *What! Have We given them a scripture prior to this,*
> *to which they are holding fast?*
> *No! They say: "We found our fathers following a certain religion,*
> *and we will guide ourselves by their footsteps." (Qur'an 43:21–22)*

In the Qur'anic worldview, the blind and unquestioning following of "the ways of our forefathers" is a folly, not a sign of guidance. In the next chapters, we shall see how Muslims would come to replace the emulation of the ways of their forefathers with the emulation of Muhammad's *Sunna*, which was described as "a lovely example" to be followed.

There were other features of pre-Islamic society beyond the notion of being custom-bound to the ways of the ancestors: the importance of loyalty to one's clan, and ultimately one's tribe, which formed the basis of social identification; the notion of honor; and the emphasis on refined language. These features were intertwined, naturally, so that honor was not merely personal but extended to one's clan. Poetry, likewise, was not merely a means of expressing one's private sentiments but was often tied to the praise of one's tribe—or mocking another tribe's sense of honor. We will deal with these key facets of pre-Islamic society in sequence, at each turn exploring how they came to be abandoned, engaged, maintained, or transformed through the Muhammadi Revolution.

Of all these features of pre-Islamic society, none was more important than its tribal nature. Society was arranged in a series of escalating social units, moving up from the family to the clan, to the tribe. The family typically consisted of the individuals inside one tent. A number of families together would form a clan and a series of clans together would form a tribe. Common descent from a shared ancestor was significant in these bonds, though alliances could also bring clans together.

The greatest determinant of one's actions was group loyalty, what some have termed "group feeling" (*'asabiyya*). The solidarity that existed among the members of a clan, and to some extent in the larger configuration of a tribe, was the key component of pre-Islamic ethics. The poetry of one Durayd, the son of al-Simmah, a member of the Ghaziyya tribe, expressed this ultimate commitment clearly:

> *I am of Ghaziyya.*
> *If she be in error, then I will err.*
> *And if the Ghaziyya be guided right, I go right with her.*[6]

The phrase "I am of Ghaziyya" is a good indication of how individuals marked their identity as part of a larger nexus. The way in which we think of our names reflects a particular model of kinship. We tend to forget that the nuclear family structure to which we are accustomed in the modern West is not universal, nor has it been historically the pattern followed by most of the world. Likewise, the notion of having a first name and a last name is a modern invention; in pre-Islamic society a person's name tended to read as follows: "Such-and-Such, the son of So-and-So, the son of . . . from the clan of . . . from the tribe of. . . ." To his companions, Muhammad himself would have been known as "Muhammad, the son of 'Abd Allah, the son of 'Abd al-Muttalib, from the Banu Hashim clan of the Quraysh tribe."

Identity was conceived of in collective terms, with the most crucial of tensions between the tribal and clan levels. For example, most of the members of Muhammad's clan (Banu Hashim) supported him, even if they did not abandon the polytheistic ways of their forefathers, whereas the staunchest opposition to Muhammad came from others in the Quraysh tribe. In other words, it should not be assumed that tribal affiliation meant absolute solidarity.

·Many facets of life were organized around the clan and tribal identity. Perhaps nowhere was this more important than in notions of honor and shame: acts were not deemed good or evil based on their innate goodness but rather on whether they were seen as bringing honor or ill repute to one's tribe. Crime was also punished in a collective fashion, and blood-revenge often was taken against members of one's own tribe. The code of blood-retaliation—which is well known of course in the biblical context—was thus also a feature of pre-Islamic Arab society.[7]

As much as later Muslims wanted to portray the pre-Islamic period simply as the canvas upon which Islam appeared, many of the traits of the pre-Islamic period lingered into the Islamic era and in fact would greatly inform the context of Islamic practices. This is a common pattern of religious traditions: they do not replace existing norms so much as adapt and modify them, transforming both the old and the new in the process. It would be easy enough to isolate aspects of the pre-Islamic culture that did not disappear and that continued into Islamic life in one permutation or another.

For instance, as we have seen, the Arabs prior to the rise of Islam took a great deal of interest in the purity of their lineage, as it was the basis for clan identity. The very names of clans were identified as "children of" the eponymous ancestor. The nobility of lineage (*nasab*), therefore, was an important feature of this society. The obsession with genealogy did not disappear altogether in the later formulations of Sunni or Shi'a Islam. The Shi'a came to associate inheritance of mystical knowledge from the Prophet with the biological family of the Prophet, albeit through his daughter. Sunnis, on the other hand, retained notions of genealogy and nobility—to the point that in some legal understandings a suitable marriage was only one in which members from families of comparable "nobility" were wed. Many of the Islamic dynasties would lay their claim to being descendants of the

Quraysh tribe, even if members of that same tribe had persecuted Muhammad during his lifetime. Such notions, with all of the inconsistencies that they entail, are of course not unique to Islam, but it is intriguing to note that they essentially represent a socially conservative reaction to the Muhammadi Revolution. One could posit that Muhammad's mission was to construct an egalitarian society in which faith and piety would be the only marker of social mobility, and that his own society refused to fully internalize that radical—yet noble— norm.

Another example of the reconfiguration rather than disappearance of a pre-Islamic virtue in the later context of Islam is the notion of honor. Honor was a crucial ethic in pre-Islamic society, whether manifested on the battlefield, in one's noble ancestry, or through lavish displays of generosity—particularly to strangers who would be impressed by the nobility of one's tribe and carry the news back to their own tribe. In other words, in the pre-Islamic culture nobility and displays of generosity were closely linked. Even today many who travel to the parts of the world where Muslims predominate come back with tales of exquisite generosity and hospitality among people whose economic standard of living surely does not match that of their honored visitors.

Whereas few are likely to complain about the legendary hospitality of Muslims, the notion of honor when linked with women is undoubtedly more problematic. In pre-Islamic societies, part of a man's honor was based on his ability to show manliness (*muruwwa*), a quality that in our age we often dismiss as mere machismo; in the Arab context, however, a man's honor is also embodied in displays of generosity, courage, chivalry, and self-sacrifice. In exchange, the male members of the tribe expected purity of lineage by being able to restrict the free movement of women, particularly their association with strange men, who, it was often feared, might render the honorable male a cuckold. Indeed, some samples of pre-Islamic poetry boast about the poet's ability to roam freely and have relations with women of other tribes:

Many's the fair veiled lady, whose tent few would think of seeking,
I've enjoyed sporting with, and not in a hurry either,
Slipping past packs of watchmen to reach her, with a whole tribe
Hankering after my blood, eager every man-jack to slay me . . .
"God's oath, man, you won't get away with this!
The folly's not left you yet; I see you're as feckless as ever."
Out I brought her, and as she stepped she trailed behind us
To cover our footprints the skirts of an embroidered gown.[8]

It is worth exploring how much of this anxiety about women's dalliance, and the resultant possibility that the purity of one's lineage could not be ascertained, might be responsible for some later rulings of Islamic law that regulated and restricted women's free movement in public arenas.

Yet to say that themes and elements of pre-Islamic society lingered and were absorbed into Islamic society is not to say that they did not undergo important transformations and transmutations. The highly ethical notion of honor itself underwent a crucial shift in the teachings of the Prophet. One of the important ways in which the ethics of honor were internalized in what we are calling the Muhammadi Revolution was in the transformation of honor from an action of outward displays of generosity and courage into a quality of the heart, where honor keeps one mindful and aware of God. This piety, which one Qur'an translator (Muhammad Asad) has termed "God-Consciousness," is the quality of *taqwa*—one of the key Qur'anic ethical concepts. The Qur'anic worldview disassociated honor and nobility from the tribal context and portrayed all of humanity as members of one super-tribe, the Children of Adam. This collective sense of identity, that of *Bani Adam*, was seen as supplanting the pride that the various Arab tribes associated with their own lineage. In the Prophet's farewell speech, he warned the Arabs:

O people, indeed God has eradicated from your minds the sense of honor and inflated pride in ancestry, which are both peculiar to the

people of Jahiliyya. You have all sprung from the common stock of
Adam, and Adam sprang from dust.[9]

This very point was also made in the Qur'an, where, in one of the
more frequently recited verses (Qur'an 49:13), we hear:

O humankind!
We created you from a single pair of one male and one female,
and made you into nations and tribes
that you may come to intimately know each other,
(not that you would despise each other).
Indeed the most honorable (akramakum) *of you*
in the sight of God
is the one who is the most God-conscious.

Here the word translated as "most honorable" is *akramakum*, that
is, "the one of you with the most *karam*." Yet in this translation the
most honorable is neither the one who is most generous nor the one
who is most lavish in bestowing gifts upon strangers and friends alike,
but the one who is simply *atqa-kum*—the most conscious and mindful of God. Honor is tied not to material generosity but rather to
remaining mindful of God in one's own heart. The quality of generosity did not disappear entirely from the Qur'anic worldview; the
most generous one is no longer the Arab hero, however, but God.
God is simply described as *al-Karim*, the Generous One who bestows
without measure. Indeed, many of the Loveliest Divine Names (*Asma*
al-Husna) in the Qur'an have to do with this divine quality of generosity. So here God, rather than particular earthly patrons, is identified
as the source of all grace and generosity.

In addition to tribal and clan affiliation and the ethics of honor,
one of the important features of Arab society was—and remains—the
emphasis on language. In fact, the most crucial forms of the Islamic
arts—Qur'an recitation, calligraphy, and poetry—deal directly with
language. After all, did God not choose the medium of language for

revealing Himself to humanity? It is no surprise that the supreme miracle of Muhammad was the Qur'an, a text that was held to be inimitable in both substance and style. Arabs had a rich tradition of poetry, and poets occupied a high social rank. The Bedouin tribes of Arabia, for example, held an annual poetry competition outside of Mecca. The poems deemed the best were woven with gold embroidery on Egyptian cloth and hung from the Ka'ba. Scholars came to think of these poems as the collection of "Hung Odes," and recently they have been translated into exquisite English at the hands of Michael Sells. These poems reveal some of the same concerns about honor and infidelity that we have examined:

> Is what you came to know,
> given in trust,
> Kept secret? Is her bond to you,
> broken, now that she is far?[10]

Some of the poems deal with the archetypal Bedouin experience of visiting the abandoned campsite of a beloved whose trace still—though barely—lingers:

> The tent marks in Minan are worn away,
> Where she encamped
> And where she alighted
> Ghawl and Rijam now left to the wild,
> And the torrent beds of Rayyan
> naked tracings
> worn thin, like inscriptions,
> carved in flattened stones.
> Dung-stained ground
> that tells the years passed
> since human presence, months of peace
> gone by, months of war.[11]

These were words of power. Arabs recognized that there was indeed something extraordinary about poetry and offered that the source of poetry was a creature called *Jinn* who took possession of the poet, rendering him jinn-ed, or, in Arabic, *Majnun*. Poets also fulfilled an important tribal role, often extolling the virtues of a tribe's reputation, and their services could even be called upon before a battle to essentially emasculate the enemy by mocking the enemy's lineage or honor. The word *Jinn* entered the English language through the more commonly known spelling *Genie*, known to many through the Aladdin story and the Genie in the Lamp. Historically, there were also connections between the Arabs' notion of *jinn* and the Roman idea of a "genius"—the spirit of ancestors that each man possessed and that provided him with inspiration.

Not only does the Qur'an also deal with inspiration, but it confidently proclaims itself the revelation of the God of Abraham, God of Moses, and God of Jesus. The word *Qur'an* literally means "recitation," and anyone who hears it cannot help but notice—and admire—its poetic quality. Many of its passages, especially the short ones that were revealed early in Muhammad's mission in Mecca, are hauntingly beautiful. Many of these passages build up a string of rhyming lines, like a wave that rises to higher and higher crescendos of drama before crashing with full force to awaken the dormant soul of humanity, as in the "Chapter of the Tearing" (Qur'an 82:1–6):

> *Idha 's-samau n'fatarat (When the sky is torn)*
> *Wa idha 'l-kawakibu n'tatharat (When the stars are scattered)*
> *Wa idha 'l-biharu fujjirat (When the seas boil over)*
> *Wa idha 'l-quburu bu'thirat (When the tombs burst open)*
> *'Alimat nafsun ma qaddamat wa'akhkharat (Then a person will know*
> *what she has given and what she has held back)*
> *Ya ayyhu 'l-insanu ma gharraka birabbika 'l-karim (O humankind,*
> *what has deluded you from your generous Lord).[12]*

The "Chapter of the Tearing" is one of the apocalyptic passages in the Qur'an, marking the End of Days when the life of this world (*dunya*) as we know it shall come to an end and the natural order of things will be overturned. The passage is marked by a series of revolutions, unveilings, openings, and scatterings, and each word rhymes and adds to the rhyming pattern in Arabic: the sky is torn (*fatarat*), the stars are scattered (*tatharat*), the seas boil over (*fujjirat*), and the tombs burst open (*bu'thirat*). What takes place in the natural realm will be mirrored inside the hearts of humanity, where another revolution will take place, overturning the state of ignorant bliss in which some are living and revealing what each soul has given and what each has held back (*akhkharat*). In each case, the hard consonants of *ra-ta* are repeated: fatarat, tatharat, fujjirat, bu'thirat, akhkharat. Sound and meaning go hand in hand in building up an expectation of something that is coming—with each passing note the drama escalates toward a zenith. Particularly when it is recited, those in the audience hold their breath in anticipation of when the rhyme will be broken and the message delivered. At long last, the dramatic change of rhythm arrives:

O humankind, what has deluded you from your generous Lord.

The rhythm pattern is broken here, the line ending instead in *birabbika 'l-karim* (your generous Lord). The new rhyme also signals the beginning of a new mode of consciousness, when nothing is veiled from God and nothing is held back from our own awareness. Truth and sin, ugliness and beauty will all be exposed in this new life, new world, new consciousness. The ending lines refer to "your generous Lord," the *karim*, a term that, as we have seen, refers no longer to an Arab hero but to God. This is one struggle in which no Arab hero can be called upon, only God. No acts of generosity can help one—only being mindful and aware of God.

In spite of this nuance of rhyme and poetry, the Qur'an deliberately distinguishes itself as something other than *mere* poetry, and

Muhammad is not presented as a poet. Assuming the majestic divine voice "We," God states in Qur'an 36:69:

We have not taught him [the Prophet] poetry,
nor is it appropriate for him:
this is nothing less than a Remembrance of God,
and a clear recitation.

In fact, the Qur'anic text had to defend Muhammad against being a poet, because it was a common accusation of pre-Islamic Arabs who were seeking to dismiss the significance of Muhammad's revelation:

And they say: "What!
Shall we abandon our gods
to follow a mad poet?" (Qur'an 47:36)

Furthermore, pre-Islamic society featured soothsayers (*kahin*) who foretold the future and spoke in rhyming prose called *saj'*—the same style of many of the Qur'anic passages. And does the Qur'an not foretell a future, albeit the Hereafter? Yet here again, the Qur'an emphatically distinguishes the prophecy of Muhammad from the task of soothsayers:

Then recall . . .
By the grace of thy Lord,
you are not a soothsayer (kahin),
nor are you a madman (majnun). *(Qur'an 52:29)*

and:

This is the word of an honored messenger.
It is not the word of a poet. (Qur'an 69:40–43)

In spite of superficial similarities with both poetry and soothsaying, however, the language of the Qur'an differs in substantial ways from both of them. Unlike poetry, the revelation of the Qur'an does not seek to glorify one tribe over another, and in fact it undermines the social privilege of Muhammad's own tribe, the Quraysh. The Qur'an presents itself as the very word, not just of the God of the Quraysh, or exclusively the God of Arabia, or even the God of the world, but the One God of all the different worlds, all the various universes (*rabb al-'alamin*). In addition, the Qur'an presents itself as a direct revelation from the universal God of the whole cosmos, something no poet had claimed before. The revelation given to Muhammad did not fulfill the functions of poetry as understood by Arabs. Instead, it called on Muhammad to act prophetically: to announce and to warn, to remind humanity of what they had been, and to awaken a spiritually dormant people. He was to serve as an echo of Abraham, and the civilization that grew up around him and the message he delivered to that people would serve as his own echo.

With this background, we are now prepared to undertake a closer study of the Qur'anic text's critique of the world of Muhammad, the society of Muhammad, and the "ways of the forefathers."

Truth vs. Ignorance: The Qur'anic Polemic Against Jahiliyya

The term most commonly given in Muslim sources for the pre-Islamic era is the *Jahiliyya*, literally meaning ignorance. A secondary meaning of the term is being rabid, like a mad dog.[13] This ignorance was taken in a double sense to imply ignorance both of God and of one's own true self. In that sense, the Qur'anic revelation is taken to be the opposite of ignorance. It is precisely meant to be a means of knowledge of God and knowledge of one's true self.

In the Qur'an, the Jahiliyya era is even contrasted with Truth as such, a contrast that is all the more stark when it is recalled how frequently Muslims came to represent God as the Truth (*Haqq*). To put it differently, the Jahiliyya is conceived of not as a time period but rather as a mode of consciousness, a state of being. It represents an anxiety in the heart due to a lack of the tranquillity that can only come from faith in God. The group persecuting Muslims are described this way:

> *Another band was stirred to anxiety by their own feelings,*
> *moved by wrong suspicions of God*
> *—suspicions due to Ignorance. (Qur'an 3:154)*

The contrast here is between Truth (*Haqq*) and ignorance (*Jahiliyya*), or to put it differently, knowledge of God arrived at through God's revelation and genuine spiritual inquiry versus the fanciful imagination that leads one to ignorance. Furthermore, in this Islamic view, knowledge of God is ultimately connected to knowledge of one's true self in Islam. You cannot know yourself without knowing God. You cannot know God without knowing yourself. This idea is usually connected to one of the Prophet's sayings: *Man 'arafa nafsahu, faqad 'arafa rabbahu.* (To know one's own self is to know one's Lord.)

The word used in this saying for knowing, *'arafa*, refers not just to discursive knowledge but to intimate knowledge. In another verbal form, *'irfan*, it refers to gnosis, the mystical form of knowledge that is a priori, immediate, unmediated. The mystics, for example, were often referred to as *'arif* (gnostic). In other words, according to this statement of Muhammad, a true faithful is one who knows God immediately, directly, and intimately. The Jahil, in contrast, would be the very antithesis of the true faithful: one who can speak only through conjecture and with no direct knowledge of or intimacy with God.

One of the characteristic features of the Qur'an is how it associates one's view of God with the state of one's heart: theology reflects on morality, and vice versa. One Qur'anic narrative brings out this point in the starkest way possible. In this verse of the Qur'an (48:26), the quality of jahiliyya is contrasted with that of peace and tranquillity:

Whereas they who are bent on denying the truth
harbored a stubborn disdain in their hearts
—the stubborn disdain [born] of ignorance (jahiliyya),
God bestowed from on high His inner peace (Sakina)
upon His messenger and the faithful,
and bound them to the spirit of God-consciousness.[14]

Here the disdain, turmoil, and heart-agony of the Jahiliyya, those who cover up the reality of God, is contrasted with the calm and peaceful serenity that comes with faith in God. This inner peace, which is identified as God's own peace, is called the *Sakina* and is easily recognizable to Jews and Christians as the same *Shekinah* that indicates the presence or indwelling of God. In other words, the difference between Jahiliyya and Islam is not merely theological but rooted in the state of the innermost chamber of one's heart.

This leads us to one of the more important ideas about the very word "Islam." It is true that the primary etymological meaning of "Islam" is wholehearted, willing, and engaged submission to God.[15] Yet a secondary meaning of the word "Islam," coming from the root S-L-M in Arabic, is also linked to the *salāma* of the heart, the quality of well-being, and wholeness. This is the move from having a heart fractured by the pursuit of this-or-that internal idol to arriving at a state of wholeness through devotion to the One God. Wholeness of the heart, spiritual integration, is becoming one internally through being devoted to the One. It is for this reason that so many of the passages in the Qur'an speak about the need to have a whole heart: Abraham is described, for instance, as coming to his Lord with a whole heart (*qalb*[in] *salim*[in]) (Qur'an 37:84). Arabic, like Hebrew, functions in a system where words that share the same three consonants have essential meanings in common. The word for a "whole heart" in the Qur'anic verse just cited (*salim*) comes from the same Arabic root as the words for well-being and wholeness (*salāma*) and even the word "Islam" itself. A pure heart is one that will literally lead one all the way to God, not just in this world but in the world to come. As the Qur'an states, a day will come when no benefit will be derived from wealth, nor from the male offspring that the pre-Islamic Arabs so treasured, but only from a whole heart (Qur'an 26:88–89).

As with so many of the other key concepts, the very narrative of the Qur'an reflects this emphasis on the connection between one's heart and faith in God. After the famed opening chapter of the Qur'an (the *Fatiha*), the second chapter of the Qur'an, the longest chapter in the whole book, starts out by talking about hearts—diseased hearts. Many who are reading through the Qur'an for the first time are put off by this discussion of diseased, troubled, and hypocritical hearts in the beginning pages of the second chapter. These pages describe the hearts of the people who, according to the Qur'an, claim that they have faith in God and the Last Day but in reality have not had their hearts illuminated by faith. There is a disease in their hearts, and they think they are cheating God—whereas in reality they are only cheating their own souls. These are stern and in some ways frightening words, yet the Qur'an has to start there because that is the starting place for most of humanity. We can start a journey only from where we are. We have to know that we are broken before we can be healed. Yet again, we are reminded of the words of the Prophet: "Speak to people at the level of their understanding." If humanity were not broken and forgetful, we would have less need of this dramatic divine intervention. It is after this reminder of the reality of hypocrisy and the disease of the heart that the Qur'anic narrative moves to the cycles of prophecy, beginning with Adam and moving through the familiar biblical prophets and ending with Prophet Muhammad.

But first, we turn to a discussion of the previous prophetic traditions, as well as polytheism, in Arabia prior to the rise of the Muhammadi Revolution.

Polytheism in Pre-Islamic Arabia

At the time of Muhammad's birth around 570 CE, the majority of Arabs were polytheists. In addition to their aversion to giving up multiple deities with tangible idols in favor of one albeit invisible deity, other aspects of their faith made them hostile to Muhammad's message. The pre-Islamic Arabs viewed humanity as a very mortal creature, without an abiding spirit. Their poetry depicted this in graphic terms: "What are we, if not a body and a soul? The body, we go down with it under the earth. While the soul passes away like a gust of wind."[16] In addition, pre-Islamic Arabs rejected the notion of a hereafter. They held that it is a personified view of time that catches up with us at the end of our days: "They say: there is nothing but this present life of ours; we die and we live, and it is only time that destroys us" (Qur'an 45:24). In one of the rare instances when God speaks in the first-person voice with Muhammad, the Divine tells humanity to not curse time, because "I am Time." In other words, what catches up with us at the end of our days is nothing less than God's plan—not an impersonal notion of time.

If there is no hereafter, and no cosmic accountability for one's deeds, what prevents society from collapsing into full-blown chaos? It would be a great injustice to assume that pre-Islamic society was simply bereft of any code of ethics. As we have seen, codes of honor, nobility, tribal loyalty, and generosity were well known. Instead, what pre-Islamic Arabs found baffling was the Qur'anic notion of cosmic and individual accountability before a singular God. The Qur'anic revelation insisted that each and every deed—famously, even one as small as a mustard seed—will be evaluated in heavenly scales of justice, with no good being unrewarded and no bad action going unnoticed. To put it differently, the Qur'an summoned Arabs to change not only their notion of theology (their view of God or gods) and their ethics (their ideas about right and wrong), but also the structure of their society. This summons became part of the consistent Qur'anic call, invitation, and polemic against Arab society: how one lives in the midst of humanity is related to how one sees God, and vice versa. Theology and humanity are forever linked.

One of the areas in which the Qur'an critiqued early Arab society is gender norms. We cannot be certain about the exact nature of gender relations in pre-Islamic and early Islamic society. Those who see the rise of Islam as elevating women's status in society depict pre-Islamic society as a bastion of misogyny, whereas those who see Islam as further restricting women's rights have sought to identify an elevated status for women prior to the rise of Islam. What is not debated is that prior to the revelation of the Qur'an, Arabs practiced female infanticide. The practice was as straightforward as it was hideous: if a family feared poverty and did not have any sons, they would bury a newborn daughter and try again for a son, because it was deemed that sons would bring a tribe honor and glory. The Qur'an confronts the pre-Islamic Arabs and this vile practice in the strongest terms possible:

When the news is brought to one of them of the birth of a female
  child,
his face darkens, and he is filled with inward grief!
With shame does he hide himself from his people,
because of the bad news he has had!
Shall he retain the child in contempt, or bury her in the dust?
Ah! What an evil choice they decide on. (Qur'an 16:58–59)

The vulgarity of this practice, based on a preference for a male child over a female child, and the practice of violence against defenseless newborns are part of the Qur'an's strong moral and ethical critique of pre-Islamic society. Yet in a way that is typically Qur'anic, the ethical and the theological overlap yet again. In other words, the Qur'an recognizes that how we deal with our fellow human beings reveals a great deal about how we see (or hide ourselves from) the Divine, and vice versa. What seems like a critique of social practices slides into a theological critique:

They show ingratitude for the favors We have bestowed upon them.
Then enjoy the brief time, for soon you shall know.
And they even assign to things they do not know . . .
By God you shall certainly be called to account
for your false inventions.
And they assign daughters to God!
Glory be to God.
And for themselves they desire sons! (Qur'an 16:55–57)

Here the narrative shifts into theological mode in a subtle way, blasting the pre-Islamic Arabs' conception that Allah had three daughters: Lat, Uzza, and Manat. Lat was the goddess in whose grounds in Ta'if (a city close to Mecca) no living creature could be harmed. Uzza was identified with the morning star Venus. Manat was seen as the goddess of destiny.[17] The Qur'anic language rejects any notion of God (Arabic: Allah) having sons or daughters. Complicating the discussion is the fact that the term "children of God" is used in a biblical context to denote people close to God (even Adam is described as a son of God in Luke 3:38), but in a pre-Islamic Arab context the notion of daughters of God was taken more literally. Perhaps recognizing that there is no feasible way of upholding a Christian language of a divine son while rejecting a pagan argument of divine daughters, the Qur'an begins by rejecting the language of both of these alternatives. In passages like the famous chapter of *Ikhlas* (sincerity) or *Tawhid* (Oneness), it is affirmed that:

Say, God is One.
God is Absolute.
He is unbegotten, unbegetting.
And there is none like Him. (Qur'an 112:1–4)

Let us return to the passage dealing with female infanticide and the misogyny of pre-Islamic Arabs. There the Arabs are critiqued not only for their polytheism but also for attributing to God what they loathe for themselves: daughters. In other words, in a typical Qur'anic stance, a theological critique (polytheism) and a social critique (misogyny) are linked together. How we deal with our fellow human beings—in this case, our daughters—is yet again connected to how we engage God, and vice versa.

The Pre-Islamic View of God

Some elements of the pre-Islamic Arab religious worldview can be gleaned from the Qur'an. They were certainly not atheists or agnostics. If anything, they believed in a well-populated spiritual cosmos. All premodern societies had faith in some conception of one or more deities, souls, or forces that transcended the visible level. For the Arabs prior to the rise of Islam, their objection was not that God did not exist, but rather that there were a multiplicity of gods. In fact, the pre-Islamic Arabs did have a view of One God, who in Arabic was called Allah (*Al-ilah*, the God). In their conception, however, Allah was not the only God, merely the Supreme God among them. This conception was similar to that of many tribal societies that had a conception of a High God or Sky God who transcended the lower deities. Likewise, the Arabs held that between Allah and our level of existence stood a whole host of lower deities who acted as intermediaries. Quite often these deities were connected to particular tribes, so that each tribe had its own representation of deity. The Ka'ba temple, established by Abraham for the One God, eventually came to be surrounded by some 360 idols—more or less one for every day of the year. The various tribes would bring their icons and idols to the Ka'ba during the pilgrimage season, creating a pantheon of tribal deities. The annual rite of pilgrimage brought many pilgrims to Mecca, and during their visits they engaged in trade as well as worship. Pilgrimage and business were perfectly intertwined for Mecca. The religion of Mecca was their business.

History cannot avoid theology, yet it cannot be reduced to theology either. In contrast to the monotheism that Muhammad proclaimed, the Arabs fundamentally did not wish to give up their conception of multiple deities. They were equally aware, however, that abandoning Mecca as a pilgrimage center for the multiple tribal deities would result in a tremendous loss in their business affairs as well. The rich and powerful elite of Mecca who had achieved their wealth through trade were loath to give up this economic privilege. In addition, they were particularly hesitant to spend any of their wealth to help the socially disadvantaged in the systematic way called for by the social justice emphasis of Muhammad's message. Part of the Qur'anic polemic against those who hoarded and "devoured wealth" that did not benefit them has to be understood in this light.

And yet, as we have said, theology cannot be avoided. The Qur'an's narrative shifts from the social and ethical to the theological with ease and grace, and it is worth exploring how it covers what the pre-Islamic Arabs already believed about Allah in order to challenge them to abandon their ways. The Qur'an tells us that these Arabs had very specific understandings of God[18]:

1. Allah was the Creator of the World.
   In the words of the Qur'an:

   If you ask them "who has created the heavens and the earth, and has imposed law and order upon the sun and the moon?" they will surely answer, "Allah!" (Qur'an 29:61)

   As is the case with many other traditions with a conception of a Supreme (or Sky) God, pre-Islamic Arabs also held that Allah created the world. The question was whether God would remain involved with creation in an intimate way, as the Qur'an asserts, or whether the Divine would step back into oblivion after creation.

2. Allah was the Giver of rain, the Giver of all life to living things on earth:

If you ask them
"Who sends down rain from the sky
and revives the Earth
after it has been dead?"
They will surely answer,
"Allah!" (Qur'an 29:63)

All the Arabian regions, with the exception of the regions next to the coast, were extremely arid. Life depended on the meager rain and the ability to reach an oasis built around a well. As such, it makes sense that the descent of rain was seen as a tangible symbol of divine mercy. No wonder that in the Qur'an, as in the Bible, part of the description of Paradise always includes a place where "rivers flow" (Qur'an 2:25 and 47:15).

3. Allah was the One who presided over the most solemn oaths.

As in biblical cultures, to swear by God's name was a serious affair, and the Qur'an recognized that the pre-Islamic Arabs "swore by Allah their most earnest oath." (Qur'an 35:40–42 and 16:40–48). Many of these oaths were taken during commercial interactions, and business ventures surely did not disappear with the arrival of Islam and its injunctions against types of oaths. Instead, documenting transactions with multiple eyewitnesses and signing written contracts replaced taking oaths in God's name.

4. Allah was an object of what might be termed "momentary" or "temporary" monotheism.

Intriguingly, when pre-Islamic Arabs found themselves in moments of great crisis and turmoil, they turned not to any of the lower deities but directly to Allah:

And when waves enshroud them
like dark clouds,
they cry unto Allah
making their faith pure for Him. (Qur'an 31:31–32)

But alas, this cry of the heart in a moment of turmoil did not result in a change in their worldview: "But when God brings them safe to land, behold! They begin to ascribe partners (yet again)" (Qur'an 31:65). In other words, their appeal to God was a momentary one, not a sign of transformation in the deepest part of their hearts. Yet the Qur'an used even this recognition to make its plea to the pre-Islamic Arabs: somewhere inside they knew they were to be calling upon God. If in moments of great crisis they could recall their connection to God (as in the old saying "there are no atheists in school on exam days"), why could they not live every breath in light of that recognition?

5. Allah was the Lord of the Ka'ba.

The Arabs already had a memory that the Ka'ba had been built by Abraham when he brought his son Ishmael to the desert. In the Qur'an, God is called "the Lord of this house" (Qur'an 106:1–3). Yet, as we have seen, the Ka'ba had been converted into a house of many idols.

What is the collective impression of this appeal to pre-Islamic Arabs? Though they did have a conception of Allah as the Supreme God and the Creator God, it is one thing to say that Allah is supreme among all the deities and quite another to say that Allah is the only deity. It is famously true that the most frequently used word in the

Qur'an is "Allah." The second most common word deals with a clus-
ter concerned with knowing, reasoning, intellect, pondering, reflecting, meditating upon, and thinking. In short, part of the Qur'anic
plea in the pre-Islamic Arabian milieu was to invite them to ponder
the truth that they already attested to in the deepest parts of their
hearts. In fact, the word that is often translated as "infidel" or "unbe-
liever" (*kafir*) in the context of the Qur'an actually means "one who
covers up." The implication, from a Qur'anic point of view, is that
all of humanity—including pre-Islamic Arabs—has already attested
to God's lordship and that we bear the imprint of that knowledge
deep in our hearts. That recognition has been merely covered up
and buried by the ideas about God that we have arrived at through
our own misinterpretations and projections. Part of the task of the
Qur'an, in other words, is not to teach humanity anything new but
rather to remove the dross on our hearts so that the illuminated jewel
that each and every human being contains can shine again.

This explains part of the ongoing Qur'anic assertion that there
is nothing new here, at least nothing new in light of what has been
already revealed to all the previous prophets. Many narratives in the
Qur'an engage polytheistic readers to move them along increasingly
higher levels of monotheistic devotions, returning them, as it were, to
the hidden but still present jewel of divine recognition within them.
The truth of one's being, what the Islamic tradition calls the *fitra*,
is always there; it can be forgotten about, but never destroyed. The
destination is the home. We aim to return to where we come from.
As the Qur'an states:

We come from God, and we are always returning to God.

Jews and Christians in Pre-Islamic Arabia

Muhammad would have to deal with the reality of a multireligious,
multiethnic audience. While much of the polemic of the Qur'an is

against the pre-Islamic Arab polytheists, Arabia was home to a scattered group of Christians and Jews who also formed part of the religious matrix of this complex society. As we shall see, the presence of Jews and Christians had a crucial role to play in raising the level of familiarity with biblical narratives in Arabia.

The Christian Middle East at this time was a house divided against itself, comprising Greek Orthodox, Egyptian and Abyssinian Monophysites, Persian Nestorians, and others. Christendom in this era was torn asunder by theological-political tensions that were often articulated in competing views of the nature of Christ—whether he had one nature that was simultaneously divine and human (the Monophysite doctrine), or whether he had a separate human and a separate divine nature (the Nestorian position). Although the Nestorian view was somewhat similar to what became the eventual mainstream Christian doctrine, the Nestorians did not accept the notion of a "hypostatic union" of the divine and the human in Christ. As tedious and hairsplitting as some of these debates may seem to us today, they were real back in the seventh century and created a bitterly divided Christendom. The Nestorian position was rejected by the First Council of Ephesus in 431 CE, and the Monophysite view met the same fate in the Council of Chalcedon in 451 CE.

To adopt one particular point of view in these theological divides also meant lining up on one side of a linguistic, political, and religious divide. Orthodox Christians, who were in a position of theological and political privilege, bitterly persecuted their coreligionists who subscribed to alternative theological views. These divisions among the Christian sects and the persecution of minority opinions led many Christians in the Middle East and North Africa to welcome both the call of Islam and the expansion of the Arab armies. It is important to note that Islam spread initially in many of the regions, such as Syria, Levant, and Persia, that were dominated by these persecuted Christian minorities. The eventual Arab conquest that established an Islamic empire over the present-day Middle East and North Africa was certainly a combination of military conquest and tribal migrations, and that element of the conquest should not be minimized. But neither can we overlook the fact that many Christian communities that had been persecuted at the hands of other Christians welcomed the more favorable conditions offered to them by their Muslim conquerors, who seemed as interested in establishing an empire and taxing the population as they were in outright conversion. In fact, in many areas it took about three hundred years for even half of the population to convert to Islam. In other words, the myth of forced conversion to Islam through the sword is largely that: a myth. It is more accurate to state that historically the Arab Empire was established through the sword, but the conversion of people to Islam was a gradual, centuries-long process.[19]

The Arab Christian tribes closer to the Byzantine Empire, such as the Ghassan tribe, were culturally under that zone of influence and subscribed to a Monophysite view of Christ. Al-Hira, the Persian vassal-state, followed the competing view of the Nestorians. In other words, Christianity was already known and practiced in Arabia among many tribes. More important for the Islamic narrative was the long-established Christian church in Abyssinia (modern Ethiopia), led by the Negus. As we saw in the opening pages of this chapter, it was the protection of the Christian king in Abyssinia that led to the survival of the nascent Muslim community. Another connection to Abyssinia was through the former black slave Bilal, who became one of Muhammad's closest companions and earned the distinction of serving as the first muezzin (*Mu'adh dhin*), the person who gives out the call to prayer. Bilal suffered from a lisp, yet Muhammad loved his sweet and melodious voice and often asked him to "refresh us, O Bilal," through the call to prayer.

Muslims cherish the memory of a handful of Christian individuals in Mecca. Unlike Jews, whose identity was often tribal, Christians in Hejaz (the region of Arabia comprising both Mecca and Medina) are usually depicted in the sources as isolated individuals. Two of them are held to have played significant roles in the life of Muhammad. One of them was a Syrian monk named Bahira. When Muhammad was a young boy, his uncle, Abu Talib, took him on a caravan journey to Syria. There the traveling caravan came across the Christian hermit, whose study of ancient manuscripts had led him to expect a new prophet sent by God to the Arabs. When he saw the caravan approach, he felt the presence of an extraordinary soul among the travelers and invited them to a meal. The travelers left Muhammad, a mere boy of twelve, behind to tend to the luggage. Bahira, not sensing among the adults anyone who matched the description he had read, asked for Muhammad to be brought to him. There, the pious monk engaged the young boy, who was not yet a prophet, or the Prophet, in conversation about his habits. He even asked to examine the boy's face and body, and there—as the tradition says, between his shoulder blades—Bahira found the sign of the Seal of the Prophets that he had learned about in his Christian texts. He entrusted Muhammad to his uncle and asked Abu Talib to look after the young boy and protect him from his enemies.[20]

Why do the Muslim sources include such narratives? A simple answer might be because they happened, and indeed, there is no reason to suspect that they did not. As Muslim sources traditionally add, *Allah^u a'lam* (God knows best). Equally important is the fact that the Muslim sources include these episodes to underscore the fact that some Christians were anticipating the emergence of a prophet and to show that the message of this prophet would represent a reaffirmation and continuation of biblical prophecy.

Lastly, we know that some of the Christians around Mecca were integrated into the polytheistic milieu around the Ka'ba. The tradition records the presence of icons of the Virgin and the Child among the idols of the Ka'ba. We shall see in the next chapter that Muhammad's handling of these two icons has been a lasting memory for Muslims' encounter with Christianity.

If Christians in the life of Muhammad are usually depicted as isolated individuals (learned and pious), Jews, who were much more numerous, are represented collectively. There were important Jewish tribes in Khaybar, Fadak, Tayma', Wadi al-Qura, and, most importantly, Yathrib. This last city, which would forever be transformed into the City of the Prophet (*Madinat al-nabi*), was the site of both fruitful and contentious interactions among the nascent Muslim community and the Jewish tribes.

One commonality among local Jews and Christians was that both groups spoke Arabic. As such, whenever Jews and Christians referred to the One God that they worshiped, the term they would have used in Arabic would have been *Allah*, derived from *Al-ilah*. *Al* is the definite article "the," and *ilah* is the Arabic word for "deity." In other words, Allah simply was the definitive noun meaning "the God." Today as in the past, Arabs (whether Muslim or Christian) use the term "Allah" to refer to the One God. Contrary to some assertions, Allah is not somehow the "Islamic" God as distinct from a Jewish or Christian deity. All Arabic speakers, both past and present, be they Christian, Jew, or Muslim, use the term "Allah" to refer to God.

After the final destruction of the Second Temple in Jerusalem by the Roman army in 70 CE, Jews were largely scattered across Eurasia. Many Jews stayed in North Africa and West Asia. Arabia in particular was a place that many Jewish tribes called home, and southern Arabia had an ancient presence of Jews. As was the case with many other Jewish communities in the Diaspora, most of the Jews were quite assimilated into their immediate communities, even to the point of having adopted Arabic, or at least a dialect of Arabic known as Yahudiyya (the "Jewish Arabic"), for their daily language. Some of the Jewish tribes of Arabia were on particularly good terms with the Persian Empire, and there are reports of the Jewish Banu Qurayza and Banu an-Nadir having served as tax collectors in Medina on behalf of the Persians.[21] This fact is yet another reminder of the multiple ways in which Arabian society was already connected to surrounding civilizations.

Perhaps a more crucial aspect of the Jewish and Christian presence was that Arabia was an overwhelmingly oral culture, with literacy largely restricted to monks, rabbis, and the occasional businessman. The more learned members of the Jewish community, of course, kept alive the tradition of Hebrew. As we shall see later on, many of these learned Jews would eventually convert to Islam and bring with them the wisdom of the biblical tradition within the Islamic fold. Even in Muhammad's lifetime, however, these communities played an important role. Given the low rate of literacy, the majority of religious education, including that of Jews and Christians, took place orally. Biblical narratives, at least in their broad outlines, were familiar to the Arabian audience, even those who were not Jewish or Christian. This partially explains why in the Qur'anic narrative the tales of Noah, Abraham, Moses, and Jesus are introduced in such an abbreviated fashion: the expectation was that the audience would already be familiar with the main parts of the narrative, and the focus was placed instead on the moral of the stories. Quite common are narratives in which the historical event is crystallized to its jeweled essence, capturing the lesson that transcends time and space. An example from the life of Noah illustrates this point:

> *Remember Noah, when he called out to us before. We listened to his prayer and delivered him and his family from the great distress.*
> *We helped him against people who rejected Our Signs: Truly they were a people given to evil. So We drowned them in the Flood all together. (Qur'an 21:76–77)*

The same episode is retold in multiple narratives, each time from a slightly different perspective. This repetition of narratives is often rather strange to readers who are approaching the Qur'an for the first time. One recent Muslim scholar, Seyyed Hossein Nasr, has justified this repetition by noting that it is as if we have become so distracted from our divine roots that the same melody needs to be played in multiple notes, so that one of them may resonate with us and restore us back to a state of wholeness. What unites the various accounts, however, is that the focus of the Qur'anic narratives dealing with biblical episodes remains on the level of the "moral of the story" rather than chronicling how many cubits wide Noah's ark was or the exact name of the species carried onboard. In other words, even when addressing the pre-Islamic Arab audience who were not Jewish or Christian, the Qur'anic revelation still assumed that they had been orally informed about the main narrative. The Qur'an positions itself as part of the unfolding of the biblical prophecy.

Traces of Abraham's Monotheism in Pre-Islamic Arabia

Jews and Christians are familiar to modern audiences, but the religious matrix of Arabia also featured groups that are largely unknown to us today. One of them was another group of monotheists known as the Hanif. It is quite difficult to establish much about the exact identity and beliefs of this movement. It seems clear that there were individuals who identified as Hanif, but beyond that it is hard to be certain because so much of our information about them comes from sources after the rise of Islam, including the poetry of Umayyah, the son of Abi al-Salt. According to these sources, the Hanifs—very much like the Muslims— were devoted to acts of worship to the One True God, declared themselves devotees of the primordial religion, forbade the drinking of wine, and traced their monotheism back to Abraham.

Whereas it is hard to be absolutely certain about the reliability of these later sources, we are on much stronger footing with the Qur'an itself. In the Qur'an, the Hanifs are seen as primordial monotheists, and the Qur'an (30: 29–30) associates them with the legacy of Abraham himself:

> Abraham was a Hanif,
> and neither a Jew nor a Christian.
> He did not belong to the idol-worshipers.

Here is part of the Qur'an's claim that it represents both a continuation of and a return to the primordial monotheism of Abraham. The Qur'an simply—and accurately—states that Abraham lived prior to the existence of a distinct people called Jews, as well as before the emergence of Christians. Yet he too related to the God of the whole world, and it is this primordial form of monotheism that, according to the Qur'an, has been the message of all the prophets from Adam through the ages—and now Muhammad.

> *God has proscribed the same faith for you*
> *as that which he revealed to Noah—*
> *And that which We sent down to you and that which we enjoined on*
>   *Abraham, Moses, and Jesus.*
> *Steadfastly uphold the faith,*
> *and do not break up your unity therein. (Qur'an 42:13)*

The connection between Abraham and Muhammad would be a cornerstone of the Islamic tradition. The ritual of the pilgrimage, for example, recalls the hardships faced by Abraham's wife Hagar, a former handmaiden, and his son Ishmael when they were left in the Arabian desert. To this day, millions of Muslim pilgrims go to the hills of Safa and Marwa to reenact Hagar's desperate search for water in the hot sun. The tale of the test that God put before Abraham to sacrifice his son is well known to Jews, Muslims, and Christians. Whereas Jews and Christians identified the son as Abraham's younger son, Isaac, Muslims were less sure. Some, drawing on the biblical tradition, also identified Isaac as the object of the sacrifice. The majority of Muslims, however, noting that the narrative refers to Abraham's "only son," argue that it must have taken place in the period when he had only one son, that is, Ishmael. Even in the centuries prior to the rise of Islam, Ishmael had already been identified as the ancestor of the Arab peoples, and it is no surprise that when God chose a prophet to deliver the message to the Arabs, it was through Muhammad, a descendant of Abraham through Ishmael—as Jesus had been a descendant through Isaac. Later on, Abraham and Ishmael together established a temple devoted to the One God. This temple, built in the shape of a cube, is remembered as the Ka'ba and continues to serve as the spiritual axis of the world for Muslims.

The Ka'ba, in the center of the Sacred Mosque of Mecca.
Photo courtesy of Majed Sultan.

In the words of the Qur'an:

Remember We made The House a place of gathering for humanity and a place of safety.
So take the Place of Abraham as a place of prayer. We established a covenant with Abraham and Ishmael that they should sanctify My House for those who circumambulate it, or use it as a retreat, or prostrate themselves in prayer in that place. (Qur'an 2:125)

The location identified as the Place of Abraham (*maqam Ibrahim*) is still venerated by Muslims during their pilgrimage to Mecca.

Muslims, generation after generation, have walked hand in hand in the footsteps of Abraham toward the Ka'ba. Photo courtesy of Nushmia Khan.

As the Qur'an had predicted, the Ka'ba has in fact served as a place for Muslims to circumambulate and prostrate themselves in prayer in the very place that Abraham established as a gathering place for humanity and as a place of safety. And a gathering place for humanity it has certainly been—the Ka'ba is arguably the most frequently visited religious site in the history of humanity. Mecca has also served as a symbol of the celestial Center for Muslims; from the beginning, the gatherings in Mecca for the pilgrimage once a year provided Muslims with an extraordinary opportunity to take the latest ideas, goods, aesthetics, and devotions back and forth from the farthest regions of the world. If the Muslim community is conceived of as a human body, Mecca is its heart. The faithful of the community are sent here for rejuvenation, before returning to the periphery.

The Qur'anic passage about Abraham and Mecca continues with the blessings offered by Abraham for this city:

And remember, Abraham said:
"My Lord, make this a City of Peace,
and feed its people with fruits—
such of them as have faith in God and the last Day."
    (Qur'an 2:126)

Lastly, the Qur'anic narrative ends with the most explicit account of Abraham's foreshadowing of the rising of a prophet from among his children through Ishmael. If the Bible provides us with the theater of God's involvement with Abraham's descendants through Isaac, it is in the Qur'an that Isaac and Ishmael share the stage equally, both receiving equal blessing. And it is in the Qur'an that Ishmael's descendants receive the blessing that is largely absent from the biblical narrative:

And remember Abraham and Ishmael raised the foundations of the
    House with this prayer: "Our Lord! Accept this from us,
For you are the All-hearing, the All-knowing.
Our Lord! Allow us to submit ourselves wholeheartedly to you,
And make of our offspring a people who will submit wholeheartedly
    to you.
And show us our places for the celebration of rites;
And turn to us in Mercy,
For you are the Accepter of Repentance, the Most Merciful.
Our Lord! Rise up from among them a messenger of their own,
Who shall rehearse Your Signs to them
And instruct them in scripture and wisdom,
And sanctify them." (Qur'an 2:129)

The God of Abraham heeded the prayer of Abraham and sanctified Abraham's descendants. As Abraham had prayed, God also raised from among Abraham's descendants a prophet who would remind humanity of the Signs of God and teach them both scripture and wisdom. The name of this prophet, this child of Abraham, was Muhammad. It was an appropriate name, because the name Muhammad literally means "one who is praised," and praised he has been for centuries by the Muslim children of Abraham.

The life narrative of Muhammad himself reiterate this organic connection between him and Abraham. One of the most convincing messages of the Qur'an is that in fact it contains nothing new. It is, for lack of a better term, original: it draws upon the same Origin from which all of creation stems, the same source of all prophetic guidance before Muhammad. Yet part of the rhythm of creation, according to the message of the Qur'an, is that humanity is bound to forget. In the presence of an Abraham, a Jesus, a Moses, or a Muhammad, all is real, all is luminous. If a prophet tells us that bones will be resurrected and those long dead will be gathered again in a place with soothing shade and flowing rivers, we believe everything this prophet says. In time, however, we forget. The task of prophecy is to remind us of that which we have known, and still know somewhere deep inside. There is no new lesson to learn; our task is only to remember, to recall what we already know, to remember who we are. Yet the recollection of who we truly are—created in God's image with the breath of God breathed inside us, as both the Qur'an and the Bible tell us—becomes covered up, as it were. We forget who and what we are.

In the life narrative of Muhammad, the same pattern of knowing, forgetting, and remembering is connected to the example of Abraham. Abraham raised the foundations of the Ka'ba and built it for the worship of the One God, but in time humanity forgot the purpose of the Ka'ba and turned it into an idol-house for the pagan deity Hubal. Jews stopped visiting this temple. Monotheism was forgotten. The Ka'ba crumbled, losing its roof, and its treasures were stolen—perhaps a sign of the lost treasure of monotheism. God's temple, according to the Qur'an, needs to be rebuilt, just as monotheism needs to be proclaimed once more. So Muhammad rises. Muhammad rises to rebuild and renew the monotheism first brought forth by Abraham.

According to the narratives of Muhammad's life, when he was thirty-five years old, and not yet the Prophet, the Arab tribes of Mecca decided to rebuild the Ka'ba. We know that this event took place around the year 605 CE and that some of the carpenters involved in this task were Coptic Christians. The tribe of Quraysh was, of course, involved in this renovation as well. A crisis arose when it came to putting the sacred Black Stone back into the foundation of the Ka'ba. The Arab chiefs were bickering among themselves: they could not agree on which tribe should be in charge of lifting up the Black Stone. As was so often the case, the reason for the conflict was tribal: the honor would not have gone to the chief but to the tribe, and all the tribes were vying for this honor. Eventually, the Arab chiefs agreed to abide by the judgment of the next person to walk in, who happened to be Muhammad. The Arab chiefs rejoiced, greeting Muhammad as the *Amin* ("the Trustworthy"). Already they had come to trust Muhammad with their caravans, and they trusted him in this weighty matter as well. Muhammad avoided showing favoritism, however, by having each of the tribes hang on to the corner of a sheet; he himself placed the Black Stone in the middle of the sheet, then had them all lift up the Stone. Muhammad thus restored the Temple, by returning the Black Stone to the corner of the Ka'ba.

In displaying this Solomonic wisdom, Muhammad avoided splitting the community apart and instead united the tribes. And there is a deeper meaning here, as there always is in these types of narratives. He had been known, even in his youth, as the *Amin*, the Trustworthy. People trusted him with their gold and their caravans. Before Muhammad was the Prophet, he was Trustworthy. The Qur'an (33:72) speaks of the *Amana*, the Divine Trust—the cosmic responsibility of being God's representative on Earth, a burden so severe that heavens and mountains dared not undertake it, but humanity did. *Amin* and *Amana* are, of course, etymologically linked. Muhammad the Amin, the Trustworthy, is the one to remind humanity of the awesome task of bearing the Amana, the Divine Trust. A child of Abraham reminds the offspring of Abraham of the God of Abraham—and their own God. Abraham would echo in the land of Abraham's offspring yet again.

Echoes of Abraham and the Names of God

We have seen how the Qur'an engages the audience in an extended plea to realize ultimate monotheism. At times this engagement is carried out in the form of a narrative. One of the more intriguing is the episode in which Abraham engages his community through a series of arguments and demonstrations. In the Qur'anic worldview, the stories of Abraham are not just about the Abraham of history but also about the Prophet Muhammad's time and about eternal tendencies in humanity's approach to God. As with Abraham, so with us.

In the beginning of Abraham's call to prophecy, the Qur'an depicts Abraham as approaching his father and warning him: "Shall you take idols as gods? For I see you and your people in clear error." Abraham then approaches his community, stands where they stand, and does what the Prophet Muhammad would identify as "speaking to people at the level of their understanding." Seeing that they worship a star, Abraham too cries out: "This is my Lord." But when the star sets at the end of the night, Abraham calls out: "I do not love those that set." He then sees the moon rise, and again he cries out: "This is my Lord." And when the moon sets, he again cries: "Unless my Lord guide me, I shall surely be among those who go astray." Lastly, he sees the sun rise in splendor. He says: "This is my Lord, this is the greatest!" When the sun sets—as all natural phenomena must eventually do—Abraham turns to his community and states:

O my people! Behold, far be it from me to ascribe divinity, as you do, to aught beside God!

Behold, unto Him who brought into being the heavens and the earth have I turned my inner being, having turned away from all that is false; and I am not of those who ascribe divinity to aught beside Him.[22] *(Qur'an 6:74–79)*

How do we account for Abraham's bowing before what is other-than-God in the earlier portions of this narrative? Throughout the centuries, Muslims have interpreted this narrative in divergent ways. Perhaps the least imaginative approach is to simply see Abraham as a great actor going through the motions with his community for one night so that he can disprove one proposed deity after another. Yet other Muslims, particularly some of the mystics, see something more honest and paradigmatic in Abraham's actions, which illustrate, in this view, the all-too-human quality of rising through higher and higher conceptions of deity. In the beginning we imagine God to be a slightly better version of ourselves, then the comforter of all that is missing from our lives, and then a king, before we finally realize that God is the Ultimate, the One, the perfection of Love, Majesty, and Beauty.

As Abraham invites his people, so did the Qur'an with the pre-Islamic Arabs. The argument moves—over a period of years—from stating that Muslims will worship only One God, to stating that the other deities have no efficacy, to finally stating emphatically that in fact there is only One God. Ultimately the Qur'anic argument rises to the level of stating that the deities worshiped by the pre-Islamic Arabs are names without reality—labels, as it were, that if removed would point not to alternative deities but simply to a vacuum. In speaking of the "daughters of Allah," the Qur'an states:

These are nothing but names which you have devised
—you and your fathers—
for which God has sent down no authority.

They follow nothing but vain conjecture,
and what their own carnal souls desire!
Even though there has already come to them
guidance from their Lord. (Qur'an 53:23)

The same critique is put in the mouth of the prophet Joseph, who in prison invites his fellow inmates to have faith in the One True God. He says to them:

O my two companions of the prison.
I ask you: are many lords differing among themselves better,
or God, the One, Supreme and Irresistible.
If not Him, you worship nothing but names which you have named
—you and your fathers—
for which God has sent down no authority.

The command is for none other than God.
He has commanded that you worship none but Him,
that is the true faith. (Qur'an 12:39–40)

The theme of the names through which the faithful are to call upon God comes up at a few different points, creating an opening into the life of piety for Muslims. In some early chapters, the notion is simply that one can call upon God through a multitude of names:

Invoke God, or invoke the Most Gracious [Rahman]:
by whichever name you invoke Him,
His are all the attributes of perfection. (Qur'an 17:110)

Eventually, however, we get litanies of what are called the Lovely Names of God (*Asma al-Husna*), whose number is traditionally put at ninety-nine, or perhaps one hundred (with one of them being hidden). These are awe-inspiring verses. In the Qur'an, they are introduced with a declaration that if God had revealed this Qur'an upon a mountain, the mountain would have been torn asunder out of awe (Qur'an 59:21). And yet God reveals the Qur'an to the heart of humanity—more specifically, the blessed heart of Muhammad. This is yet another indication that a heart purified and perfected is not simply a lump of flesh in the chest, but none other than the earthly throne of God, perfect for receiving the Word of God, the Spirit of God. One of the secret conversations between Muhammad and God in fact alludes to this very point: "My heaven cannot contain me, nor can my Earth. But the heart of my faithful servant contains me."

One of the most commonly recited examples of a litany of the Divine Lovely Names, the Beautiful Names of God, is the following passage in the Qur'an:

He is God,
other than He there is no other deity.
The knower of the Hidden and the Manifest
He is most-merciful [Rahman], tenderly compassionate [Rahim]
He is God, other than He there is no other deity.
The Sovereign
The Holy One
The Source of Peace
The Faithful
The Preserver of Safety
The Exalted in Might
The Irresistible
The Supreme.
Glory be to God above the partners they ascribe to Him.
He is God,
The Creator
The Evolver
The Bestower of forms.

To Him belong the Loveliest Names.
Whatever is in the Heavens and on Earth praises Him.
And He is Exalted in Might, the Wise. (Qur'an 59:22–24)

The recitation of these Loveliest Names of God forms an essential part of the spiritual tradition in Islam. In fact, the cornerstone of both the theory and the practice of Islamic spirituality is embedded in the recitation of many such descriptions from the Qur'an. For example, one such verse in the Qur'an (2:115) proclaims:

To God Belong the East and the West.
Whichever way you turn, there is the Face of God.
For God is All-Encompassing, All-Knowing.

Up to now, we have seen a glimpse of the world before Muhammad, a world that still recalls Abraham without heeding the God of Abraham, a world in which the One God is removed from creation and relegated to a realm of transcendence beyond approach. The society is not bereft of ethics, but all ethics are practiced in a tribal context. Muhammad was born into this world, which was the setting for what we call the Muhammadi Revolution, as we shall see in the next chapter.

This revolution took effect not by discarding all that had come before, but rather by modifying, editing, subverting, and reorganizing what came before. We have already seen the movement in the Qur'an from stating that Muslims will only call upon God to the neglect of the deities of the polytheists, to stating that affairs in the end will return to God, to stating that there is emphatically One deity and the other alleged deities are names with no reference points. If all Muslims agree that there is One, and only One, God, verses like "Whichever way you turn, there is the Face of God" open up new possibilities. In subtle and complicated ways, there is ultimately One:

God is One.
Reality is One.
Humanity is One.
Guidance is One.
Existence is One.

For Muslims who recognize this reality, *Tawhid* is not merely the assertion that there is only One God, but the imperative toward the integration of all reality. All that is broken must be made whole again. It is not God that is fractured, but us as human beings. God is already one—we as humanity must be made One. We have to heal our internal fractures, our fractures as one humanity, our fractures with the natural cosmos, and our sense of separation from the Divine. Some Muslim mystics, the advocates of the notion of Oneness of Being (*wahdat al-wujud*), saw themselves as following in the footsteps of the Prophet Muhammad. Before getting to their tale and the multiple ways in which Muslims engaged the legacy of Tawhid, however, we will return to the tale of the Prophet whose footsteps so many sought to follow in.

CHAPTER TWO

The Muhammadi Revolution

SOME SIX HUNDRED YEARS AFTER the time of Christ, in an age when the teachings of the prophets were mostly forgotten, and in a region of the world where no prophet had been sent by God before, a young man named Muhammad found himself unwilling to worship the gods of his forefathers and unable to bear the injustices of his own society. Troubled by the suffering of the poor and the downtrodden in his society, Muhammad was in the habit of climbing a mountain called Light and retreating into a cave called Hira to ponder meaning and existence. Before he was the Prophet, the Messenger of God, Muhammad was known to be a sensitive man and a trustworthy soul, and those around him trusted their goods to him to take for caravan-led trades at far distances. Soon almost all the members of his society would find themselves entrusting Muhammad with much more than their goods. This time it would be their hearts and souls that they entrusted to the one they had come to call the *Amin*, "the Trustworthy."

Revolution as Heart-Transformation

In our own age, when we think of a "revolution," most of us imagine violence. We often begin by thinking of political acts in which one faction overthrows an established regime through a coup d'état. Even when the revolution is viewed in a positive sense (the American Revolution, the French Revolution), we largely think of revolution in a political sense, that is, as a process that begins with the transformation of a government. Yet the word "revolution" has an older sense as well. The oldest usages of the term in English implied the movement of a celestial body, like the sun in an orbit. That sense of an orbit was often accompanied by the notion of the return of an epoch. Already in 1597 there were mentions of "the day . . . changed in regard of a new reuolution begunne by our Sauiour Christ."[1] Other meanings of the word "revolution" included the notion of "revolving" around an axis or a center, as well as the more intellectual process of pondering, reflecting, and considering. It was not until the seventeenth century that the term "revolution" came to be primarily associated with a political transformation.

Some of this same tendency to think of revolution as something that begins with "turning things over" internally is also reflected in the languages that Muslims speak. One of the more common terms used for "revolution" in Arabic is *Inqilab*. Although the term is now associated with political revolution, etymologically it too comes from the root Q-L-B, which connotes both "the heart" and "change" or "transformation." A true revolution was initially deemed in both Western and Islamic sources to be an affair of the heart.

It is in this sense that we speak here of a Muhammadi Revolution. It is true that the revelation bestowed upon Muhammad—which began in the cave he used as a retreat—did bring about a full-scale social and political transformation of Arab society, and ultimately much of the world from Asia and Africa to Europe. As we saw in the last chapter, those changes represented a sometimes successful, sometimes compromised, attempt to transform tribal and patriarchal pre-Islamic society into an egalitarian community of faith-fellowship, where, as Muhammad famously said, human beings would be equal like the teeth of a comb. Yet just as with the term "revolution," the origins of the Muhammadi Revolution (*Inqilab*) began with a much more interior affair, a transformation of the heart (*qalb*). The Muhammadi Revolution cannot be understood apart from the internal matter of changing hearts and souls. If the word "revolution" initially referred to the orbit of heavenly bodies around a center and the return of an epoch, the Muhammadi Revolution was ultimately a reminder to humanity to return to orbiting around the Center. It represented a return of humanity to a wholesale surrender before the Divine and a mindful correction of what was deemed our forgetful tendencies: forgetting about the message of previous prophets, forgetting about God, and forgetting about our own true selves.

One of the commonalities of every revolution, whether of heavenly bodies or social transformations, is a sense of movement. It is hard to be a revolutionary—in the original sense of the word—by standing still, and Muhammad's revolution certainly implied this sense of movement, dynamism, and transformation. In this chapter, we trace some of the significant "movements" of Muhammad's life.

This point is particularly important to remember given the common tendency to speak of an "Islamic tradition": the word "tradition" and, even more so, the adjective "traditional" convey the impression of something static and frozen. Like the word "revolution," the concept of "tradition" has also lost much of its original meaning. "Tradition" originally referred to the notion of "handing over" and "transmission." Whether we speak of an Islamic, Jewish, or Christian tradition, to conceive of these traditions as eternally unchanging systems that simply preserve "traditional" sets of values is to lose the sense of dynamic movement, transmission, and transformation inherent in all of them.

A key component of the Muhammadi Revolution—as imagined in this sense of dynamic transformation, beginning with the heart and ultimately transforming society—is a sense of movement, and here we look at some of the key movements in Muhammad's life. These movements are key to understanding the ethos of Islam, and each represents not just a shifting from one point to another but also the awakening of a sense of purpose—moving from how things are to how they should be, and raising up humanity to resonate with that ideal.

In this chapter, we discuss three movements of Muhammad's life:

- Muhammad ascending the Mountain of Hira, receiving the revelation (*wahy*), and descending the mountain to deliver the message to humanity.
- Muhammad ascending from Mecca to Jerusalem and unto Heaven (*mi'raj*), having a direct encounter with God, and returning compassionately to humanity.
- Muhammad leaving his homeland of Mecca to migrate to Medina (*Hijra*), establishing a multireligious community there, and eventually returning triumphantly to Mecca.

Muslims have come back to these movements over and over again to gain a sense of their place in the cosmos and to both ask and answer the ultimate questions of where we come from, what we are here to do, and how we return to our Origin. These pivotal movements from Muhammad's life are the keys for understanding the Muhammadi model of being with and returning to God, as well as the Muhammadi Revolution of returning humanity to the orbit of a God-centered life.

Perhaps a word should be added here about the word "Muhammadi" in relation to these movements. During Muhammad's own lifetime, his wife, A'isha, used to refer to him as "the walking Qur'an." In other words, divine guidance is not simply sent to humanity as if through a UPS delivery. Guidance is more than simply a book—it is a book internalized by illuminated teachers whose ethics, behavior, and manners become the embodiments of the teaching. It is for this reason that I refer to this revolution not simply as an Islamic revolution, or even as a Qur'anic revolution, but as the Muhammadi Revolution. Ever since the time of the Prophet Muhammad, to be a follower of Muhammad, to be a child of Muhammad, has entailed in some sense being, or aspiring to become, Muhammad-like, or Muhammadi.

Before beginning the analysis of these Muhammadi movements, it is worth pondering that the first two movements are what we might

THE MUHAMMADI REVOLUTION | 101

call "vertical": ascending the mountain to receive revelation, and ascending to Heaven to encounter God. Each ascension also has a descending movement—to complete the orbit, as it were, and bring the lessons of revelation/encounter back to humanity. That movement is significant, since it reminds Muslims to keep the ascension/mystical component engaged with the dimension that seeks to live the teachings in the midst of society.

Equally important is the notion that Muhammad establishes what is the model human community in Medina through the Hijra, the migration from Mecca to Medina. This third movement, which we may think of as "horizontal," comes after, not before, the ascent to Heaven. In other words, before there can be a social movement, there has to be a spiritual awakening. This is one of the lasting lessons of the Muhammadi Revolution: it is both impossible and futile to attempt to better the condition of humanity without first tending to the spiritual process of awakening. That awakening does not take place in isolation from humanity—as we have seen—but it cannot be bypassed. In fact, one could say that attempts to ameliorate the lives of human beings by forgetting about the spiritual need to uplift humanity simultaneously are doomed to be counterproductive and in fact lead to the further fracturing of humanity. One must uplift all of the human being, including the heart and soul.

With that reminder, we return to the cave where the Muhammadi Revolution began.

The First Movement: To the Mountain of Light and Back

In the lives of religious luminaries, every detail is held to be sacred and symbolic. It is surely no accident that the mountain Muhammad climbed to meditate was called the Mountain of Light (*Jabal al-Nur*), since it is light that leads to the illumination of humanity (for Ottoman depictions of Muhammad meditating on the Mountain of Light, see below). Also rich with symbolism is the cave, which represents an opening inward. In the Greek tradition, the parable of the cave is well known as one of Plato's teachings on the need to look beyond the shadowy realm and see things as they are, a teaching that is almost verbatim a prayer of Muhammad:

O Lord, show me things as they are.

Ottoman miniature depicting Muhammad meditating on the Mountain of Light. Courtesy of the Topkapi Palace Museum.

In the later tradition, the cave would always be connected to the heart, another opening inward where one can contemplate the realities and seek illumination. The poetry of Muslim mystics like Rumi would state:

Consider this heart as a cave,
the spiritual retreat of the friend.[2]

The practice of going on spiritual retreats was not unknown among Arabs, and even prior to the Qur'anic revelation there were always the select few who gravitated to a meditative life. Muhammad himself stated that he began having powerful spiritual experiences, which he compared to the "breaking of the light of dawn," an inward illumination.[3] In time, these experiences became more dear to Muhammad. As a result, he went to the mountain-top more frequently on his meditative sojourns. He recalled that, as he left town, he would hear the following words clearly: *al-Salamu alayka ya Rasul Allah* ("Peace be upon you, O Messenger of God").[4] Muhammad would look to the right and the left, yet no speaker would be in sight.

Muhammad ascended. For pre-Islamic Arabs, Ramadan was the month for a practice known as *tahannuth*, a spiritual retreat. Here Muhammad would retreat for prayer in the privacy of the Mountain of Light. In preparing for his retreat, he would feed the poor and the needy. Even before he was the Prophet, Muhammad's spiritual practices linked inner reflection with social action. It was during one of these meditative retreats, in the year 610 CE, that the angel Gabriel appeared to him in the shape of a human being. Gabriel appeared to Muhammad and said: "Recite." Muhammad said: "I am not a reciter." The traditions of Muhammad report that the angel "took me and whelmed me in his embrace until he had reached the limit of my endurance."[5] Gabriel released Muhammad and said: "Recite." Again Muhammad said, "I am not a reciter," and again Gabriel embraced Muhammad tight and said: "Recite." This time the words of revelation—the first verses of the Qur'an to be revealed—came to Muhammad freely:

Recite in the name of thy Lord who created!
Created humanity from a clot of blood.
Recite, and thy Lord is the most Generous,
and has taught by the Pen—
taught humanity that which they knew not. (Qur'an 96:1–4)

Muhammad stated that after this experience, it was as if his heart were a tablet upon which the words of the Qur'an were being inscribed.[6] At this point Muhammad began to descend the mountain, completing the first orbit of this Muhammadi movement. He now recognized the angel Gabriel, filling the sky from horizon to horizon, in his cosmic form. Gabriel greeted Muhammad by saying: "O Muhammad, you are the Messenger of God, and I am Gabriel."

What was Muhammad's response to this vision of an angelic figure and having the awesome experience of receiving the revelation for the first time? According to most early sources, Muhammad—like any pure soul—was overcome. The famed tenth-century historian Tabari, who collected some of the most reliable accounts of the Prophet's life, records that Muhammad feared that he might have become one of the jinn-possessed poets he had disliked so much, until Gabriel reappeared to him and assured Muhammad that indeed he was the recipient of God's revelation through an angel.[7] We saw in the previous chapter that in Muhammad's world the powerful rhymed words uttered by poets were believed to be inspired by supernatural creatures (*jinn*). The words of the jinn-possessed (*majnun*) poets were most often in praise of their tribe. The words of the Qur'an flowing through Muhammad were also rhymed, but the content could not have been more different than jinn-inspired tribal praise: the rhymed words traced back not to a jinn, but to the God of the Universe. In fact, the Qur'an assures Muhammad's audience that their "esteemed companion" (Muhammad) is not a jinn-possessed poet and that the revelation is "nothing short of a Reminder of God for all of the cosmos" (Qur'an 81:22–27). The content of this Qur'anic revelation dealt with the Omnipotence, Justice, and Mercy of the One God and was an emphatic departure from tribal ethics in holding each individual singularly accountable before God in a cosmic judgment in the Hereafter.

It is worth pausing to reflect on the significance of the way in which the most reliable of Islamic sources depict Muhammad at this crucial juncture. Far from depicting a cosmic Muhammad (which we will see in the next chapters), early sources depict Muhammad at this point as a human being who is in awe of and even dazzled by the cosmic vision he has had. These early sources do not shy away from depicting this awed experience. Over the centuries, this very human image of Muhammad would be downplayed. In fact, some of the recent biographies of Muhammad have cast great aspersions on this narrative and prefer to see Muhammad as having been providentially prepared for the task of receiving revelation, to the point that no shock or awe would have been necessary.[8]

Yet if we do take the oldest and most reliable biographical accounts seriously, after his awe-some encounter with the angel Gabriel, Muhammad was in need of comfort and reassurance. According to the standard biography of Muhammad from Ibn Ishaq, which was composed around 150 years after the time of Muhammad and provides the basis of all later biographies, God provided this comfort through his wife, Khadija. She was the first to have faith in God through Muhammad and to believe in the authenticity of Muhammad's experience. She was, to put it more bluntly, the first Muslim of the Muhammadi path.

Khadija's support is not left in the abstract. Rather, the biographical account of Ibn Ishaq provides two different narratives in which she comforts and shelters Muhammad from his spiritual storm. Continuing his descent from the Mountain of Light after receiving the awe-inspiring revelation, Muhammad went to his wife. No longer just Muhammad but now the Prophet, he approached Khadija and sat close to her. The Prophet confided in her that he was concerned that he might become like those poets possessed by the jinn. Khadija responded in compassion:

I take refuge in that, Father of Qasim [the son of Khadija and Mu-
  hammad].
God would not treat you thus,
since he knows your truthfulness,
your great trustworthiness,
your fine character, and your kindness.
*This cannot be, my dear.*⁹

Khadija assured Muhammad that he had indeed had a visionary experience, and her faith brought comfort to Muhammad's heart. Muhammad told Khadija what he had seen, and she responded: "Rejoice . . . and be of good heart. Verily, by Him in whose hand is Khadija's soul, I have hope that you will be the prophet of this people."¹⁰ Khadija goes on to consult her cousin, Waraqa, the son of Nawfal, who was a learned Christian. Waraqa compared the visionary experience of Muhammad with that of biblical prophets and rejoiced by saying: "Holy, Holy! By Him in whose hand is the soul of Waraqa, there has come unto Muhammad the same angel that had come to Moses. Verily Muhammad is the Prophet of this people. Bid Muhammad to be of good heart."¹¹ Going to Muhammad, Waraqa conveyed the same sentiment to him and sealed it by kissing Muhammad's forehead. Again, as we saw in the episode of the monk Bahira in the previous chapter, Muhammad's biography did not shy away from having Christians in Muhammad's time affirm his prophethood and see in him the confirmation and affirmation of biblical prophecy.

The second narrative in which Khadija comforts Muhammad is even more tender, even more intimate. It bears repeating in full here, especially because it is these types of narratives that have conveyed to Muslims a full sense of the humanity of Muhammad—that of a human who was transformed through the encounter with the Divine, no doubt, yet remained human, became fully human. This narrative is quoted from Khadija herself. She asked Muhammad to inform her when the agent of revelation, Gabriel, visited him, so that she could help him determine if indeed it was the angel or a demon of the type that possessed poets. Muhammad told Khadija the next time Gabriel came to him. Khadija asked Muhammad to sit by her left thigh, which Muhammad obliged her by doing. She asked Muhammad: "Do you still see him?" Muhammad answered in the affirmative. She then asked Muhammad to sit by her right thigh, and she repeated the same question, which Muhammad again answered in the positive. She then asked him to sit in her lap and asked him if he still saw the angel. Muhammad yet again answered: "Yes." She then loosened the knot on her robe and unveiled her body while Muhammad was still sitting in her lap. At this point she held the Prophet in the naked embrace of a husband and wife, which the biography describes as "the Messenger of God—peace and blessings of God be upon him—was between her and her slip dress."[12] She then asked him: "Do you still see him?" Muhammad answered: "No." Khadija responded: "Rejoice, and be of good heart. By God he is an angel, and not a satan."[13] Had Gabriel been a demonic being, he would not have fled the scene of a beautiful naked woman, whereas the angel of revelation, full of modesty, had left the husband and wife alone.

It is one thing to speak of Muhammad as the Prophet, the Messenger of God, in terms of his relations to God. Muslims have also imagined Muhammad as the model human being who also illustrates the perfection of every human relation. He is not merely the Prophet; he also demonstrates, in episodes like the one just described, how to be the ideal husband and father, which is crucial in portraying the life of intimacy and affection. Far from illustrating a model of patriarchy, in which the wife's duty is to provide unquestioned obedience, here Khadija shelters her husband and comforts him, as he would do for her in other circumstances. Some modern Muslims, framing their critique of Islam in the context of gender issues, have been quick—perhaps too quick—to point out that Muhammad was fifteen years younger than Khadija and that she was a successful and independently wealthy businesswoman who employed Muhammad first to run her caravans to Syria. Indeed, Khadija has provided many modern Muslim women with an example of a self-sufficient woman who entered into an intimate marital relation with a man. Khadija in fact proposed marriage to Muhammad, something unheard of in Muhammad's age and rare even today.

Khadija proposing to Muhammad. From the Qisas al-anbiya'.

There is something else about the marriage of Muhammad and Khadija that deserves further examination as the very model of an intimate marital life in Islam. What is remarkable about Khadija is not merely that she was a successful businesswoman, but also that she and Muhammad embodied a nurturing and loving relationship that lasted for twenty-five years, until her passing. The narratives of Muhammad's life praise her as they do no other companion of Muhammad's:

> She was the first to believe in God and His messenger, and in the truth of his message. Through her, God lightened the burden of His prophet. He never met with contradiction and charges of falsehood, which saddened him, but God comforted him by her when he went home.
>
> She strengthened him, lightened his burden, proclaimed his truth, and belittled men's opposition. May God Almighty have mercy upon her![14]

This support and affection between Muhammad and his wife Khadija, even their erotic relation, would undoubtedly shape many of his views toward women. One of his statements that would be cited by many later Muslims was the following *hadith* (saying of the Prophet Muhammad):

> Three things from this world of yours
> have been made lovely to me:
> perfume,
> women,
> but that which brings delight to my eyes
> is prayer.[15]

Here perfume may be taken as an appreciation of all that is natural and beautiful—indeed, the entirety of the natural cosmos. Women are the connection, the linchpin, between the natural realm of beauty and the spiritual domain. Later Muslim mystics, such as the thirteenth-century Ibn 'Arabi, interpreted this saying of Muhammad's to mean that the spiritual and the sacred ("prayer") enter this world ("perfume") through women.

A positive appreciation of relations between men and women would also be reflected in the legal code that was eventually built around Muhammad's teachings. In the *Shari'a*, the Islamic legal code, there is no indication that the sole purpose of sexual relations in a marriage is reproduction. While the scope of sexual relations is naturally limited, there is a frank appreciation of sexuality as a good in and of itself in the context of marriage. In fact, Muslim scientists in the premodern period developed a sophisticated array of birth control technologies with the full approval of the juridical authorities.

But before there would be Muslim jurists and Muslim scientists and even Muslim erotic poets, there had to be a prophet. Up to this point, the rank of Muslims consisted only of Muhammad and his faithful wife Khadija. Support would grow very slowly. This ocean was one that would form drop by drop, wave by wave, as the Qur'an states: "And you see people entering God's religion wave by wave" (Qur'an 110:2). In the beginning, the waves were smaller—so much so that the personality of the individual drops could be identified.

After Muhammad and Khadija, the next to enter the faith was Muhammad's cousin Ali. It would be this same Ali who eventually married Fatima, the beloved daughter of Khadija and Muhammad. It would be this Ali who became the model of Islamic chivalry and the darling of Islamic mysticism in later centuries. A generation after the passing away of Muhammad, it was the succession dispute between Ali and other followers of Muhammad that eventually (though not immediately) led to the sectarian strife between Sunni and Shi'i Muslims. It is this sectarian division among the followers of Muhammad that still erupts today in conflicts in Iraq and elsewhere. Yet at this point Ali was still a mere boy, not even a teenager. Muhammad had taken Ali into his own household to alleviate the pressures of a large family on his uncle, Abu Talib. Thus, Ali was raised by Muhammad and knew the Prophet as no one else did. In the earliest biography of Muhammad, Ibn Ishaq wrote: "It was a special favor to Ali from God that he was in the closest association with the Messenger before Islam."[16]

In his first task of religious instruction, teaching the prayers, Muhammad provided a lovely model of transmission. According to this story, Gabriel taught Muhammad how to pray, and Muhammad taught Khadija. Gabriel instructed Muhammad how to perform the ritual washing before the prayers, and Muhammad passed on these teachings to Khadija. In a real sense, Khadija is the first Muslim to follow Muhammad, as Muhammad followed the angels. Here is a model of transmission, of tradition-in-making, acted out between the husband-prophet and the wife. The young boy Ali would join them in prayer. The first full congregational prayer was thus performed around the Ka'ba, consisting of the Prophet, the Prophet's wife, and the Prophet's cousin. And so it has been for the Prophet's community as it has kept the tradition of prayer ever since. In fact, one of the re-markable aspects of Islam has been the way in which the transmission of rituals has preserved their form through the centuries, across the entire Muslim community from Indonesia to America. Muslims of all languages, races, and social classes can line up next to one another and participate in a shared ritual of prayer.

Muhammad then invited his family members to answer God's call. In the spirit of generosity, he made a spread for them in which mirac-ulously, out of one lamb and one cup of milk, he fed the whole clan. He then invited them to Islam with the following words:

> O sons of 'Abd al-Muttalib,
> I know of no Arab who has come to his people
> with a nobler message than mine.
> I bring you the best of this world and the next.
> God has commanded me to call you unto Him.
> Which of you, then, will help me in this,
> and be my brother and my successor among you?

The gathering fell silent, and only the thirteen-year-old boy Ali rose up to answer by stating that he would be the Prophet's helper. The prophet then put his hand on the back of Ali's neck and said:

"This is my brother and my successor among you. Hearken unto him, and obey him."[17] The men of the tribe rose to their feet and mocked Ali's father, saying that he had been called to obey his own son. Surely even they recognized that there was something radical and indeed antitraditional at work. What Muhammad had stated represented a "revolution" vis-à-vis their own cultural norms, according to which a son was expected to follow in the "ways of the forefathers." But Muhammad was privileging a mere boy of thirteen over the elders of a tribe on account of his faith. It was this attachment to a mere boy that would lead some members of Muhammad's community to form a distinct Shi'i identity after Muhammad's passing.

During this time Muhammad continued to preach his call, and he gradually gained more followers in Mecca. The aristocracy of Mecca kept a watchful and concerned eye on the growing movement. Recognizing the challenge not just to their religion but indeed to their social customs, they went to Abu Talib—Ali's father and Muhammad's uncle—and stated: "By God, we cannot endure that our fathers should be reviled, our customs mocked and our gods insulted. Until you rid us of him we will fight the both of you until one side perishes."[18] Abu Talib, who had not at this point adopted the faith of Muhammad, went to his nephew and spoke to him out of his concern: "O son of my brother, spare me, and spare thyself. Lay not upon me a burden greater than I can bear."[19] Muhammad's response was legendary:

> I swear by God, if they put the sun in my right hand and the moon in my left on condition that I abandon this course before He has made it victorious, or I have perished therein, I would not abandon it.[20]

Abu Talib, moved by the sincerity of his nephew, rose up with tears in his eyes and pledged his support. As an elder of the tribe, Abu Talib could provide some moral support and protection for his beleaguered nephew, but even he could not always protect the Prophet. Particularly venomous toward Muhammad was a Meccan leader named Abu Hakam

("Father of Wisdom"), whose name the Muslim tradition changed to Abu Jahl ("Father of Ignorance"—the same root as Jahiliyya). Abu Jahl was fond of walking up to the Prophet when Muhammad was sitting by the Ka'ba and casting all the insults he could muster at Muhammad. The Prophet's response was to sit in silence and stare at Abu Jahl without uttering a word. This too is part of Muhammad's legacy. At a later point in his life, Muhammad would provide a model of the warrior and a model of the civic leader, but his reaction at this point was also a Muhammadi model of nonviolence—of not returning evil for evil.

This phase of Muhammad's life lasted much longer than most remember: thirteen long, grueling years. In fact, for the first thirteen years of his prophecy, the Muslims were a beleaguered, harassed, and persecuted minority in Mecca. During this time, the small community of Muslims was subjected to various dispossessions, bans, and trade embargoes. For a while they were exiled from their homes into a nearby valley. Those who lacked tribal and clan protection were especially targeted. In the last chapter, we were introduced to Bilal, the Abyssinian slave who became the first muezzin of Islam. Bilal was physically tortured by his master, Umayya, the leader of the Jumah. Umayya would have Bilal dragged to the hot Arabian desert, where he would place large stone blocks on Bilal's chest and threaten to leave him there until Bilal renounced God and accepted the goddesses Lat and Uzza. Bilal simply repeated: "Ahad, ahad" (One, One).[21] One of the great ironies of Islamic history, as we shall see later, is that this same torturer became the ancestor of the first Islamic dynasty, the Umayyads.

The Second Movement: Mi'raj and Back

It was around this time that Muhammad sent waves of his followers to Abyssinia to live under the protection of the Christian king Negus. This move ensured the survival of the community, yet such a temporary measure could not be a lasting solution. Even though those who were sent to Abyssinia included many of the most vulnerable, the abuse in Mecca was no longer restricted to the slaves and the downtrodden of Muhammad's community. Muhammad himself was increasingly targeted. The abuse intensified in a year that Muhammad called "the Year of Sadness." Over a brief period in the year 619, he suffered two great losses: his closest friend and confidante, his lover and partner, Khadija, as well as his uncle Abu Talib, who had protected him from the Meccans. The death of Khadija was particularly devastating for Muhammad. After all, they had been married since Muhammad was twenty-five (and Khadija was forty) until Muhammad reached fifty and Khadija sixty-five. During this time they had four daughters and two sons, both of whom perished in their youth. No man or woman would subsequently take Khadija's place in Muhammad's heart.

The abuse of Muhammad intensified during this year. Once when he was praying in his own house, a man threw a sheep's bloody uterus on Muhammad. On another occasion, the Meccans threw dirt in his face and all over his head. It was Muhammad's daughters who cleaned up his face, washing it with their tears. Such sadness, persecution, and grief can break human beings or it can polish their souls to the point of illumination. The Year of Sadness forced Muhammad to turn inward even more. Some of his tenderest prayers were uttered during this time:

> *O God, unto Thee do I complain of my weakness, of my helplessness, and of my lowliness before men.*
> *O Most Merciful of the merciful, Thou are Lord of the weak. And You are my Lord.*
> *In whose hand will You entrust me? Unto some far-off stranger who will ill treat me? Or unto a foe whom You have empowered against me? I care not, so You be not wroth with me.*
> *But Your favoring help—that were for me the broader way and the wider scope!*

I take refuge in the Light of Your Countenance whereby all darknesses are illuminated and the things of this world and the next are rightly ordered.[22]

If the Muhammadi Revolution was to start in the heart before transforming a society, it had to replicate the rhythms of the heart. Life is sustained through the beating of the heart, and a heartbeat consists of both contractions and expansions. The contraction of the heart—what might be called the "dark night of the soul" in Christian spirituality—is also part of the path. This is one of the differences between any genuine spiritual path and New Age spiritual fluff, which promises abundant happiness and fulfillment without any parallel process of suffering, penitence, and repentance along the path. After experiencing the Year of Sadness, Muhammad and his community were persecuted and harassed to the utmost degree, but they were soon rewarded with the most magnificent of spiritual gifts.

It was at this period of Muhammad's life that he experienced the heavenly ascension, the *Mi'raj*. Because the Mi'raj is as crucial to understanding the spiritual life of Islam as the crucifixion of Jesus and the enlightenment of the Buddha are to those traditions, we devote a separate discussion to it in the next chapter. If the ascent to the Mountain of Light and the descent to proclaim the message represented the first movement of the Muhammadi Revolution, the Mi'raj represents the second, and central, movement. It is the Mi'raj that marks Muhammad not merely as the Prophet but also as a mystic. Without the Mi'raj, Muhammad is the Warner who is sent to admonish society to abandon its heathen ways and return to God's path. With the Mi'raj, Muhammad also charts a path for humanity to ascend to the Divine. As we saw with the first movement to the Mountain of Light, the Mi'raj also includes both an ascent and a return. Both signal an engagement with humanity after an intimate experience with God.

The Mi'raj, as we shall see, would include a series of movements, from Mecca to Jerusalem, and from Jerusalem to Heaven. In Heaven,

Muhammad would have a direct encounter with God and a powerful mystical experience. And yet, after all of this, he would return to
humanity. The return of Muhammad is paired with an episode that,
depending on the reading, is comical, compassionate, or both. Prior
to returning to this realm of existence, Muhammad met up again with
Moses and announced to his own community: "And what a fine friend
of yours he [Moses] is!" Moses asked the Prophet how many daily
cycles of prayers God had enjoined on Muhammad's community.
Muhammad responded that God had required Muslims to perform
fifty prayers a day. Moses, apparently drawing on his experience in
dealing with his own community, retorted that humanity would never
accept having to offer fifty prayers a day, and he urged Muhammad
to go back to God to renegotiate. Muhammad returned to the Divine
and beseeched God to reduce the burden on humanity. God agreed.
Upon Muhammad's return, Moses asked how many prayers humanity would be expected to perform now, and Muhammad responded
that God had mercifully agreed to reduce the required daily prayers
to forty. Again, Moses impressed upon Muhammad that this would
never do. Each time Muhammad went back to God, and each time
God lowered the burden on humanity until only five prayers a day
were required. Muhammad mentioned that it was his modesty before
God that kept him from bargaining more, and yet, for those who perform those five prayers, it is as if they have performed fifty.

There are some crucial implications in this narrative. First, this
episode takes place at the end of the Mi'raj, and Muhammad would
comment later that for ordinary believers the daily prayers are their
version of the heavenly ascension. The prayers are not simply words
to be read, much less a gymnastic cycle of bows and prostrations.
Rather, they are the occasion for the ordinary faithful to come face-
to-face with the God of the whole universe. In other words, encountering God is not the sole prerogative of Muhammad, but rather the
destiny of all humanity. Second, Islam is intended to be a practical
matter—that is to say, one that can be woven into one's practice.
Here we are reminded of the Qur'an verse: "God does not burden

any human being any more than he is well able to bear" (Qur'an 2:286). According to the Mi'raj narratives, this verse from the end of the second chapter of the Qur'an is one of the blessed ones that had never before been revealed by God to a prophet. God had reserved those blessed verses to honor Muhammad. Third, and most importantly, these narratives provide a model of human negotiation with the Divine, even in matters so lofty as religious obligations. Religion is not a matter of God simply handing teachings to humanity, but the engagement of humanity with the Divine.

There would be one more lesson to be learned from this most sublime of ascensions. Upon his return, Muhammad was received with both awe and disbelief by his community. There would be important differences of opinion among the members of the community about Muhammad's experience, and these differences are recorded in the most reliable sources about Muhammad. The sources that would eventually shape the opinion of the majority insisted that the heavenly ascension took place both physically and spiritually. For them, humanity would someday be resurrected both physically and spiritually, and the life to come would be one of integration of body, mind, and spirit. Others had very different perspectives. Some, including Muhammad's wife A'isha, whom he married after the death of Khadija (we deal with the issue of Muhammad's polygamy later in this chapter), insisted that the whole episode was a visionary experience, one in which the Prophet had a dream-vision (*Roya, Ru'ya*). For them, the realm of the Spirit would always take precedence over the physical realm; to enter the heavenly realm, in their view, one had to cast aside the terrestrial. Regardless, the whole episode is described as one of guidance and mercy for the faithful.

Yet even in the Prophet's age not all were so eager to accept his awesome experience. Some disputed that a being who had gone to sleep in their midst could have been taken to Jerusalem—and up to Heaven. Muhammad's old friend Abu Bakr rose to his defense, stating: "If Muhammad says so, then it is true. And what is so surprising in that? He tells me that communications from God from heaven to earth come to him in an hour of a day or night and I believe him, and that is much more extraordinary than that at which you boggle!"[23] It was at this time that Abu Bakr earned the honorific *Siddiq*, meaning "the one who testifies to the truth." The Qur'an states that God tests humanity with the good and with the bad. Testing with the bad is easy to imagine, as humanity has often been tested with oppression and injustice, exile and poverty. And yet we are also tested with the good, in terms of how we respond to demonstrations of God's grace. Muhammad's Mi'raj represented the highest good bestowed upon humanity, and this "ladder" of grace—the literal meaning of *mi'raj*—has led to humanity both rising up spiritually and falling down.

The Third Movement: Hijra

It was after these experiences, combining profound hardship with unspeakable joy, that Muhammad's last major movement began. This was the emigration to Yathrib, the city that would be renamed Madinat al-nabi ("the City of the Prophet") and forever after known simply as Medina ("the City"). In human history, some religious personages and places have achieved such iconic status that within their own religious world they are referred to as a proper noun. There are many who have been spiritually awakened, for instance, yet to speak of "the Awakened One" is to speak of the Buddha. In the Bible there are many who are anointed, and yet "the Christ" is a reference only to Jesus. And so it is with "the Messenger." There have been innumerable prophets and messengers, but in this spiritual cosmos, to speak of the Messenger of God is to speak of Muhammad, and "the City" in this spiritual cosmos can only refer to Medina. Earlier we used the analogy of Mecca as the heart of the Islamic community, the place to which the community returns to be rejuvenated. In this analogy, Medina's role is to serve as the lungs of the community, as the place the community returns to in order to get in touch and be inspired—literally filled with spirit (etymologically linked to our word "respiration")—not only through God but also through the very being of Muhammad. Even today, many pilgrims describe the pilgrimage to Mecca as a dramatic and awe-inspiring experience, but add that Medina has a charm and sweetness all its own, a "flavor" that they associate with the Prophet. Many Muslims, especially those from South Asia, have written tender and heartfelt poems expressing their prayer to be given the opportunity to visit Medina just once and to be filled with the Muhammadi presence. For many of Muhammad's followers, Medina will always be "the City of the Prophet."

The Mosque of the Prophet in Medina.
Photo courtesy of Farnaz Safi.

Muhammad's migration to Medina would be known as the Hijra, and it is the quintessential marking point of Islamic history. It is worth noting that the Islamic calendar does not begin with the year of Muhammad's birth (as the Christian calendar begins with the birth of Christ), nor does it begin with the commencement of revelation to Muhammad. Rather, it begins with this movement, the third and final movement of the Muhammadi Revolution. This horizontal movement from Mecca to Medina would establish the model community under Muhammad's rule and Muhammad's care. And yet, like all revolutions in the original sense, it had a sense of orbit to it, a circularity, a going forth and then a returning. It entailed, as it had to, an eventual return home and a cleansing of that origin as well.

The pagans of Mecca were stepping up their persecution of Muhammad and his followers, who realized that hostilities were escalating. Whereas in the beginning the persecution was directed at the marginalized members of Muhammad's community, now there were clear indications that Muhammad's own life was in grave danger. In fact, the Meccans were planning the imminent assassination of the Prophet. It was at this time that providential grace provided an opening: a community of people from Yathrib, a city two hundred miles away from Mecca (and not yet known as "the City"), came to Muhammad, offering their allegiance to him and asking him to come to their city to help them settle their tribal disputes. They had been long impressed by Muhammad's qualities as the Amin (the Trustworthy) and saw him as having the Solomonic wisdom to arbitrate among them. Muhammad first sent a few of his followers to Yathrib, while he stayed behind. Amazingly enough, many of the same people who harassed and persecuted Muhammad still trusted him with their belongings. After all, Muhammad was known as Amin even to his enemies. Muhammad would not leave Mecca until he had returned the goods that had been entrusted to him.

After Khadija passed away, Muhammad's two closest friends were Ali—now a strapping young man—and Abu Bakr, a respected elder of the community. Both would play crucial roles in this migration. Muhammad had Ali assume the dangerous task of sleeping in his stead in his bed while the band of assassins waited outside the Prophet's house. The pagans of Mecca had come up with a seemingly ingenious plan: a young man from each of the clans would join the assassins' gang to make sure that no single clan could be targeted in retribution. Yet, as the Qur'an states:

And [remember, O prophet], how those who were bent on denying the truth were scheming against you, in order to restrain you, or to slay you, or to drive you away: thus have they schemed. But God brought their scheme to nothing—and God is above all the schemers. (Qur'an 8:30)

Here was the gist of God's scheme: Muhammad would escape to Yathrib under the cover of the night, while the chivalrous Ali assumed the Prophet's place in bed and bore the risk of his own assassination. Muhammad covered Ali in his green shawl and had him repeat a verse of Surah Ya-Sin as protection. According to tradition, Muhammad sprinkled dust on the heads of the assassins' group, rendering them momentarily blind. This is said to be the meaning of the verse of the Qur'an (36:9) that states: "We [God] have enshrouded them in veils so that they cannot see."[24] Meanwhile, Muhammad and Abu Bakr took to the road, heading toward Yathrib. Standing outside the city, Muhammad looked back lovingly on Mecca and said: "Of all God's earth, you are the dearest place unto me, and the dearest unto God. Had not my people driven me out from you, I would not have left you."[25] The Hijra was neither an abandonment of Mecca nor the forgetting of where one had come from. It was the determination to rise up from oppression, with the intention of returning eventually to redeem even the oppressor.

The pagan assassins followed Muhammad and Abu Bakr and came very close to finding them. Some traditions report that during the Hijra, Muhammad and Abu Bakr hid in a cave for three days. According to these accounts, God miraculously covered the front of the cave with a spiderweb and placed a dove on a tree branch near the cave. In other words, it appeared to be an entry that had not been disturbed. Surely there is something symbolic in these accounts as well: the spiderweb is simultaneously ornate and transparent—yet made from one of the strongest substances in the natural realm. Such is part of God's design: the same creature can be a parable of blessing or of ruination. Here the spiderweb saved the life of the Prophet, and elsewhere in the Qur'an the house of spiders is taken as a parable for those who call upon beings other than God for protection (Qur'an 29:41). The same metaphor can have multiple meanings in a scripture that has infinite layers of meaning. As for the dove perched at the entrance to the cave, as far back as biblical times the dove had been a symbol of the Spirit.

Muhammad and Abu Bakr eventually arrived in Yathrib and were received with joy and beautiful poetry composed in honor of the Prophet. Ali too would join them in a few days. It had taken him three full days to disperse all the goods that Muhammad's enemies and others had entrusted him with, a further indication of the level of trust all had had in the very soul they were persecuting. When Muhammad arrived in Medina, his address there was simple, and a reminder of the need to connect acts of worship with care for the poor:

> *O people, give unto one another greetings of Peace;*
> *feed food unto the hungry;*
> *honor the ties of kinship;*
> *pray in the hours when men sleep.*
> *Thus shall you enter Paradise in peace.*[26]

The first communal action in Medina was establishing the Mosque, truly the first Muslim mosque. It was a simple mosque, built through the cooperation of many of the faithful. The trunks of a few palm trees were used as pillars to support the palm branches that provided shelter from the sun, but most of the courtyard was left open—the model that would be followed in most of the Islamic world.

Muhammad himself joined in the building task, and he was fond of reciting a line of poetry as he worked:

> *No life there is but the life of the Hereafter,*
> *O God, have mercy on the Helpers and the Migrants.*[27]

One of the ways in which God's mercy rained down on the Helpers (the *Ansar*, those from Medina who received the Prophet) and the Migrants (the *Muhajirs*, those who accompanied Muhammad from Mecca) was through a bond of brotherhood. Muhammad's first declaration was to alter the social fabric of the Yathrib (now Medina) community. He had each member of the Helpers pair up with a member of the Migrants, establishing a bond of faith that bypassed, transcended, and inverted tribal connections and socioeconomic class status. Muhammad's own faith-brother would be none other than Ali.

In one of his first speeches, Muhammad preached the following sermon:

> *Praise belongs to God whom I praise and whose praise I implore.*
> *We take refuge in God from our own sins and from the evil of our*
>   *acts.*
> *He whom God guides none can lead astray;*
> *and whom He leads astray none can guide.*
> *I testify that there is no God but He alone,*
> *and He is without comparison. . . .*
> *Love what God loves.*
> *Love God with your hearts,*
> *and weary not of the word of God and its mention.*
> *Harden not your hearts from it. . . .*
> *Love one another in the spirit of God.*
> *Verily God is angry when His covenant is broken.*
> *Peace be upon you.*[28]

This community was one based on faith in God and love for one another "in the spirit of God," as this speech enjoined them to do. It was in Medina that the general moral outlines of Muhammad's teachings became linked with a full set of ethical, legal, and social injunctions. Muslims had prayed ever since the time of Muhammad, Khadija, and Ali, but it was in Medina that the communal prayers were offered on Friday. The Arabs had been familiar with the image of pillars that prop up a tent, and Muhammad used this image to describe the way in which faith is propped up and supported. If faith in God (*Shahada*) was the pillar of the faith, it was in Medina that the pillar became transformed into a whole abode—the abode of Islam.

Even the verses revealed to Muhammad began to change in nature in Medina. The verses in Mecca had been short psalms; often apocalyptic in nature, they spoke of the End of Days. In Mecca the Qur'an spoke poetically and powerfully about how the Earth would be overturned, both a literal description of the events anticipating the Day of Judgment and a symbolic description of how the Muhammadi Revolution was overturning and subverting Arab tribal patterns and the religious polytheism of "the ways of the forefathers."

Yet it was not enough merely to overturn; something had to be offered in return, something more generous, more compassionate, and more beautiful. It was in Medina that these teachings would be offered. The verses of the Qur'an revealed in Medina addressed the very immediate questions that the young community confronted—questions of marriage and death, inheritance and divorce. If in Mecca Muslims were confronted primarily by pagans, here they had to come to terms with the presence of Jews and Christians. As such, many of the verses of the Qur'an revealed in Medina deal with the biblical narratives of the prophets that are familiar to us from the Bible. In fact, Qur'an scholars later would divide the Qur'an into those verses revealed in Mecca (*Makki*) and those revealed in Medina (*Madani*). The implicit assumption is that one cannot understand the meanings of the rich verses of the scriptures without knowing something about the contexts in which—and often against which—they were revealed.

Many who read the Qur'an for the first time are astonished to find that alongside all the verses that discuss God's infinite mercy and compassion—mentioning that God is closer to us, for instance, than our own jugular vein (Qur'an 50:16)—are verses revealed during Muhammad's time in Medina that deal with "the hypocrites": those who lied and cheated and deceived and those who sought to stab the nascent community in the back while pretending to be sympathetic to Muhammad's mission. Without the context, these verses can seem odd, or even cruel. We now turn to the turbulent context of the contentious politics in which Muhammad found himself embroiled in the very city that would be forever remembered as his City.

Muhammad, Hypocrites, Jews, and Pagans

The community in Medina was a complex one, made up of the various Helpers in Medina, the Migrants from Mecca, and the Jews of Medina. While many of the Helpers and Migrants had accepted Muhammad's call, most of the Jews of Medina had maintained their autonomy. One of the extraordinary arrangements that Muhammad undertook was a written covenant with all the tribes in Medina—the Arab tribes as well as the Jewish tribes. The covenant recognized the existing tribal structures and named the various tribes. Each tribe was to be led by its own chief and governed by its own laws, and each tribe agreed to come to the aid of the other tribes if one was attacked. Consequently, a betrayal of the agreement by any member of the tribe would have ramifications for the whole tribe. This framework was key for understanding the tensions that developed later between Muhammad and some of the Jewish tribes. Although the Jews were recognized as Jewish, they were primarily recognized as a tribe, in the same way the Arabs of Medina were recognized as tribes that had willingly entered into this legal agreement.

This covenant, which some historical texts refer to as the Constitution of Medina, is a great model that set up Medina as a multiethnic and indeed multireligious society in which Muhammad was accepted as the supreme authority while also ensuring the autonomy of each religious community. Muhammad's authority was derived from his status both as the Messenger of God and as the "Trustworthy" leader who had inspired the leaders of Yathrib to invite him to the city in the first place to mediate conflicts even among those who were not his followers. The covenant itself—which scholars have for the most part accepted as a historically valid document—is what we would term a secular political treatise that spelled out alliances and promises of mutual protection among a number of tribes, some Arab and some Jewish. It is worth looking at some of its salient features[29]:

> *In the name of God the Compassionate, the Merciful.*
>
> *This is a document from Muhammad the prophet [governing the relations] between the believers and Muslims of Quraysh and Yathrib, and those who followed them and joined them and labored with them. They are one community* (umma) *to the exclusion of all men. . . .*
>
> *The believers shall not leave anyone destitute among them by not paying his redemption money or bloodwit in kindness.*
>
> *A believer shall not take as an ally the freedman of another Muslim against him. The God-fearing believers shall be against the rebellious or him who seeks to spread injustice, or sin or enmity, or corruption between believers; the hand of every man shall be against him even if he be a son of one of them.*
>
> *A believer shall not slay a believer for the sake of an unbeliever, nor shall he aid an unbeliever against a believer.*[30]

As this excerpt articulates, one of the characteristics of this community is that the Muslim *umma* was defined by bonds of faith, which would take precedence over previous tribal affiliations. Equally important was the notion that no one—no matter how destitute—should be left behind. In other words, in this community, faith, not wealth or ancestral nobility, would be the marker of distinction. As the document states, the community of Medina was one community (*umma*). The word *umma* is derived from *umm*, for "mother." The Muslims were to be as if born from one mother in terms of their intimacy toward each other.

The Constitution of Medina goes on to detail the relations with the Jews, who made up a significant population of the City prior to the Hijra.

> *To the Jew who follows us belong help and equality. He shall not be wronged nor shall his enemies be aided. The peace of the believers is indivisible. No separate peace shall be made when believers are fighting in the way of God. Conditions must be fair and equitable to all.*[31]

Here is one of the loftiest ethical commitments of this document: peace and justice are to be conceived of in a holistic fashion, not parceled out to this or that group: "The peace of the believers is indivisible." The Constitution of Medina goes on to define what we might think of as citizenship in a way that would not take hold anywhere else in the world—and not in Europe—for another one thousand years: the notion that Muslims and Jews were equal in this community.

> *The Jews shall contribute to the cost of war as long as they are fighting alongside the believers. The Jews of the Bani 'Awf are one community* (umma) *with the believers—their freedmen and their persons except those who behave unjustly and sinfully, for they hurt but themselves and their families. The same applies to the Jews of the Bani al-Najjar, Bani al-Harith, Bani Sa'ida, Bani Jusham, Bani al-Aws, Bani Tha'laba, and the Jafna.*[32]

It is evident from this description that the Jews were not dealt with as one monolithic entity, but rather as distinct tribes. Some of these tribes would have very harmonious relations with Muhammad, and others would align themselves with Meccan pagans and thus enter into a state of conflict with Islam. Yet both tension and coexistence would be handled on a tribe-by-tribe basis, not through any monolithic policy toward all Jews.

The document further states specifically that "Jews of al-Aws, their freedmen and themselves have the same standing with the people of this document in pure loyalty from the people of this document."[33] In an age when no place in the world defined citizenship on the basis of a constitution, this document—agreed to and signed by Muhammad and the citizens of Yathrib, both Arabs and Jews—stands as a remarkable social contract. While each community was to maintain its religious distinctions, Jews and Muslims were to constitute one umma in their political loyalty to one another.

The Constitution of Medina details the hoped-for ideal in the governing of relations between the Muslims, the residents of Medina, and Jews. What ensued at times measured up to this lofty and laudable ideal, and at other times fell tragically short. The Muslims' tensions with the Jews of Medina were always part of a larger struggle: the increasing hostility between Muhammad's followers in Medina and the pagans of Mecca. The Meccans came to realize that the Muhammadi Revolution presented not only a theological challenge to them but a full-blown social and political challenge as well. As such, they waged a series of wars on Muhammad's community. The Battles of Badr, Uhud, and Khandaq ("the Trench") are well documented in the sources. Each battle would end in a Muslim victory, but present different lessons to be learned. Muhammad's biography by Ibn Ishaq covers the details of each battle in full glory, down to the lists of the 314 Muslims who fought in the Battle of Badr and the 50 Meccan pagans who were killed. The emphasis the biography places on these battles is consistent with a remnant Arab custom of pre-Islamic times: the celebration of the bravery of Arab warriors.

More important than the details are the morals of each battle. Previously, Muslims had been commanded by God to avoid fighting, and yet there came a time when oppression and injustice had to be confronted. As the Qur'an stated at this point:

Permission to fight is given to those against whom war is being wrongfully waged—and indeed, God has the power to aid them to

victory—those who have been driven from their homelands against
all right for no other reason than for them saying: "God is our Lord."
(Qur'an 22:39–40)

In Mecca, Muhammad had preached nonviolence and resistance
vis-à-vis Meccan religious practices. The teachings of Muhammad at
this later phase of his life, however, turned away from pacifism and
recognized that there was a time for peace and a time for war—as
the Bible had recognized. The Qur'an attests that Muhammad was
predisposed by nature to despise war, but that God commanded him
to undertake it when necessary: "Fighting is ordained for you, even
though it be hateful to you" (Qur'an 2:216). The Qur'an emphasizes
that when one has to confront the enemy—those who, in the words
of scripture, have driven one from one's home and oppressed a whole
community—then the fighting must be undertaken in a noble fashion, with set bounds not to be exceeded.

And fight in God's cause against those who wage war against you, but
do not commit aggression—for verily, God does not love aggressors.
(Qur'an 2:190)

Muhammad himself would specify further restrictions on what
could and could not be done in the context of a war. Women, children, and the elderly were not to be killed—so long as they were not
trying to kill Muslims.[34] Religious leaders, like monks and hermits,
were also exempt. Another restriction—of tremendous modern significance—was to avoid killing noncombatant civilians. At one point
Muhammad found a woman who had been slain on the battlefield
and said of her: "She was not one who would have fought."[35] Many
have surmised from this that those who were not directly engaged
in warfare were not proper targets of attacks.[36] According to some
narratives, Muslims were also prohibited from cutting down trees
and poisoning water wells—although scholars have debated these
points.

The picture that emerges from this set of restrictions is that warfare was not to be abandoned to the law of the jungle—or in this case, the law of the desert. Even warfare had to be brought under divine guidance. It might seem strange to some modern sensibilities to overlap war and religious guidance, yet it is worth remembering that when war was largely detached from religious ethics and the throes of nationalism prevailed, humanity ended up with the single bloodiest century ever: the twentieth. If bringing war under religious guidance has not resulted in a nonviolent paradise, detaching it from religious guidance has surely led us into hellacious genocides and holocausts.[37]

The paradigmatic battle in a way was the first one, the Battle of Badr. In that battle, the Muslim armies, vastly outnumbered by the superior Meccan forces, were aided by a cloud of angels riding on stallions whose hooves did not touch the ground. This is how the enemies described the scene, which cast such fear into their hearts that some perished on the spot. This promise of heavenly help is reflected in a verse of the Qur'an in which God promises Muhammad's community:

> *I shall, verily, aid you with a thousand angels following one upon another. (Qur'an 8:9)*

This pattern of God's aid is familiar, of course, to a biblical audience, for at a time of real persecution God's aid has to be real. Muslims have traditionally taken this angelic aid at the Battle of Badr to have been both spiritual and physical, yet some rationalist Muslims in both the premodern and the modern eras have insisted that the angelic aid was purely spiritual. This is how the philosophically inclined Razi took it six hundred years after Muhammad, and how the twentieth-century modernist Rashid Rida and the Qur'an translator Muhammad Asad interpreted it. Regardless of whether one believes this angelic aid to have been spiritual or physical, in the pages of the scripture it is typically connected to the affairs of the heart. In the very next verse after the one quoted here, God offers the faithful a coolness and a delight in their heart:

> *And God ordained this only as a glad tiding,*
> *and that your hearts should thereby be set at rest*
> *—since no victory can come from anyone other than God;*
> *indeed God is Almighty, Wise. (Qur'an 8:10)*

Muhammad, accompanied by angels, leading the battle against the pagans of Mecca. Courtesy of the Topkapi Palace Museum.

Two details about the battle have lingered in the memory of Muhammad's community: one episode from the battle, and one from prior to the battle. During the battle Muhammad took a few pebbles (or dirt) and cast them toward the enemy. The Qur'an insists:

When you threw,
It was not you that threw—
but God that threw. (Qur'an 8:17)

This verse from the very midst of battle—showing how human agency, when the heart has become transformed and the ego-self alchemically transmuted to the point of illumination, can become transparent in the face of divine will—would become a favorite of mystics of Islam. Here the human becomes simply an instrument of God's will. This is, after all, one of the consequences of perfect and total engaged surrender (*islam*), when the human will and the divine will are superimposed. One of the sacred statements of Muhammad (*hadith qudsi*) in fact reflects on this phenomenon. According to this saying, which spiritually oriented Muslims never tire of meditating on, when faithful servants approach God by means of prayers and acts of worship beyond what is required, God loves them. God becomes the sights through which they see, the ears through which they hear, the feet with which they walk, and the hands by which they act. They are granted anything they ask for from God, and God offers them their protection. Appropriately enough, this Sacred Tradition is contained in a chapter of the sayings of Muhammad (the hadith collections) called "Sayings to Make the Heart Tender" (*al-riqaq*). By casting a few pebbles at the enemy during the battle, Muhammad embodied this lofty spiritual station. Even battle, if carried out for the sake of the heart, can lead to the softening of the heart.

The other significant episode took place before the battle. On the way to Badr, Muhammad had his forces disembark close to some water wells. One of the men of Medina—Hubab, the son of Mundhir—went to the Prophet and asked him whether the location was one that the Prophet had chosen merely through his own intuition or whether it was directly inspired by God. The Prophet answered that he had arrived at his choice of location through his own intuition. Hubab then suggested a better and more strategic stopping point that would offer the smaller Muslim army a greater advantage. The Prophet readily agreed to Hubab's suggestion.[38] Here is another indication that not every action of the Prophet is intended to be worthy of direct imitation and emulation and that even Muhammad himself distinguished between things he did that were inspired by God and other actions he took that were open to improvement by knowledge to which others had access. These episodes may be of crucial significance to Muslims in the post-Muhammad age as they figure out how to latch on to the memory of Muhammad, like a child clinging to a mother's breast, while also incorporating into their lives and practice the knowledge they have acquired since his time.

The victory at Badr had a further consequence for Muhammad's community. The more the pagans of Mecca recognized Muhammad as a threat, the more they reached out to factions inside Medina to form alliances to subvert and weaken Muhammad's position there. The Meccans targeted two groups in particular as potential allies: a group the Qur'an called "Hypocrites" (*Munafiqun*) and some Jews. The Hypocrites, so soundly criticized in the second chapter of the Qur'an, were those who pretended to be Muslim while in fact they remained loyal to the pagans. They were led by some of the Khazraj tribe, like Ibn Ubayy. For example, the following harsh passage in the second chapter of the Qur'an is taken in the biography of Muhammad to refer to these Hypocrites:

And there are some who say: "We believe in God and the last day" when they do not believe.
They would deceive God and those who have attained to faith—but they deceive none but themselves, and perceive it not.
In their hearts is disease. (Qur'an 2:8–9)

The heart-disease of the Hypocrites is often contrasted in the Qur'an with the peaceful and pure heart of the faithful. What is more, the biography of Muhammad is replete with accounts of the Hypocrites mocking the Qur'an and the Prophet, in contrast to the faithful, who are commanded to be truthful to God, to the Messenger, and to their own selves.

The response of the Jews of Medina to Muhammad was much more mixed. Ibn Ishaq's early biography of Muhammad speaks of many Jews in glowing terms. Some Jews joined Muhammad's faith, but not all those who are praised did so. Some, like 'Abdullah, the son Salam, saw in Muhammad signs of the foreseen Prophet whom the Jews had also been expecting. Some, like Mukhayriq, even defended Muhammad during a battle that happened to fall on the Sabbath, stating that it was meritorious to do so even if it meant engaging in activity during the Sabbath. Ibn Ishaq's biography of the Prophet is perhaps deliberately ambiguous on the question of whether Mukhayriq formally became Muslim, or whether he was a righteous Jew who had affection for Muhammad.[39] What is known is that Muhammad referred to this learned rabbi as "the best of the Jews" and that after the passing of Muhammad many of the alms that were given to the needy of Medina came from Mukhayriq.

Relations with other Jews, however, were decidedly more tense, or so it seems from some of the readings of our sources. Virtually every one of the episodes that documents tensions between Muhammad and Jews is open to some measure of historical suspicion. These tensions escalated after the Battle of Badr. The main reason seems to have been that many Jews could not believe that the God of their ancestors would have chosen to send a prophet to the Arabs instead of to the Children of Israel.[40] Some Jews from the tribe of Banu Qaynuqa openly mocked the Muslims after the Battle of Badr, stating that the Meccan pagans who had died in the battle and were buried were superior to those aboveground (that is, the surviving Muslims).[41] Furthermore, the Banu Qaynuqa rejected Muhammad's invitation to join him after the battle, stating:

Don't deceive yourself, Muhammad. You have killed a number of inexperienced Quraysh who did not know how to fight. But if you fight us you will learn that we are men and that you have met your equal.[42]

According to the biography of Muhammad by Ibn Ishaq, the Banu Qaynuqa were the first Jewish tribe to annul the agreement that had been made between them and Muhammad.[43] The Banu Qaynuqa had between 400 and 750 armed men and presented a clear danger to the young Muslim community. Muhammad responded by summoning a large force and defeating the Banu Qaynuqa, who were exiled from Medina and had to relocate to a settlement closer to Syria.

But was it actually so? This is how the main narrative of Muhammad's biography presents the tensions with the Banu Qaynuqa. Yet we are led to question this narrative by some scholarly evidence that the main traditions of Muhammad—those preserved in the two most authoritative hadith collections, one composed by Bukhari (d. 870 CE) and the other by the scholar known as Muslim ibn Hajjaj (d. 875 CE)—seem to locate the expulsion of the Banu Qaynuqa as taking place *after* the death of Muhammad.[44] In other words, it seems clear that the Jewish tribe was in fact exiled to the region near Syria, but it is possible that the event took place after the Prophet's passing and was attributed in the sources to the Prophet in order to give a contentious decision some measure of legitimacy.

Tensions with both the Meccans and some of the Jews would continue to escalate. The next conflict, the Battle of Uhud, was even grander in scale. Among the Muslims who went out to the battlefield was a woman, Nusaybah of the Khazraj tribe, who tended to the sick and wounded of the battlefield. And there would be many for her to tend to in this battle. In this decisive engagement, Muslims initially prevailed, chasing the bulk of the Meccan army off the battlefield. Then, tragically, a series of archers whom Muhammad had positioned on a strategic hill abandoned their posts to gather arms left behind on the field by the fleeing Meccan army. Another flank of the Meccan army circled the hill and dove into the Muslim army, killing many and wounding more. Had it not been for the courage of a small band of the closest of Muhammad's companions who remained and protected him (Ali, Talha, Zubayr, and Wahb), the Prophet would have been killed. As it was, Muhammad was severely wounded, with blood running down his cheek. This small band showed such devotion to him that later on Muhammad would look back on that moment, in the shadow of the Mountain of Uhud, as one in which grace and mercy poured down upon the community even in the midst of a battle against all odds. The Meccans outnumbered this small band of companions four to one, and yet could not make any headway in getting closer to the Prophet. When a Meccan horse rider, Ibn Qami'ah, rode close to Muhammad and brought down his sword with full force, Talha threw himself between the sword and the Prophet. Talha would never again use the fingers of his hands for the rest of his life—yet his bravery spared the Prophet's life. It is said that another companion, Wahb, before giving his life as a martyr, single-handedly shot arrows at the pagan army so rapidly that they thought a whole army was protecting Muhammad. Here is an episode in early Islamic history in which the memory of those who gave the greatest sacrifice—their own lives—is commemorated. In fact, in the Qur'an the words for martyr (*shahid*) and a witnessing of faith (*Shahada*) are etymologically linked. The sanctification of martyrs, of course, is well known to Christians as well, since almost all the early Christian saints were martyrs. The Christian martyrs were typically not killed in battle but rather died from persecution, but they too, like the Muslim martyrs, paid the ultimate price for their faith. It is of such souls that the Qur'an says: "Do not think that those who are slain in God's cause are dead—for they are alive with their Lord" (Qur'an 3:169).

In the aftermath of the battle, the Meccans showed their utter disregard for the Muslims by mutilating the bodies of the fallen Muslims. The most notorious of the pagans was a woman named Hind, who was married to Abu Sufyan, the leader of the Meccans. Abu Sufyan belonged to the clan that labeled itself "the Slaves of the Sun," and its members were among Muhammad's primary persecutors. Hind had hired a mercenary to kill Muhammad's uncle, Hamza, who had been one of the Prophet's main protectors. When Hamza fell in the battle of Uhud, Hind had his body mutilated, and she took a bite out of Hamza's still bloody liver. This was an act of unbridled rage and passion, since in ancient Arabic culture the liver—not the heart—was the center of a person's emotions and passions. Abu Sufyan himself hit the side of the face of Hamza's corpse with a spear, mocking the dead soldier by saying: "Taste that, you rebel." How ironic it is that this bloody couple, Abu Sufyan and Hind, would give birth to Mu'awiya, the first emperor of the first Islamic dynasty, the Umayyads. Here is one instance of the Islamic era not being completely disentangled from pre-Islamic power structures.

After the Battle of Uhud was over, Muhammad heard about the mutilation of his uncle and experienced an anger like he had never felt before—yet God's next revelation specifically forbade the mutilation of human bodies, even in revenge. Ever since then, both the letter and the spirit of Islamic law have insisted on the sanctity of human bodies, in life and in death. Any mutilation of human bodies cannot but violate the specific injunctions of the Qur'an and the example of the Prophet[45]:

If you have to respond to an attack, respond only to the extent of the attack leveled against you; but to bear yourself with patience is indeed better for you, since God is with those who are patient in adversity. (Qur'an 16:126)

As was the case after the Battle of Badr, tensions between Muslims and the Jewish tribes that had allied themselves with the Meccan pagans intensified after the Battle of Uhud. Another tribe, the Banu Nadir, made designs on Muhammad's life by attempting to poison him. Once again, this violation of the Constitution of Medina led to the banishing of a Jewish tribe. Muhammad did, however, allow the Banu Nadir to take with them their considerable wealth—at a time when the Muslims were greatly impoverished and Arab customs would have allowed them to plunder the assets of the Jewish tribe.

Other battles with the Meccans would follow, such as "the Trench," in which the Muslims dug a trench around Medina, thus thwarting the attack of the large pagan Meccan army. The ingenious idea for this trench came from a Persian companion of Muhammad's named Salman, who had been raised Zoroastrian and had explored Christianity before attaching himself passionately to Muhammad. Muhammad reciprocated this affection by claiming Salman as a member of his own family (*ahl al-bayt*). Salman's presence demonstrates that Muhammad's community, even in his own lifetime, was not purely an Arab one, including as it did the Persian Salman and the Abyssinian Bilal. This was a foreshadowing of the growth of Muhammad's following after his passing into a worldwide, multiethnic community that went far beyond its Arabic roots.

It was after the Battle of the Trench that one of the most ambiguous and potentially problematic events took place: the clash with the Jewish tribe Banu Qurayza. There is a great deal of scholarly debate about the authenticity of what took place, and given the clashes between Arabs and Jews in the twentieth century, this is one instance in which the question of what actually happened is of paramount importance. According to one version of the story, when Muhammad suspected the Banu Qurayza of disloyalty, he offered them a chance to enter Islam, but they refused. So the compound of the Banu Qurayza was surrounded until they surrendered. At that point they were handed over to the former rabbi of another Jewish tribe, the Banu Qaynuqa. Because this Jewish tribe had formerly been allies of the Aws tribe of Medina (one of the main tribes in Yathrib prior to Muhammad's migration there), the fate of the Banu Qurayza was entrusted to a leader of the tribe of Aws, Sa'd, the son of Mu'adh. Sa'd ruled that the Banu Qurayza would be dealt with harshly—and according to the ruling of Deuteronomy 20:12. Namely, their men would be slaughtered, and their women and children would be made captive.

If such an episode did in fact take place, it represents a harsh reminder of both the biblical and Arab legacy when it came to dealing with the vanquished in an age before the Geneva Conventions and our modern notion of human rights. And it surely serves as a contentious episode that is brought up by those Muslims and Jews (and alas, those Christians!) who like to point to a fundamental tension between Islam and Judaism—or between Muslims and Jews. One could naturally counter by pointing to the innumerable occasions on which Muslims and Jews in fact lived side by side in peace and harmony, yet the symbolic power of these episodes cannot be simply dismissed.

Important scholars in the field have doubted the authenticity of this episode, however, for a number of reasons. There are no indications in the Qur'an that the People of the Book (Jews and Christians) can be dealt with in such a gruesome way. More importantly, if Muhammad had consented to this harsh treatment, his consent would have carried the weight of precedence for later Muslims. Had there been a large massacre of Jews carried out with the tacit approval of Muhammad, we would expect to find ample references to it in the early legal tradition—which we do not. This has led some of the leading scholars of early Islam, such as Wael N. Arafat, to conclude that this episode represents a later fabrication, not from the time of Muhammad, but from a few centuries later, when there was in fact tension between some Muslims and some Jews.[46] It is hard to speak with certainty about this issue, so perhaps the best that we can do—aside from acknowledging profound discomfort about whatever happened—is to say alongside premodern Muslims: God knows better than we do (*Allah" a'lam*). There are simply situations whose historical veracity we cannot ascertain, but God knows what truly happened. It is, furthermore, a statement about God's knowledge of an event, not about divine sanction for that event.

Perhaps the most measured conclusion has been reached by Gordon Newby, the leading historian of the Jews of Arabia, who says that, while there were important tensions between Muhammad and the Jews, Muhammad's underlying policy was not anti-Jewish, since many Jews remained in Medina and the surrounding regions.[47] The fundamental issue seems instead to be one of political loyalty: were the Jewish tribes fundamentally loyal to Muhammad's community—and to their own political covenant with that community—or were they allied with the pagans of Mecca?

Muhammad's Family Life

Somehow, in the midst of all these conflicts and difficulties, Muhammad and his family thrived in Medina. The years in the City were joyous ones for Muhammad personally, and he settled into a very different type of a life than he had had in Mecca. Some things never changed—the communion with God and being surrounded by a small and adoring inner core of companions. The simplicity of Muhammad's lifestyle remained unchanged as well. Here was a man who could have lived as a king had he wanted to, but he insisted on turning over the resources of the community to the poor and the needy. Many verses of the Qur'an in fact associate the most intense spiritual experiences of God with direct action aimed at alleviating poverty in society. Inward and outward concerns would remain not opposites but rivers that flowed into each other and comingled:

Truly pious is the one who has faith in God
and the Last Day and the angels
and the revelation, and the prophets
and spends of his substance
—however much he may cherish it—
upon his near of kin and the orphans and the needy,
and the wayfarer and the beggars

and for the freeing of human beings from bondage;
and is constant in prayer and renders the purifying dues.
  (Qur'an 2:177)

In other words, true piety links faith in God, the angels, and the Prophet with direct action aimed at helping the most marginalized members of society. What is rendered "purifying dues" in this translation is the *Zakat*, a pillar of Muhammad's teachings. Zakat was the alms charity that one gave and that purified one's heart and soul in the process, and no one mirrored this kind of giving better than Muhammad himself. When he was asked, as he often was, what he took pride in, he would say nothing—but if he had to take pride in something, it would only have been his voluntary poverty (*al-faqru fakhri*). As the Qur'an reminds us, all of humanity stands in need of God's generosity and largess.

Muhammad did not simply preach modesty and voluntary poverty but lived it. His close disciple Umar reported that when he went to Muhammad's house, he would be struck each time by the bareness of the room. The furniture consisted of only one mat on the floor with three leather cushions.[48] The rest of the decoration was simply the presence of the Prophet, and the presence of the One who sent the Prophet.

In Medina, Muhammad's household was attached to the Mosque, which was also the gathering place for all the poor and destitute in the City, many of whom had come to Medina from far away to meet the Prophet whose fame was growing around Arabia. Those who resided in the Prophet's household were used to sharing their food, as meager as it was, with the poor who congregated there. As Muhammad was fond of telling them, "Food for one person suffices two persons, and food for two persons suffices four persons, and food for four persons suffices eight persons."[49]

It is one thing to preach voluntary poverty for one's self—as Muhammad and Jesus did, in addition to many other prophets—but it is another thing to watch one's beloved family members suffer through poverty when one could remove all of their material needs. Muhammad's tenderest love was reserved for his daughter Fatima. Fatima was something of a hostess to the poor and destitute of Medina; she ground up so much grain to make bread for them that her hands were covered in blisters. Her husband, Ali, Muhammad's cousin and the first male convert to Islam, was as poor as he was scrupulous, and he used to draw water from wells to earn some income for his family. When they reached the zenith of their poverty, Ali asked Fatima to beseech her father, the de facto ruler of Medina, for some assistance. Fatima went to Muhammad, who asked his daughter: "What has brought you here, my little daughter?" Fatima, overcome with the modesty and shyness that have always been a sign of Muslim piety, could only answer her father, "I have come to offer you greetings of peace," and returned to her husband empty-handed. When Ali saw that she was empty-handed, he returned to the Prophet with her to ask for aid, but Muhammad said that as long as there were poor and destitute people in Medina, he could not bring himself to give aid to his own daughter and son-in-law. That night Muhammad visited the household of Ali and Fatima and sat beside them. He told them that he had brought them something better than what they had asked for: a prayer taught by Gabriel himself. He told them to repeat "Glory be to God" (*subhan Allah*) ten times after each prayer, "Praise be to God" (*al-hamdu lilah*) ten times, and "God is most great" (*Allahu akbar*) ten times, and then, before going to bed, to repeat each formula thirty-three times. This formula, which is still associated with Fatima in Islamic piety, has remained one of the most popular chants among Muslims ever since. No less a person than Ali himself stated that he did not once fail to repeat this prayer formula after the Messenger of God taught it to him.[50]

The same household of Fatima and Ali also brought Muhammad one of his greatest sources of joy—his grandchildren. His love of children became legendary, particularly his love for his grandchildren Hasan and Hossein (also spelled Husayn), who would run through the ranks of the supplicants to jump on their grandfather's back during prostrations. It was these two children whom Muhammad would frequently proclaim as "the dearest unto me of the people of my house."[51] Also beloved was another grandchild, Umamah, whom Muhammad would perch on his shoulders during prayers, putting her gently on the ground during the bowing down and prostrations before restoring her to his blessed shoulders for the recitation of the Qur'an.[52] Quite often he would say of his grandchildren: "O God, I love them—Thou, love them."[53]

Another aspect of his life at this period was marriage. As noted earlier, Muhammad had married Khadija when he was twenty-five and she was forty—and they had stayed married in a monogamous relationship for twenty-five long and happy years. All the children of the Prophet who survived were descended from this marriage, and Khadija, as we have seen, was clearly a supportive, nurturing, strong, and equal partner to Muhammad. Yet after Khadija's passing, Muhammad entered into another model of marriage, one that was consistent with both the biblical and Arabian models. At this point in his life, Muhammad took on multiple wives. Yet even here he broke with custom. As the leader of Medina, he could have married the youngest and the most beautiful—and certainly only virgins—had he wanted to. Yet for the most part he insisted on marrying women who had become widowed or were without protection. More in keeping with the norms of his world was the fact that these marriages were also a means of fortifying friendships and alliances: Muhammad's wives included the daughters of his close friends Abu Bakr and Umar, and his own daughters were married to Ali and Uthman.

Yet even in the household of the Prophet, a polygamous relationship was bound to lead to some tension and jealousy—especially when the wives competed for the Prophet's attention. When Muhammad married Safiyya, a Jewish woman who was young and beautiful, his wife A'isha inquired about the new wife. Upon being told that Safiyya was in fact beautiful, and that the Prophet in fact loved her a great deal, A'isha was consumed by jealousy. The Prophet asked A'isha what she thought of the new bride, and A'isha curtly answered: "I saw in her a Jew like any other Jew." Muhammad patiently corrected her by saying: "Say not so, for she has entered Islam and made good her Islam." When the other wives of Muhammad would tease Safiyya on account of her Jewish ancestry, Muhammad counseled her to respond by saying, "My father is Aaron, and my uncle is Moses."[54] Muhammad used his wit to defuse the jealousy as best he could. On one occasion he brought a necklace to the attention of his wives and informed them that he would place it around the neck of "she whom I love the most." The wives whispered among themselves as to which wife would prove to be the favorite, with most guessing that it would be A'isha. Muhammad placed the necklace around his precious granddaughter's neck, to the amusement of all.

Muhammad bringing together his daughter Fatima and Imam Ali in holy matrimony. Courtesy of the Topkapi Palace Museum.

Over the centuries Muhammad's polygamy would be a topic of frequent discussion for Christians—and, increasingly, Muslims. For many Christians—who conveniently overlook the polygamy of biblical figures like David and Solomon—Muhammad's polygamy provides a licentious contrast to the ascetic and celibate life of Christ (according to the accounts favored by the Church). As in most such discussions, it is hard to transcend the cycle of polemics and apologetics in this one—yet we must try to do precisely that.

The Qur'an itself restricts the number of women a man can marry to four. This marks a severe restriction of the limitless number of spouses a man could have in both the biblical and Arabian traditions. Furthermore, the Qur'an attaches conditions to multiple marriages:

Then marry from among women such as are lawful to you—[even] two, three, or four; but if you have reason to fear that you might not be able to treat them with equal fairness then [only] one. (Qur'an 4:3)

In recent times, Muslim scholars—particularly many women scholars whose voice of Qur'anic interpretation is now being heard clearly—have pointed out two previously ignored aspects of this verse. First, the verse is not about marrying any women a man might desire. Rather, the verse immediately prior to the one quoted here, and even the beginning of the verse quoted earlier (which is almost always quoted only partially, as in this citation, and not in its entirety), deals with another issue: providing for orphans. In other words, this verse does not license polygamy as such, but rather spells out provisions for women whose fathers died when they were young—surely among the most disenfranchised and marginalized members of Muhammad's society. The verses read in full:

Hence, render unto the orphans their possessions, and do not substitute bad things [of your own] for the good things [that belong to them], and do not consume their possessions together with your own.

This, verily, is a great crime.
And if you have reason to fear that you might not act equitably
towards orphans, then marry among women such as are lawful
to you—two, three, or four. (Qur'an 4:2–3)

The linkage between orphans and marriages becomes a bit clearer if we recall the patriarchal and tribal nature of the society into which Muhammad was born. Girls who were orphaned would have lost their immediate financial and tribal protection. When they reached the age of maturity, they would have been considered the least desirable candidates for marriage because they had no surviving parent whose nobility, wealth, and generosity could reflect on their character. They were, in short, among the most marginalized and stigmatized members of society. In some ways, orphaned women in Muhammad's society carried some of the stigma and some of the real financial burden borne by teenage single mothers in our own society. Here is another instance of Muhammad, himself born an orphan and passed around from family to family, providing instruction in real and meaningful solutions for the outcasts of society. In pre-Islamic Arab society, there was no government per se, and no systematic welfare institution. Muhammad's solution was to direct men to marry women who had become orphans as girls—and thus financially and emotionally provide for them.

Returning to the same Qur'anic verses that are often taken as a license for polygamy, yet another obstacle stands out. Other verses in the same chapter suggest that men will never be able to deal justly with multiple wives:

And it will not be within your power
to treat your wives with equal fairness,
however much you may desire it. (Qur'an 4:129)

If the context of these verses is indeed the instruction to marry multiple women should any happen to have become orphans as girls, then it changes one's reading of polygamy—and in that context, the Qur'an would seem to seriously condemn Muslim men who take what should be instruction in tending to the most downtrodden members of society as a license to take on multiple partners. In other words, the passage seems intended to be a directive for providing care for those in need. But this assertion should give us pause. Even allowing for the fact that only a small percentage of Muslim men have ever taken on more than one wife, what does it mean to state that Muslims have misunderstood or abused a verse of the Qur'an? Is one in fact stating that Muslims have misunderstood a verse of scripture for 1,400 years? One cannot answer that question in the affirmative without opening oneself up to the charge of hubris.

In the case of Muhammad himself, it seems clear that most of the women he married did in fact fit the category of the marginalized. Muhammad's cousin Abu Salamah had been married to a woman named Hind (no relation to the liver-eating woman of the same name), whom tradition remembers as Umm Salamah. When Abu Salamah was mortally wounded at the Battle of Uhud, he offered the prayer that a man better than himself would come along to marry his wife. Four months after Abu Salamah died, the Prophet asked Umm Salamah for her hand in marriage. Umm Salamah answered: "I am a woman whose best time has gone, and I am the mother of orphans. What is more, I have a nature of exceeding jealousy, and you, O Messenger of God, already have more than one wife." Muhammad answered:

As to age, I am older than you. As to your jealousy, I will pray God to take it from you; as to your orphan children, God and his Messenger will care for them.[55]

Another wife, Safiyya (whom we met earlier as the object of A'isha's jealousy), was of a Jewish background. Her husband had been killed during the Battle at Khaybar, and she herself was reported to have been of a deeply pious nature. Muhammad offered her a choice of remaining Jewish and going back to her people or becoming Muslim and marrying him. Her answer was: "I choose God and his Messenger."[56] Another beautiful woman of Muhammad's household who was not from a Muslim background was Mariya the Copt; she bore Muhammad a precious son named Ibrahim (Abraham), who perished in infancy.[57]

Other wives were marginalized not on account of their ancestry but because of their status. Muhammad's wife Juwayriya, the daughter of Harith, had been made captive by the Banu Mustaliq tribe. Muhammad paid for her redemption and also offered to rid her of the contract and marry her.[58]

Some of Muhammad's marriages, in a typical Near Eastern pattern, were made to cement bonds of friendship and loyalty. Muhammad married Hafsa, daughter of Umar, as well as A'isha, daughter of Abu Bakr. As was also common in the ancient world, A'isha was betrothed to Muhammad at a young age. There are conflicting reports about her exact age when the marriage was consummated, and this too is a topic of great controversy among both Muslims and polemicists against Islam.[59] A great many of the traditions reported to be from Muhammad were in fact transmitted from A'isha, who figures prominently in the transmission of hadith.

In detailing the reasons why Muhammad took multiple wives—ranging from firming up bonds of friendship to securing the freedom of slaves—we should avoid the modernist trap of minimizing or dismissing Muhammad's own function as a sexual being. The traditional Muslim sources do emphasize that Muhammad saw attraction between men and women as a positive force. In fact, Muhammad rebuked those of his followers who wished to castrate themselves in order to be freed of marital obligations and instead devote themselves wholeheartedly to a life of prayer. He famously said: "Marriage is part of my Sunna." Muhammad elaborated that a well-balanced life was one in which one-third of the day was spent in work, one-third in worship, and one-third with family.

The Return to Mecca

By this point in Muhammad's life, his fame and following had grown to the point that he was able to subdue the Meccan forces. The movement of the Hijra had also come full circle, and the time for leaving his home was over. It was time for Muhammad to return to his earthly home, Mecca, where he had been born, where the first revelation had come, and where the House of God (Ka'ba) would be the central pilgrimage site. Medina was and would remain the City of the Prophet, but it was time for Mecca to be returned to the fold of monotheism, as had been intended when Abraham and Ishmael built the Ka'ba there. Muhammad assembled an army of ten thousand people and began marching toward Mecca. Less than a generation earlier, all that had stood between him and certain death was a cave hidden by a spider-web spun by God's plan. That was part of God's plan, and the return, too, was part of the divine plan. Mecca, where Abraham's temple had been built, was about to be redeemed. This redemption had to be one bathed in mercy.

The mercy of the return home would be shown in ways large and small. On the way to Mecca, Muhammad saw a female dog that had given birth to a new litter of pups. Concerned that the commotion of an army of ten thousand might disturb them, Muhammad bid one of his followers to stand guard over them, sheltering them.[60] After all, the Qur'an (21:107) states that Muhammad was sent as a mercy to all the cosmos, all the creatures, and all the universes. These creatures too followed God's will, and Muhammad was sent as a mercy to them as well.

The mercy that Muhammad showed the dogs of the desert—typically the most despised of all animals in Arabia—he also showed the Meccans who had persecuted him and his followers for a generation. By both Arab and biblical tradition, he had the right to march into Mecca and slaughter all the men and take their women as slaves. Yet Muhammad declared a general amnesty for all, establishing a paradigm for forgiveness at the height of his political power. It is one thing to preach nonviolence and forgiveness when one is politically inferior, and entirely another to mercifully forgive when one has the power to demolish. On the way to Mecca, one of Muhammad's companions named Sa'd, who had been chosen as a standard-bearer, began rejoicing that this was "a day of war, and sanctuary no more." Muhammad ordered Ali to take the flag from Sa'd to make a point about the merciful nature of the day.[61] His old nemesis Abu Sufyan, who had risen up against Muhammad so many times in war, feared for his safety, and yet Muhammad specifically declared Abu Sufyan's house a sanctuary. There is a time to win people over in war, and there is a time to win people over by the charm of one's personality. This was a time for mercy.

The law of revenge and retribution was laid aside, for as Muhammad said: "This is the day of mercy, the day on which God has exalted Quraysh."[62] On this day, Muhammad even forgave an ex-follower who had apostatized and returned to paganism.[63] With his companions around him, Muhammad marched into Mecca and entered the sanctuary around the Ka'ba. It was time to complete the orbit, to finish the circle. Faith in God had been restored in Arabia, and now it was time to recover God's temple in Mecca. As Jesus had cleansed the Temple, now Muhammad would cleanse the Ka'ba. Muhammad stood at the temple that Abraham had built and began restoring the temple of Abraham to its pristine condition, even as he had already restored monotheism to its original message. Since the age of Abraham, some 360 pagan idols had been placed around the Ka'ba. One by one Muhammad pointed to them, and one by one they fell down.[64] The verse of the Qur'an on everyone's lips was this one:

Truth has come,
And falsehood has vanished.
Indeed the false always vanishes. (Qur'an 17:81)

A poet composed a line on this occasion of the smashing of the idols: "You would have seen God's light become manifest."[65] The rest of the conquest of Mecca, the Opening of Mecca, was also a tale of forgiveness and amnesty. Muhammad recited this merciful passage in the Qur'an:

God forgives you, and He is the Most Merciful of the merciful. (Qur'an 12:92)

It is one thing to forgive a faceless enemy, but quite another to reconcile with those who have persecuted us and our loved ones. Muhammad came face-to-face with Hind, who had devoured the liver of Muhammad's uncle Hamza. When she declared her intention to embrace Islam, Muhammad simply said to her: "Welcome." When the son of his former nemesis Abu Jahl entered the area, Muhammad bid his companions to not speak ill of Abu Jahl, for "reviling of the dead gives offense to the living, and reaches not the dead."[66]

One last episode from this day of mercy deserves to be recalled. The idols of paganism were all smashed. According to one report, recorded by the biographer Ibn Ishaq, Muhammad personally spared two images, one of Jesus Christ and the other of Mary.[67] According to the historian al-Waqidi, Muhammad indicated that these two icons were not to be destroyed by protectively putting his hands over them.[68] As had been the case with Judaism, Islamic teachings did not approve of graven images in places of worship. Yet Muhammad's action demonstrates that he and his followers could and did distinguish between idols devoted to polytheistic deities and icons of previous revelations, such as Christianity. Throughout the centuries, Muslim artists have honored Muhammad's decision by not creating icons or images that bear the likeness of the human form in places of worship, though beautiful and reverent miniatures depicting the prophets and saints have been a part of the Islamic arts.

At the conclusion of this blessed day, Muhammad made two speeches that have been preserved. Both emphasize the transformative nature of what the people had witnessed. He told them that aside from the honor of being the custodians of the Ka'ba and providing water for the pilgrims, "every claim of privilege or blood or property [is] obliterated by me."[69] It is hard to overemphasize the revolutionary nature of this pronouncement in an Arab context where nobility of lineage was an obsession. Muhammad reminded his audience that all of humanity came from Adam, and Adam himself came from dust. He concluded by reciting for the people the verses of the Qur'an affirming that honor and nobility are associated only with piety and being mindful and conscious of the presence of God:

> O humankind!
> We created you from a single pair of one male and one female,
> and made you into nations and tribes
> that you may come to intimately know each other,
> (not that you would despise each other).
> Indeed the most honorable of you
> in the sight of God
> is the one who is the most God-conscious. (Qur'an 49:13)

Another companion recorded that after the struggle to liberate Mecca came to an end, Muhammad declared that the grounds of Mecca were sacred territory and that there was to be no more bloodshed there until the Day of Resurrection. He stated: "God made Mecca holy the day He created heaven and earth, and it is the holy of holies until the resurrection day. . . . Now it has regained its former holiness." One of his last statements to the audience was a command to transmit: "Let those here now tell those that are not here."[70]

The community of Muhammad has been fulfilling these vows and, in commemorating Muhammad, continues to share these teachings with those who were not there on that day, but who still receive God's grace.

Completing God's Favor

Toward the end of Muhammad's life, an episode occurred that was intended to teach the Muslim community lessons that had been revealed to them bit by bit. According to this narrative—which appears as the very first statement of Muhammad preserved in the rigorous hadith collection compiled by the scholar Muslim ibn Hajjaj—the Messenger of God was sitting with a small group of companions when a traveler came upon them. The assembly marveled at the origin of this mysterious guest, for his clothes were radiantly white, as if there were no sign of travel upon him. He came up to Muhammad and sat so close to him that their knees touched. He then placed the palms of his hands on Muhammad's thighs and said: "O Muhammad, tell me: what is the meaning of surrender (*islam*)?" Muhammad answered:

> *The surrender is to testify that there is no god but God and that Muhammad is God's messenger, to perform the prayer, bestow the alms, fast Ramadan, and make, if you can, the pilgrimage to the Holy House.*

The questioner said: "You have spoken truthfully." All the companions were astonished that this stranger would first approach Muhammad in such an intimate way, and then proceed to confirm the Prophet's answers. He then said: "Tell me, what is the meaning of faith (*iman*)?" Muhammad answered:

> *To have faith in God and His angels and His scriptures and His messengers and the Last Day, and to have faith that no good or evil comes but by His Providence.*

Yet again the speaker affirmed, "You have spoken truly," and proceeded to ask: "What is spiritual excellence (*ihsan*)?" Muhammad responded:

It is to worship God as if you see Him,
and if you see Him not,
to recall that He sees you.

After a question about the End of Days, the questioner departed. Muhammad turned to his companions and asked: "Do you know who the questioner was?" The companions answered, as was their custom: "God and His Messenger know best." Muhammad said: "It was Gabriel, who had come to teach you your religion."[71]

There are a number of instructive points to be made about this narrative. The pedagogical model of instruction, from God to the angel Gabriel, Gabriel to Muhammad, Muhammad to his immediate companions and ultimately to the listener or reader of the narrative, is yet another example of the transmission of grace and teachings. Also important is the way in which faith, action, and spirituality go hand in hand. It is not enough to have faith in God and the Messenger—one must also feed the poor and perform the prayers. The goal of a religious life, of course, is to see God—as Muhammad saw God. If we cannot—and most of us cannot—then we are reminded to be mindful of how we act by remembering that God nonetheless sees us. Over the centuries some Muslim spiritual teachers have put this injunction even more directly: How would we act if we imagined that the Prophet was watching us, or rather, if we visualized the Prophet (*tasawwur-e rasul*)? How would we act if we imagined that our spiritual teacher was watching us (*tasawwur-e pir*)?

The first set of answers identifies what are commonly called the Five Pillars: the testimony of faith, prayers, alms, fasting, and pilgrimage. The pillar analogy worked well in a society that was used to tents, as they were what propped up everything else. The prayers in particular were identified as crucial to the upkeep of a religious life. Ultimately, the whole of existence was to be transformed into a prayer. But if one could not remain mindful of God with every breath, then at least one could pray five times a day. Yet there had to be more, much more, to a religious life than just the five pillars—just as there is more to a house than the pillars that hold it up. That other component of the religious life was the etiquette, the mannerisms, and the model of selfless and polite behavior that Muhammad embodied and the community has sought to follow.

There is an even more radical assertion in this narrative. What is commonly thought of as "religion" here—that is, Islam—is identified as the first, and only the first, level. Above religion is the level of faith. Religion is the foundation, but not the utmost. One verse of the Qur'an (49:14) addresses the pre-Islamic Arabs who boasted that they had faith (*iman*). God admonishes them that while they have indeed surrendered (*islam*-ed), true faith has not yet entered their hearts. Faith transcends religion even as it permeates it. And there is yet another rank above faith: *ihsan*, the tradition rooted in the qualities of loveliness and beauty (*husn*), is the ultimate path of sanctification. This is the rank of the Friends of God (*Awliya*), the saintly ones who embody the perfection of humanity. All Muslims imitate Muhammad. The faithful have faith in the God of Muhammad. The Friends of God encounter the God of Muhammad directly. These Muslim saints are the ones who ultimately bear the fragrance of Muhammad. If all aspire to God's Paradise, these Friends of God aspire to no less than God.

This too was addressed in some of the teachings of the Friends of God, who devoted themselves above all else to the embodiment of ihsan. One of them, Dhu 'l-Nun Misri, had a vision in which God had gathered all of humanity. They were presented with the riches of the material world, and nine out of ten looked away from God, being absorbed in the affairs of this world. God then presented the remaining with Paradise, and of those who remained, nine out of ten gravitated toward Paradise. To those who remained, God showed the torment of hellfire, and nine out of ten who had remained fled. A small handful remained. God asked them what they wanted, since they had not been attracted by earthly riches, the promise of Paradise, or the threat of hellfire. These few, who represented those who aspire not just for salvation but for sanctification, answered that God knew best. These were the ones who, like Muhammad himself, had been offered a choice between the riches of this world, the riches of the next world, and God Himself, and had chosen God.[72]

The quality of ihsan, this spiritual loveliness, has been embodied by the women and men of God whose particular spiritual fragrance in the Islamic world would be Muhammadi—those who have aspired to be Muhammad-like and to rise to meet God as Muhammad rose to meet God. The most famous of the women was Rabi'a, whose heart burned with the love of God. In one of her best-known prayers, she calls out to God:

> *O Lord, if I worship you for fear of Hell*
> *Burn me in Hell*
> *If I worship you in hope of Paradise*
> *Exclude me from Paradise*
> *But if I worship You for Your own sake,*
> *Do not withhold from me Thy everlasting beauty.*[73]

Illuminated beings like Rabi'a and Dhu 'l-Nun were reminders of the Muhammadi legacy: the potential to rise up to God's throne, experience God face-to-face, and yet out of compassion for humanity choose to return. Through the centuries, Muslim poets came up with a beautiful metaphor for this experience. Paradoxically, it used the imagery of wine intoxication, which Muslims would have understood metaphorically given that alcoholic beverages are forbidden in Islam. Through this imagery, love and spiritual experiences are spoken of as a kind of intoxication, and the one who brings us the "wine" (typically God, a beloved, or a spiritual teacher) is seen as the *Saqi* (the cup-bearer). In the words of these poets, the saintly souls who follow in Muhammad's footsteps love the wine less, and the Divine Cup-Bearer more. They have returned to humanity for the sake of God, not for the sake of spiritual experiences.

The Return Home

Toward the end of Muhammad's earthly life, he began to receive divine indications that he was at the end of this cycle of existence. One of the clearest signs came from the angel Gabriel. In the hadith collection compiled by Bukhari, Muhammad states that each year, in the holy month of Ramadan, Gabriel would visit Muhammad to go over the recitation of the Qur'an that had been revealed up to that point. In the last year of the Prophet's life, Gabriel made Muhammad repeat the recitation twice. Muhammad revealed to his daughter Fatima that he was certain this double-checking of the Qur'an indicated that his time to meet his Maker had come.[74]

After Ramadan came the season of the pilgrimage, and this pilgrimage would be unlike any Arabia had seen. Some thirty thousand people accompanied the Prophet to Mecca, where they circled the Ka'ba. Medina was to remain Muhammad's home, the place where Islamic teachings had shaped a community, but Mecca was fully marked as the pilgrimage (*Hajj*) site for Muslims because it contained the Ka'ba, the House of God. As in the days of Abraham, it was now a temple devoted to the One God, cleansed of all idols. Monotheism had been restored, and the religion of Abraham had prevailed. To this day, 1,400 years later, Muslims dress as Muhammad did on that day and emulate the rituals that Muhammad inscribed. Furthermore, many of the rituals of the Hajj are connected with the legacy of Abraham. It is not enough for the pilgrims to have faith in the God of Abraham—they follow literally in Abraham's footsteps during the Hajj.

On the way back from Mecca to Medina, Muhammad paused and delivered what would be his last major sermon:

> *O people, listen to my words.*
> *I do not know whether I shall ever meet you in this place again after*
>   *this year.*

Your lives and your property are sacrosanct until you meet your Lord,
  as this day and this month are holy. You will surely meet your
  Lord and He will ask you of your works.
I have told you. He who has a pledge let him return it to him who
  entrusted him with it; all usury is abolished. . . .
Wrong not, and you shall not be wrong. . . .
All bloodshed in the pagan periods is to be left unavenged.[75]

The Prophet recognized that the cycle of bloodshed and revenge from the days of the Jahiliyya was rooted in the tribal social structure; in declaring those cycles over and done with, he was asserting the completion of the Muhammadi Revolution. He went on to talk about other aspects of social relations, namely, the family structure. He reminded husbands that they had rights over their wives, and wives that they had rights over their husbands. The one who had been known as the Amin ("the Trustworthy One") and who had delivered God's Trust to humanity reminded men that women are a trust from God (*amanat Allah*), meaning that men would be held accountable and responsible for how they had borne this trust.[76] Some versions of the speech also extend Muhammad's oration to the political realm by stating that he told his community to heed the rule of a ruler who obeyed God's word, even if the ruler was an Abyssinian slave—the lowest of the low in the eyes of the pre-Islamic Arabs. This declaration would have marked Muhammad's final attempt to replace pre-Islamic Arabia's attachment to genealogy and ancestral nobility with piety and faith.[77] Muslims throughout the centuries have not always lived up to this lofty ideal, but Muhammad's egalitarian intentions in issues of race, class, gender, and ethnicity stand clear. Many Muslims have commented that during the annual pilgrimage to Mecca the equality of all humanity is made palpably real to them.

Muhammad concluded his sermon by reminding his community of the importance of heeding God's word—the Qur'an—as well as the beautiful example he himself had left behind for his community. Lastly, he turned to his community and asked them to bear witness:

"O people, have I faithfully delivered unto you my message?"

A powerful murmur of assent, "O God, yea!" arose from thousands
of throats and the vibrant words Allahunna na'm *rolled like thunder*
through the valley. The Prophet raised his forefinger and said:

"O God, bear witness!"[78]

And so the cycle was now complete, and the Muhammadi Revolution had completed a full orbit. Muhammad had attested to God's unity and delivered the message to humanity. He had ascended to God and then returned to deliver humanity from oppression and polytheism, to form the community among humanity, and to remind humanity to bear witness that they had received the message. Muhammad's message echoes the same Qur'anic testimony in which God has humanity bear witness to God's Lordship (7:172), as we shall see in the next chapter. So humanity bears witness to God's Lordship, and humanity bears witness to Muhammad's delivery of the message.

To embrace Islam, a person must publicly utter the Declaration of Faith (*shahada*), which has two components:

La ilaha illa Allah ("There is no deity other than the One God")
Muhammadun rasul Allah ("Muhammad is the Messenger of God")

Islam—literally, a wholehearted engaged surrender to the Divine—is rooted in testifying that there is only one Absolute Deity—God—and bearing witness that this same God has guided humanity through the sending of prophets and messengers, from Adam to Muhammad. Humanity bears witness to God's Lordship prior to the existence of Heaven and Earth, and humanity bears witness here on Earth. The cycle is complete. This completion was attested to in what was perhaps the last of the Qur'anic verses Muhammad received. God said to him:

On this day I have perfected for you your religion,
and completed my favor upon you.

It has been My good pleasure
to choose Islam for you as your faith (Qur'an 5:3)[79]

On the way back to Medina, Muhammad made one more stop. This stop, in a place called Ghadir Khumm, would be of monumental importance in understanding the later direction of Islamic history. There Muhammad ascended a hill once more, as he had ascended the Mountain of Light countless times. This time he ascended not alone but with Ali—his faith-brother, who would later be seen by the Shi'a segment of his community as Muhammad's intended successor and deputy. The Prophet stood on the hilltop and raised Ali's arm so high that the whites of both of their armpits were visible, and he said:

Man kunto mawlahu,
fa 'ali mawlahu.
(For whomever I have been his master,
Ali is his master.)

This episode was attested to in a number of sources, both Sunni and Shi'a alike. Its significance would be open to interpretation, yet it remained a model of transmission of spiritual authority among both Sunnis and Shi'a down through the centuries.

Time would be short. After returning to Medina, Muhammad whispered something in the ear of his daughter Fatima that made her cry. He confided in her that soon he would be passing away. Not being able to stand to see her cry, he whispered something else in her ear that made her laugh. This time he shared with her that, of all his family, she would be the first to join him. Muhammad's love for his daughter was legendary; he was fond of saying that "Fatima is a part of my own body," that he liked whatever she liked, and that whatever hurt her hurt him.[80]

In the last days of his life, he was overcome with a fever. Once, when his condition had improved slightly, he came out of the house

to the communal prayers. His old friend Abu Bakr, who was leading the prayers, out of respect for the Prophet tried to step back to
let Muhammad lead them. The Prophet placed his hands on Abu
Bakr's shoulders and had him continue to lead the prayers. Having
blessed Abu Bakr, and having earlier declared Ali his heir, he sanctified both Ali and Abu Bakr, who later would be the choices of various factions of his community to succeed him. Those who became
the Shi'a would insist on Ali's supreme qualifications to succeed the
Prophet, whereas those who became the Sunni Muslims recognized
Abu Bakr.

Muhammad's last moment was spent with his favorite females—
with his daughter Fatima, according to some, and with his wife A'isha,
according to others. He was offered a vision of his place in Paradise
and given a choice of staying on Earth or departing to his Lord. Earlier, in the Mi'raj, he had returned to humanity to deliver the message
and lead others to sanctification. But now all that had been done.
The Messenger had delivered the message and, even more, he had
embodied the message. His wife A'isha often said of Muhammad that
"his nature *was* the Qur'an." He had become the living embodiment
of this tradition, and there was nothing more to be done. This time
he recited a verse from the Qur'an and returned to his Lord. With his
passing breath, he murmured:

> *With the supreme communion in Paradise, with those upon whom
> God has showered His favor, the prophets and the saints and the
> martyrs and the righteous, most excellent for communion are they.
> (Qur'an 4:68–69)*[81]

One last time he repeated, "With the supreme communion in Paradise," and then closed his eyes.

Those around him began to weep, for they felt as if a gate of mercy
had been closed to them. They sought to console themselves by remembering that, as the Qur'an taught them, the God of Muhammad
was alive and would never die. They rebuked each other for weeping,

even as they themselves wept. Umm Ayman, a woman who was very close to the Prophet, put it best:

Know I not that he has gone to that
which is better for him than this world?
But I weep for the tidings of Heaven
which have been cut off from us.[82]

And yet those who were attached to the memory of Muhammad would never be truly cut off from him. The Messenger was gone, but the message would remain. Muslims have always seen the Qur'an as God's words, but it has also always borne the fragrance of the heart of Muhammad, the channel through which it entered this world. One part of the Muhammadi Revolution was completed. The other part remained: bearing testimony to the message that Muhammad had delivered to them. The rest of the history of Islam has been, in effect, the playing out of this testimony. This history shows us that the Muhammadi community has both fulfilled and failed the trust from Heaven that the Trustworthy Muhammad brought to them. To keep this gate of Heaven open, they have had to keep alive the memory of Muhammad.

The door to the Mosque of the Prophet. Photo courtesy of Farnaz Safi.

A family pilgrimage to commemorate the Prophet. Female pilgrims
Pourandokht Ashtari Safi and Farnaz Safi. Photo courtesy of Farnaz Safi.

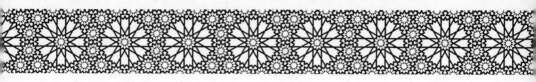

CHAPTER THREE

The Ascension of Muhammad:

FACE-TO-FACE WITH GOD

MUSLIMS, PARTICULARLY IN MODERN TIMES, make a sharp delineation between the authority of the Qur'an and that of other sources, even the words of Muhammad (*hadith*). Yet it is worth noting that while Muslims have always privileged and prioritized the Qur'an as the supreme source of authority, the Qur'an has never been for Muslims the sole source of authority. To put it differently, prior to the last few decades, Muslims had not historically adopted the *Sola scriptura* ("by scripture alone") notions that came to characterize the Protestant Reformation approach to reading scripture. It is only very recently that some Muslims have become so suspicious of all non-Qur'anic Islamic texts that they have sought to abandon everything but the Qur'an as a reliable source for Islamic thought. Before the present day, Muslims' understanding of God, humanity, and reality was always shaped by the Qur'an, but never solely by it. In this way, Muslims have been more similar to Jews and Catholics, who have always looked at scripture through the multiple lenses of the later tradition—a tradition that for Muslims was shaped by the words of Muhammad, extra-scriptural stories

("Tales of the Prophets"), oral narratives, mystical tales, and other texts. In addition, with the exception of select groups like the Kharijis, who were deemed extreme, Muslims always approached the Qur'an through the authority of interpreters. In other words, they understood that scripture never speaks by itself but is always interpreted and mediated through human voices. Another way of saying the same thing is to point out that until the twentieth century, no Muslim would have looked at the index of the Qur'an (or done a Google search) to find out what was expected of them. Divine guidance began with the text, but was always mediated through authoritative—human—teachers.

With the exception of scholars, most Muslims historically may not have even been able to differentiate exactly which parts of their understanding came directly from the Qur'an and which parts were derived from the later tradition. This is not unusual in religious history. For example, the understanding of many Christians in the West of the creation narrative (especially regarding the role of the snake/Satan) has been shaped by later sources, such as Milton's *Paradise Lost*, as much as from any narrow reading of Genesis. Likewise, much of the Jewish understanding of the Bible historically was mediated through the lens of later Midrashic and Talmudic material. When Muslims look back on Muhammad, much of their understanding of his heavenly ascension comes from the tradition that developed around the Qur'an. The prominent Muslim understanding of the heavenly ascension (*mi'raj*) narrative provides a good way to get a sense of how this surrounding tradition fleshes out the occasionally elliptical Qur'anic narratives.

Focusing on this particular narrative is also apropos because, for Muslims, it was Muhammad's most important spiritual experience—it made him worthy of emulation and it inspired a group of mystically inclined Muslims to achieve their own face-to-face encounter with God.

Jacob's Ladder and Muhammad's Mi'raj

Muhammad's heavenly ascension actually comprises a few different journeys. The narrative begins in Mecca and ends with a return to Mecca. In the middle, Muhammad ascends to the heavens to meet with the previous prophets, visits both Heaven and Hell, and has a profoundly mystical face-to-face encounter with God. We explore the details of the narratives one by one and examine the meanings they contain for Muslims.

In the account from the biography of Muhammad, during his heavenly ascension the Prophet was taken up to Heaven on a ladder, the same biblical motif we have seen in the case of Jacob. In the Bible, Jacob put his head down on a stone,

> *And he dreamed.*
> *And behold, a ladder set up on the earth,*
> *and the top of it reached to heaven.*
> *And behold, the angels of God ascending and descending on it.*
>   *(Genesis 28:12)*

When Jacob awakened from his dream, he realized that the Lord was "surely in this place," and he was filled with a sense of awe. Muhammad's experience was quite similar, except that rather than angels ascending the ladder, it was Muhammad himself who ascended to—and descended from—Heaven. And like Jacob, Muhammad too becomes immediately aware of the pervasive presence of God. The ladder (*mi'raj*) in fact lends its name to the whole episode, as well as providing the crucial imagery of ascending. If God is "within," He is also surely "above." Today we conceive of the infiniteness of the universe in a horizontal fashion, measuring space and time in unfathomable light-years. Religiously, humanity has always imagined infinity through the vertical dimension. Divine presence both permeates and transcends this realm of reality. Muhammad ascended this ladder—described as the ladder all of us will climb up at the moment of death—to demonstrate how he transcended this terrestrial realm.

What would it mean to experience death before one has died? One of the most famous statements of Muhammad invites his followers to "Die before you die." Here life and death stand not as opposites but rather as lenses through which the inner meaning of each can be contemplated. What would it mean to live one's life as if one had already tasted death? If we knew that we were going to die tomorrow, how would we treat our loved ones? How would we say our prayers? How tenderly would we hold our children? Would we spend this last series of breaths in spreading war and mischief or accumulating belongings that we could not possibly live long enough to enjoy? Or would we live in compassion and harmony with others? We all have to die at the end of our earthly existence, but what would it mean to live again after the "death" of one's selfishness and the annihilation of the "me-first" part of one's being? These questions provide a taste of the spiritual experience that Muhammad embarked upon. Muhammad was not dead, yet he climbed the ladder that mere mortals climb only after death. His experience is no less than a call for spiritual death—and rebirth—before one has to experience physical death. For Muslims, the memory of the Mi'raj is nothing short of a mandate to recall the reality of the eventual face-to-face encounter with God and to strive for it here in this life as it is promised in the afterlife.

From Mecca to Jerusalem and Meeting with the Prophets

The narrative starts in a quite ordinary way. Muhammad had gone back to the Ka'ba to perform the nighttime prayer. He loved the solitude and the peaceful nature of the Ka'ba at nighttime and often used it as a place of retreat. This night, however, he would be visited by the angel Gabriel, who was to be his companion on an extraordinary journey. That journey would not lead him directly "heavenward" from Mecca, but would first take him to Jerusalem. Thus, before the heavenly ascension proper (*mi'raj*) from Jerusalem to Heaven, there is first the night journey (*isra*) that takes Muhammad from Mecca to Jerusalem. The *isra* emphasizes the commonality of the revelations of Muhammad, Jesus, and Moses, thus reiterating the sanctity of all Abrahamic faiths. It was Jerusalem that served as the first direction of prayer for Muslims, before the decision to change to Mecca. The choice of Jerusalem as the initial site and the ultimate redirection to Mecca indicate both the shared origin of Islam as part of the Abrahamic family and the particularity of Islam.

The isra is alluded to in the Qur'an in the following narratives:

> *Glory to the one who took his servant on a night journey from the sacred place of prayer to the furthest place of prayer upon which we have sent down our blessing, that we might show him some of our signs. (Qur'an 17:1)*

The "sacred place of prayer" (*masjid al-haram*) is the vicinity of the Ka'ba, whereas "the furthest place of prayer" (*masjid al-aqsa*) is the famed Al-Aqsa Mosque, today situated adjacent to the Dome of the Rock in Jerusalem. This narrative connects Mecca, the city of the Ka'ba, built by Abraham and renovated by Muhammad, to Jerusalem, the biblical city of King Solomon.

By Muhammad's time, the Temple of Solomon in Jerusalem had long been demolished. Palestine had gone through multiple hands as the Persians, the Ptolemaic dynasty, the Seleucid Empire, the Romans, and the Byzantines took turns ruling the land of Palestine. By this point in history, the majority of Jews had been exiled from Palestine. Jerusalem played a central spiritual role in the religious life of Judaism, though politically and culturally most Jews were assimilated into their local cultures outside of Palestine. Jerusalem and the surrounding regions, of course, would be sacred to Jews and Christians, and God's plan in transporting Muhammad from Mecca to Heaven via Jerusalem would forever link Muslims with the biblical heritage. For better and for worse, the spiritual destiny of Muslims, Jews, and Christians would be linked in this small piece of land—a place the size of Rhode Island.

The Dome of the Rock in Jerusalem. Photo by Lars Jones, 1994.
Courtesy of the Aga Khan Visual Archive, MIT.

Muslims emerging from Al-Aqsa Mosque in Jerusalem after Friday prayers. The picture is taken from the adjacent Dome of the Rock, indicating its proximity to Al-Aqsa. Photo courtesy of Nagihan Haliloglu.

The Heavenly Ascension of Muhammad. Unlike most images, which veil the Prophet's face with light, in this fine sixteenth-century Persian miniature, Muhammad's face is uncovered. Photo by Schecter Lee. Image copyright © The Metropolitan Museum of Art, New York, NY, U.S.A.

The journey from the Ka'ba to Jerusalem became one of the favorites of Muslim artists, who often depicted Muhammad riding what can only be described as an angel-horse (*buraq*). Some of the extraordinary miniatures even depict Muhammad's face. More widespread are the versions in which his face and whole visage are engulfed in a halo of light and flame. We learned in the previous chapter that Muslims do not produce graven images to be displayed in places of worship. In many parts of the world, however, such as Persia, Turkey, Central Asia, and India, the production of miniatures depicting these sacred narratives was always a treasured courtly art.

According to Ibn Ishaq's biography of Muhammad, when Muhammad was led to Jerusalem, he was taken to a reunion with

Abraham, Moses, Jesus, and other prophets. This was nothing less than a reunion of monotheistic prophets. The prophets joined each other in prayer, again affirming that, from an Islamic point of view, all the prophetic traditions are one and all come from the One. Muhammad, in his capacity as the last of the messengers, led the prophets in prayers, acting as their *imam* (prayer leader).

After seeing the prophets during the meeting in Jerusalem as they had each appeared on Earth—though not in their earthly forms but rather in their spiritual and cosmic reality—Muhammad began the next phase of the journey: the step-by-step ascension to Heaven, the beginning of the Mi'raj proper. Having already seen and prayed with the prophets in Jerusalem, Muhammad again experienced a prophetic sense of fellowship as he visited different prophets in each heavenly sphere. Many in the ancient world believed that the heavens consisted of seven layers and that our own Earth occupied the layer beneath that of the moon. Muhammad's visionary experiences are articulated through this very model of a seven-layered heaven. Upon ascending from the Earth, Muhammad climbed through Heaven layer by layer: Adam was in the first Heaven, greeting the souls of humanity. Jesus and John the Baptist were in the second heavenly sphere. In the third Heaven, Muhammad met Joseph, who is described as a man so beautiful that his face was like a full moon. In the fourth level was Idris (Enoch), and in the fifth Aaron. Moses was in the sixth heavenly sphere, and in the seventh heaven, right before the gates of Paradise, was Abraham. Underscoring the connection to Abraham, Muhammad said: "Never have I seen a man more like myself. This was my father Abraham."[1] We have seen the depictions of Muhammad as recapitulating the monotheism brought forth by Abraham; in Paradise Muhammad came face-to-face with his spiritual—and genealogical—ancestor. As we shall see in the next chapter, Muslims would often link Muhammad and Abraham, devotionally sending blessings on both.

The Choice Between Milk and Wine and the Inner Jewel of Primordial Nature

One of the characteristic features of Islam is the way it intertwines theology and history, mystical insight and biography. In the midst of the biographical narrative of Muhammad's heavenly ascension we are introduced to an episode that contains profound theological meaning for Muslims. At this point in the narrative, Muhammad is brought two vessels, one filled with milk, and the other with wine. Both options are blessed, as both liquids are to be found among the rivers of Paradise, according to the following verse of the Qur'an:

> *Here is the parable of the paradise*
> *which the God-conscious are promised—*
> *In it are rivers of water incorruptible,*
> *and rivers of milk of which the taste never changes,*
> *and rivers of wine, a joy to those who drink it,*
> *and rivers of honey, pure and clean. (Qur'an 47:15)*

There is a choice in Paradise between milk and wine, and yet during the ascension Muhammad picks the cup filled with milk and drinks from it. Gabriel praises Muhammad: "You have been rightly guided to the way of the primordial path, and have thus led your people thereunto. Wine is forbidden to you."[2]

What is this "primordial path," referred to in Islam as the *fitra*? It is one of the keys to a true understanding of Islam. The Qur'an emphasizes the need for us to remember who and what we are— made in the image of God and intended to know God. From this fitra-perspective, the goal is more than merely being saved from sin. It is to return to that state of primordial purity and illumination in which each human being has already been created. According to the Qur'an, there was a period before the entities of time or space existed, a period of pre-eternity (*azal*) when God gathered up the souls of all of humanity and asked them the ultimate rhetorical question:

Alastu bi-rabbikum? (Am I not your Sustaining Lord?)
   (Qur'an 7:172)

The question is one that resonates through Islamic spirituality, as does humanity's answer, the emphatic "Yes!" (*bal*). The Qur'an never pauses to question the existence of God, a reality that it simply takes for granted. Rather, it bears the testimony of humanity's covenant with God's Lordship. There is a difference between divinity and lordship: lordship (*rabbubiya*) is the relationship between humanity and the Divine. God is always God—divinity precedes, permeates, and endures after eternity—but lordship is different. For lordship to exist, humanity has to exist so that the relationship between the lord and the servant can be established. It is well known that humans, as God's servants, need God, yet even the lord "needs" servants if the lord is to assume the quality of lordship. Before humanity enters the cosmic picture, God is God, but until then even God has not yet fully assumed and realized the potential of lordship. Human creation is not an accident, nor is it meaningless. Before creation, God is God, but the quality of lordship has not yet been actualized. Our creation has cosmic consequences even for God, as it enables God to perfect the attribute of lordship through relationship with humanity. An analogy might illustrate the point more clearly. Before a man and a woman have a child, they may be tender and compassionate, but the quality of parenthood has not yet been expressed and actualized. Having a child brings out those latent qualities in parents. That might be an analogy for how lordship creates a situation in which the divine qualities of lordship are expressed. Our creation is not an accident, but a necessary part of the process of divine self-fulfillment.

If this covenant is significant for God, how much more so for humanity: the imprint of this testimony, this witnessing to the lordship of the Divine, is left upon the hearts of humanity. We are created for a purpose: to know God, to be fully human, and to mirror God's attributes in this realm. It is one thing to ask the question of the meaning of life and existence. It is another to state that the creation of humanity is a necessary part of the very process of meaning. The knowledge of this primordial covenant (the 'ahd-e alast, which the mystics of Islam never tire of referring to) is imbedded deep in the human spirit. Here is the ultimate key to understanding Islam: when the Qur'an speaks of "infidels," the term refers not simply to those who have rejected faith, or Muhammad's message. To be an infidel (kafir) in the Qur'anic worldview is literally to cover up something—to cover up the realization of what we are created for. It is the covering up of our own inner jewel of primordial nature, fitra, that is the egregious error of kufr (infidelity).

With that theological connotation of the narrative in mind, let us return to Muhammad's choice between wine and milk. Celestial wine is permissible—even the Qur'an mentions the existence of wine in Paradise, albeit a wine that does not hamper one's judgment or cause drunkenness (Qur'an 37:47)—but wine is forbidden on Earth, as it leads to the clouding of cognition and remembrance. As we have seen, Muhammad picks milk—the drink of babes, the drink that is closer to the primordial sustenance, the maternal sustenance—over wine. In the Islamic tradition, Muhammad is called the Ummi, which all too often is translated as the "unlettered" prophet. Muslims have generally sought to emphasize the miraculous nature of the Qur'an by pointing to Muhammad's lack of formal education, even in reading and writing, prior to receiving the revelation. It is true that Muhammad did not have earthly schooling and that his knowledge of God came to him through revelation. But the word Ummi has another meaning that is much more immediate and intimate than "unlettered." The word comes from Umm, meaning "mother." So Muhammad is also the maternal Prophet, the one who chose the milk of the mother over the wine. Likewise, Muslims who follow in his footsteps choose the innocence of babes, a return to the pure spiritual innocence of the fitra. In a remarkable gender-bending narrative, the Persian mystic poet 'Attar even asks the Prophet to be like a mother, nursing the infantlike umma—also derived from Umm (mother)—from his breast of mercy.

Shir deh mā rā az pestān-e karam
(Give us milk from the breast of generosity.)[3]

Muhammad's Visit to Heaven and Hell

In a way that is characteristic of Islam, the mystical and the social again comingle in Muhammad's experience of Heaven and Hell. Those spiritual experiences of witnessing the joys of Paradise and directly encountering God take place, not in isolation, but right alongside social reflections. Even though Muhammad rises through the seven layers of Heaven and has a direct vision of God, not all celestial realities prove to be beatific. As Heaven is real, so is Hell. Muhammad was also taken on a tour of Hell to show him the punishment that awaits the sinful. One episode in particular impresses upon the reader the dire and serious consequence of evil actions. Throughout his visit Muhammad is greeted by smiling prophets and cherubic angels, but when he meets the Keeper of the Gates of Hell he finally confronts the one angel who does not smile upon meeting him. Yet the ascending Prophet is assured that, if this angel, named Malik, were ever to smile, he would smile upon meeting Muhammad.

While Muslim artists have commonly focused on depicting Muhammad's ascension through Paradise, a few have also imagined Muhammad's visit to the torment of hellfire.

Muhammad's look inside Hell reveals the suffering of the Children of Adam to be real and tangible. Evil is not left abstract, but connected in a most direct way to earthly abominations. When Muhammad sees men who take a firelike stone into the pit of their stomach, he is informed that these are those who usurped the wealth of orphans. Muhammad's vision literally acts out and confirms what the Qur'an has described, comparing the usurping of orphans' property to devouring hellfire:

Those who unjustly devour the property of orphans,
devour a fire into their own bodies.
They will soon be enduring a blazing Fire. (Qur'an 4:10)

Time and again, the Qur'an speaks out on behalf of the disenfranchised, the poor, the needy, the traveler, and always, always, the orphans. The orphans, who in a tribal society were among the most vulnerable, were close to Muhammad's own heart because his own father had passed away prior to his birth.

The Miraj-Nama, *Persian, fifteenth century. Gabriel shows Muhammad*
how those who devour the property of orphans on Earth are punished in hell
by having molten lead poured down their throats.
Courtesy of Bibliotheque Nationale, Paris.

Usurping the property of orphans is not the only sin whose punishment Muhammad witnesses. He also sees the punishment of those who grew rich through usury on earth, and of those who chased after illicit sexual relations and betrayed the good partners God had given them. In each case, God had provided a way that was good and beautiful but some chose to pursue their own passions. In Hell the very thing they pursued is transformed into a hideous punishment they must literally devour. Lastly, Muhammad also witnesses the punishment of those who transgressed against the bonds of familial relations.

The horrors of hellfire in this narrative are directly attributed to our own vices. In other words, injustice, lust, greed, and cruelty are the very source of hellfire. We are the fuel of our own burning. The Qur'an repeatedly talks about how we "send forth" our actions to the Hereafter. The reader is left to ponder what would happen to hellfire if we stopped feeding it with our sins.

If the description of Hell is graphic and painful, the imagery for Paradise depicts a garden of delight. Consistent with the spiritual nature of these passages, the joy of Paradise is first described through Muhammad's encounter with different prophetic figures at various layers of Paradise. Some of the loveliest of all Islamic miniatures depict the scenes of Muhammad ascending through Paradise.

In seeking to convey the beauties of Paradise to an earthly audience, Muhammad states:

> A piece of Paradise the size of a bow is better than all beneath the sun, whereon it rises and sets.
>
> If a woman of the people of Paradise appeared unto the people of earth, she would fill the space between Heaven and here below with light and with fragrance.[5]

A Direct Encounter with God

As we have seen, Jerusalem would not be the destination of Muhammad's journey, but rather the Lord of Jerusalem, the Lord of Mecca, and the Lord of all the worlds. Likewise, Heaven and Hell would not be the end of the journey, but rather the Lord of Heaven. The

Qur'anic narrative gives us another passage that broadly outlines the zenith of Muhammad's heavenly ascension toward a direct encounter with God.

Muhammad ascending through the heavens, accompanied by angels.
From Nezami's Khamsa, *produced in Tabriz, Iran, 1539–43.*
©The British Library Board.

By the star when it sets
Your companion has not gone astray nor is he deluded
He does not speak out of desire
It is nothing less than an inspiration inspired
Taught to him by one of great power
And strength that stretched out over
While on the highest horizon.
Then drew near and descended

At a distance of two bows' lengths or nearer
He revealed in his servant what he revealed. (Qur'an 53:1–10)[6]

This passage, simultaneously vibrant and veiled, has captured the spiritual imagination of Muslims for over one thousand years. The narrative here, like a great Hitchcock mystery, works precisely by allowing the imagination of the audience to supply the details as it leaves things suggested, indeed unsaid. The combination of saying, unsaying, and imagination provides an inviting context in which the reader is not just reading words on a page but participating in the production of the meaning. In the passage, the phrase "Your companion" clearly refers to Muhammad: it is affirmed that Muhammad is not going astray, and that the words do not arise out of Muhammad's own desires or delusions. Then the picture becomes elliptical and mysterious. In response to this mystery, Muslims have offered varying opinions about the precise meaning of these verses. These different opinions tell us a great deal about how different Muslims have come to conceptualize the relationship not just between God and Muhammad but between God and humanity. To appreciate these differences, we turn to a close reading of these verses.

What we know from the verse is that Muhammad has been taught by "one of great power" who sends down the inspiration (*wahy*) to Muhammad. But who is this mysterious character? Is it God? Is it Gabriel? Does it make a difference in the meaning of the episode? The difference is as great as the difference between God and angels. Different Muslims have come up with different ways of imagining the identity of this unnamed character identified simply as "one of great power," and those differences tell us a great deal about their assumptions vis-à-vis God and humanity. A dominant tradition has been to state that the unnamed character is in fact Gabriel, since Gabriel is the angel of revelation. According to this reading, Muhammad is said to have had a vision of Gabriel during his spiritual journey. This type of narrative has appealed to those Muslims who theologically like for God to remain God and humanity to remain humanity, with the twain never meeting. This has been a popular interpretation of the passage among many Muslim theologians and rationalists.

Yet other Muslims have read the same narrative and imagined this encounter in powerfully different ways. These are the Muslims who yearn for nothing less than seeing the very face of God. For them, the "one of great power" who teaches the Qur'an is none other than God. In this reading of the Qur'an—which the rules of Arabic grammar make equally plausible—Muhammad has a face-to-face encounter with the Divine. What is more, if Muhammad ascended to God—if it is indeed possible to have a direct encounter with God—then this possibility is open to all of humanity, including modern Muslims. The Muslims who gravitate toward this reading of the ascension are usually known as the mystics (Sufis) of the Islamic community. For them, these narratives are not just about accounts of the time of Muhammad but descriptions of reality even now: as it was then, so it is now. As with Muhammad, so with us. In fact, for these mystical Muslims the very model of a spiritual life becomes nothing short of first aspiring to and then attaining (God willing) a direct encounter with God.

This difference of interpretation also tells us a great deal about the ways in which these various groups of Muslims see and emulate Muhammad. All Muslims emulate the Prophet. It is in how the Prophet's ascension is interpreted that Muslims differentiate themselves. If Muhammad went to see God, then ordinary Muslims want to emulate the one who saw God. The mystics of Islam, on the other hand, want to follow Muhammad completely by stepping in his footsteps. Not being content to merely imitate Muhammad, they want to experience what Muhammad experienced, and embody what he embodied. If Muhammad saw God, they want to see God. If Muhammad ascended to heaven, they want to ascend to heaven. All of these interpretations have something very important in common, namely, the reverence for Muhammad who shows Muslims the path to God. The first group so reveres Muhammad that they believe he attained spiritual experiences—like direct encounter with God—that are not open to most human beings. The second group so reveres Muhammad that they wish for a Muhammadi encounter with God of their own. Paradoxically, these mystics take following in Muhammad's footsteps literally. Here is one of the intriguing aspects of a religious tradition in which God is revealed through a sacred language: mystical readings of scripture, and of God, emerge not by going around the literal meaning—that is, by arguing that literal interpretations are not the most important readings—but rather by going through them. The literal meaning of scripture does not close off the possibility of deeper meanings—it leads to them.

Meeting God (or Gabriel) Face-to-Face

Almost every part of the passage has been subject to further elaboration and unpacking over the years. How close did Muhammad come to God/Gabriel? According to the narrative, it was two bows' lengths (*qab qawsayn*), or even nearer (*aw adna*). The first commentaries that grew up around the verse speculated on the meaning of "two bows' lengths." Those who are more theologically inclined and who like to keep God and humanity at arm's length from each other interpret this phrase as twice the distance that a bow can shoot an arrow—thus, about the length of a football field. Others read it as the length of two bows, that is, a few feet. Yet others, more mischievous, imagine a bow whose string has been pulled—as in the distance between the two ends of the bow, a few inches apart. What matters in the end, of course, is not the actual distance intended by the phrase but the involvement of the human being in imagining increasing levels of intimacy between humanity and God.

And after books have been written speculating on this question, after words have been exhausted—as the Qur'an says, if the oceans were ink and trees were pens, the praise of our Lord still could not be exhausted—in one short phrase the Qur'an points simultaneously to the limitation of language and the invitation to dream more: "or nearer." God—or Gabriel—came as close as two bows' lengths (however that is understood)—*or nearer*. This is what great literature has in common with scripture, with *The X-Files*, and with Hitchcock: the power of suggestion. The Qur'an repeatedly warns humanity about baseless conjecture (*zann*) in attributing to God falsehood. Yet there is another type of imagination that the tradition identifies as beatific (*khayal*), and as one that can lead humanity closer to God.

The concluding lines of this Qur'anic verse state:

The heart did not lie in what it saw.
Will you then dispute with him on his vision?
He saw him descending another time
At the lote tree of furthest limit.
Therein was the garden of sanctuary
When there enveloped the tree what enveloped it
His gaze did not turn aside nor did it overreach.
He had seen the signs of his lords, great signs.[7] *(Qur'an 53:13–18)*

Here again the mystery of the passage continues: Muhammad sees not with his eyes but rather with his heart (*fu'ad*). The heart spoken of here is not just the lumpy muscle in the chest but the very throne of God's spirit. Did God not reveal to Muhammad in a private communication that the "Heavens and the Earth do not contain me, but the heart of my faithful servant" does? Of all the human faculties, it is the heart that is most suitable for beholding the Divine. When humanity was created, God breathed into humanity something of Divine Spirit. As the Qur'an states in one of those rare and marvelous verses in which God speaks in the first-person voice:

Wa nafakhtu fihi min ruhi.
(I breathed into humanity something of My own Spirit.)
   (Qur'an 38:72)

The spirit, whose seat is always the heart, is that in humanity which is from God, closest to God, and thus most suitable for perceiving and beholding the Divine.

Traditional Accounts of Muhammad's Encounter with God

As we have seen, the Qur'anic narratives about Muhammad's heavenly journey are rich, yet elliptical. These verses invite us to engage them using the faculty of imagination. And this is precisely what Muslims have done throughout the centuries, taking these Qur'anic passages and fleshing them out by weaving them together with the teachings of the Prophet, the commentary of scholars, and the inner intuition of Muslims who reflect on God's word. The first layer, as always, came from Muhammad's own memory, as preserved through the standard biography of the Prophet. Subsequent layers came from the later sources that attempted to fill in the elliptical Qur'anic nuggets and create a more complete narrative. Here we examine one such later, fuller narrative of the ascension.

The full description of Muhammad's encounter with the Divine is told in slightly different versions in different treatises. One of the most explicit is the version from the fifteenth-century scholar al-Suyuti, whose *al-La'ali al-masnu'ah* details the following:

> *Now when I was brought on my Night Journey to the [place of the] Throne and drew near to it, a green rafraf [a silk brocade] was let down to me, a thing too beautiful for me to describe to you, whereat Gabriel advanced and seated me on it. Then he had to withdraw from me, placing his hands over his eyes, fearing lest his sight be destroyed by the scintillating light of the Throne, and he began to weep aloud, uttering tasbih, tahmid and tathniya [words of praise] to Allah.*
>
> *By Allah's leave, as a sign of His mercy toward me and the perfection of His favor to me, that rafraf floated me into the [presence*

of the] Lord of the Throne, a thing too stupendous for the tongue to tell of or the imagination to picture. My sight was so dazzled by it that I feared blindness. Therefore I shut my eyes, which was by Allah's good favor. When I thus veiled my sight Allah shifted my sight [from my eyes] to my heart, so with my heart I began to look at what I had been looking at with my eyes.

It was a light so bright in its scintillation that I despair of ever describing to you what I saw of his majesty. Then I besought my Lord to complete his favor to me by granting me the boon of having a steadfast vision of Him with my heart. This my Lord did, giving me that favor, so I gazed at him with my heart till it was steady and I had a steady vision of Him.[8]

A key aspect of this narrative deals with how Gabriel brings Muhammad from Earth through the levels of Paradise but is unable to enter into the direct divine presence. There the intensity of divine light and love is too great for Gabriel, who, as some later Muslim poets would put it, is afraid that the intensity of divine love will burn his feathers. Muhammad alone disembarks and enters into the divine presence. Here is the full promise of what it means to be human: we can ascend to a height and a level of intimacy with God that angels dare not attempt. This is the return to one's Origin—to be transformed into the very light of God at the core of our *fitra* (primordial nature). Only light can enter into light—only that which comes from God can enter into divine presence. The Mi'raj exemplifies the astonishing capability of humanity to enter into this communion, this mystical experience with God. As Muhammad ascends, so too does the community of Muhammad aspire to ascend. As Muhammad goes, so goes the Muhammadi community.

Gabriel's shielding of his eyes and Muhammad's awe correspond to what some religion scholars have called *mysterium tremendum*. We have seen this same quality acted out in the Bible when Isaiah shouts out that he is a man unworthy of beholding the Divine. Before one enters into the tender presence of God, there has to be awareness of the awesome quality of God (*mysterium tremendum*) and the complementary quality of *mysterium fascinans* that draws one toward and into the Divine. Without the awesome, majestic quality of God, the Divine is nothing more than a cosmic Santa Claus. With it, the cosmic dance of majesty and intimacy continues. These dual qualities of the Divine are what Muslims have referred to as the qualities of *jalal* (majesty, glory, might, power, awe-inspiring) and *jamal* (beauty, mercy, compassion, tenderness). The key, as always, is not to abandon the *jalal* (glory) or the *jamal* (beauty)—not to sublimate the *mysterium tremendum* or the *mysterium fascinans*—but rather to go through them and harmonize them, arriving at what Muslims have called *kamal* (perfection). The harmony of jalal and jamal leads to kamal—yet another series of rhyming words whose sound resonates in the meaning.

As we have said previously, for the Muslim the goal of human creation is for humanity to reflect divine qualities onto this realm. If God is perfect, then there is a way for the human being to reflect the perfection of God on this Earth. It is this quality of perfection that the later mystics would summarize as the attributes of *Insan al-Kamil* (the perfected and completed human being), the one who brings together all of the divine qualities and attributes. And naturally, in the Islamic tradition the very model of the perfected and completed human being is recognized as Muhammad. Muhammad's ascension replicates this complete and perfect encounter with the Divine.

Whereas the Qur'an leaves Muhammad's encounter with God to the imagination, the biographical tradition fleshes it out. The Mi'raj narrative continues to open up the corresponding verses of the Qur'an. It is worth mentioning that the very word for commentary, *sharh*, literally means "to open up." These commentary traditions are seen as opening up the inner meanings of scripture:

> *"There He was, when the veil had been lifted from Him, seated on His Throne, in His dignity, his might, His glory, His exaltedness, but beyond that it is not permitted me to describe Him to you. Glory be to Him! How majestic is He! How bountiful are His works! How*

exalted is His position! How brilliant is His light! Then He lowered somewhat for me His dignity and drew me near to Him, which is as He has said in His book, informing you of how He would deal with me and honor me:

> *One of great power*
> *And strength that stretched out over*
> *While on the highest horizon.*
> *Then drew near and descended*
> *At a distance of two bows' lengths or nearer"*
> *(Qur'an 53:5–9).*

This means that when He inclined to me He drew me as near to Him as the distance between the two ends of a bow, nay, rather nearer than the distance between the crotch of the bow and its curved ends. "He revealed in his servant what he revealed" (Qur'an 53:4), that is, which matters He had decided to enjoin upon me.[9]

In this telling of the ascension, the narrative has already identi-fied the "one of great power" directly with God. Here is a potential drawback of these narratives that flesh out the ambiguity and nuance of the Qur'an: some of the possibilities have to be laid aside in order to clarify the other possibilities. Yet these texts in general do not aim to dismiss the other possibilities; instead, each provides one possible point of view. This text goes on to record in even more glorious detail Muhammad's most personal encounter with God:

Now when He—glory be to Him—lowered His dignity for me He placed one of His hands between my shoulders and I felt the coldness of His fingertips for a while on my heart, whereat I experienced such a sweetness, so pleasant a perfume, so delightful a coolness, such a sense of honor in [being granted this] vision of Him, that all my terrors melted away and my fears departed from me, so my heart became tranquil.

Then I was filled with joy, my eyes were refreshed, and such delight and happiness took hold of me that I began to bend and sway to right and left like one overtaken by slumber.

Indeed, it seemed to me as though everyone in heaven and earth had died, for I heard no voices of angels, nor during the vision of my Lord did I see any dark bodies. My Lord left me there such time as He willed, then brought me back to my senses, and it was as though I had been asleep and had awakened.

My mind returned to me and I was tranquil, realizing where I was and how I was enjoying surpassing favor and being shown manifest preference.[10]

The coolness and delight in his heart that Muhammad describes upon meeting God—recall that in Arabic coolness of the eyes and heart denote the utmost joy, whereas in English we speak of "warming" the heart—come to epitomize spiritual ecstasy and joy. Later mystics who engaged in intense spiritual experiences referenced even their own swaying to Muhammad's motions. As for Muhammad himself, he summarized this "time" with God by saying: "Indeed I have with my Lord a Moment (*waqt*)."

Note that he does not say "I had" a moment with my Lord, but rather, "I have" a moment. This encounter with God—*this* moment—becomes a relationship that never entirely disappears. Muhammad returns to the moment (*waqt*), and so do the later mystics of Islam, who come to identify themselves as *ibn al-waqt*, Children of the Moment. All mystical paths speak of the need to "live in the moment"—that is, to be unattached to past suffering and unconcerned about the anxieties and hopes of the future. For the Muhammadi mystics, a goal of the spiritual path is to be with God here and now—in the very moment, as they say, when the breath has gone into the chest and has not yet departed.

Mystical Tales of Ascending in Muhammad's Footsteps

Even the minute details of Muhammad's ascension would be emulated by these Children of the Moment who followed in the Muhammadi path of grace. One of the last details of the ascension mentioned in the Qur'an is that "his gaze did not waver nor did it stray. Truly did he see some of the most profound of his Sustainer's symbols" (Qur'an 53:17–18). Here Muhammad is revealed as a mature spiritual being, whose eye-of-the-heart can behold God and not turn away and not be distracted in the awe of the moment. As Muslims through the centuries have emulated Muhammad in their own spiritual lives, this quality is one that they have sought to replicate and duplicate. Since Muhammad went on an ascension, a select group of saintly beings, referred to in the Islamic tradition as the Friends of God (*Awliya*), also had spiritual experiences of ascension. One of the early Friends of God whose fame would travel down through the centuries was Bayazid (Abu Yazid) Bistami, a ninth-century Muslim mystic from Persia. Bayazid was among the first to pattern his spiritual experiences of ascension after Muhammad and to describe his own tale as one of the annihilation of his ego-self in God, with the permanence of only that which is God. Echoing the common cosmology of his day, Bayazid described having ascended through seven layers of Heaven. At each layer of Heaven, he meets a different prophet or angelic figure in Islam's spiritually populous cosmos. Each dazzlingly beautiful, these angels offer the Friend of God (*wali*) "gifts of every kind" and "dominion over every Heaven." Yet following in the footsteps of Muhammad, Bayazid turns down these offers by stating: "O my dear one, my goal is other than what you are showing me."

Bayazid ascends as Muhammad did, in the footsteps of Muhammad, until he too reaches God, who addresses him, as Muhammad had been addressed:

To me, to me!
O my chosen one,

Come near to me,
And look upon the plains of my splendor
and the domains of my brightness
Sit upon the carpet of my holiness . . .
You are my chosen one,
My beloved. . . .[11]

Even Bayazid's response is like that of Muhammad: "Upon hearing that, it was as if I were melting like melting lead. Then he gave me a drink from the spring of graciousness with the cup of intimacy." Affirming the connection to the Prophet, in this last phase Bayazid is received by the spirit of each prophet, in particular that of Muhammad, who receives him, welcomes him, and blesses the saint who has literally followed in his footsteps to reach God. This is one of the unique aspects of Islamic spirituality: a combination of the call to follow the Muhammadi path with the necessity of ascending to meet God directly.[12] It is, paradoxically, following the Muhammadi path that leads one to have an immediate, unmediated encounter with the Divine.

Let us return one last time to Muhammad's own narrative, as recorded in these later biographies. Some record a conversation between God and Muhammad about spiritual "degrees" and "excellences." God reveals that the degree of one's spiritual development is a reflection of how well one conducts religious observances, like prayers and ablutions, even in the face of hardship. In the full articulation of the Islamic tradition, the legal and spiritual dimensions always exist side by side, like the two wings of the angelic creature that carried the Prophet into the presence of God. Ritual is not characterized as mindless, repetitive acts, as modern critics of religion have asserted, but rather as the very substance and structure that a spiritual path requires. As for the "excellences" that God reveals to Muhammad, they are more socially significant acts such as feeding the hungry and spreading peace. Yet again in the sublime moments of utmost mystical experience, the concern for social justice never disappears.

The concluding lines of the Mi'raj narrative place Muhammad in the context of the prophetic chain of messengers and detail the gifts that God will bestow on the community of Muhammad:

> *Never have I heard anything sweeter or more pleasant than the melodious sound of His voice. Such was the sweetness of His melodious voice that it gave me confidence, and so I spoke to Him of my need. I said:*
> *"O Lord, You took Abraham as a friend,*
> *You spoke with Moses face to face,*
> *You raised Enoch to a high place,*
> *You gave Solomon a kingdom such as none after him might attain,*
> *and You gave to David the Psalms.*
> *What then is there for me, O Lord?"*
> *He replied:*
> *"O Muhammad,*
> *I take you as a friend just as I took Abraham as a friend.*
> *I am speaking to you just as I spoke face to face with Moses.*
> *I am giving you the Fatiha [the opening chapter of the Qur'an] and the closing verses of al-Baqara [Qur'an 2:284–86], both of which are from the treasuries of My Throne and which I have given to no prophet before you.*
> *I am sending you as a prophet to the white folk of the earth and the black folk and the red folk, to jinn and to men thereon, though never before you have I sent a prophet to the whole of them."*

After promising Muhammad's community success on earth, God sends down a promise to exalt Muhammad's name, "even to the extent of conjoining it with My name, so that none of the regulations of My religion will ever be mentioned without you being mentioned along with Me."[13]

And so it has remained for 1,400 years, Muhammad's name conjoined with God's name. Most of the honorifics that Muslims bestow on the Prophet link his name with God's name: Muhammad is the

Messenger of God (*Rasul Allah*), the Prophet of God (*Nabi Allah*), the Beloved of God (*Habib Allah*), the Servant of God (*'Abd Allah*), the Intercessor before God (*Shafi' Allah*), and so on. Muslims are often described as the recipients of the *Shahadatayn*—the two testimonies, the two *shahada*s—which testify that there is no deity except the One True God and witness that Muhammad is the Messenger of God. In other words, Islam is not simply about the existence of one Absolute Deity (*la ilaha illah Allah*), but also about the fact that this deity is related to humanity through the sending of messengers (*Muhammad^un Rasul Allah*). Just as the statement *la ilaha illah Allah* is about so much more than simple monotheism, referring also to *Tawhid* (Oneness, Unity) in all its theological and mystical connotations, the idea of *Muhammad^un Rasul Allah* encompasses all the ways in which Muhammad, as the embodiment of the ideal of humanity, is himself connected to Allah, and in turn connects humanity to Allah.

The Return to Humanity

As powerful as the narratives of ascension are, grace for the community does not end with the ascension. To every ascent, there is a descent. Although most Muslims focus on the experience of ascension, it is important to realize that there has to be grace in both the ascension and the return. The Qur'an is explicit on this point: the word most frequently chosen for "revelation" deals with the idea of being "sent down." There is mercy in Muhammad being elevated to heaven, and there is mercy in the lowering down of the Word of God. Muhammad ascends to heaven and has the direct encounter with God. The question remains: Why return to humanity? If Muhammad found himself in that utmost position of bliss, why detach himself from immediately beholding the Divine and return to this realm?

The answer has to be connected to the reason this world was created: compassion. Like a bodhisattva who postpones his own entry into Nirvana, Muhammad returns from the awesome mystical experience of being with God for the sake of his community. This selfless compassion, indeed sacrifice, is not a choice that most mere mortals would have made. Even the great sixteenth-century Muslim saint of South Asia, 'Abd Al-Quddus Gangohi, is remembered as having said: "I swear by God that if I had reached that point, I should never have returned."[14] And yet, thanks be to God, the Prophet returns. This movement has remained a key part of Islamic life: the true test of the women and men of God is not just ascending but also being able to return to humanity, to eat and sleep in the midst of the people, to conduct trade and human interaction, to live a family life—and yet not for one moment to become unmindful of the presence of the Ever-Merciful.

CHAPTER FOUR

Islam as an Abrahamic Tradition

IF THE MI'RAJ REPRESENTS THE zenith of Muhammad's spiritual experiences, and if the conquest of Mecca represents the earthly conclusion of the Muhammadi Revolution as it came to terms with the pagan tradition of the *Jahiliyya* (pre-Islamic polytheistic Arabia), a larger question remains: what is the nature of the complex relationship of Muhammad's revelation to its fellow traditions in the Abrahamic family, Judaism and Christianity? It is to this relationship that we now turn.

Islam as Universal Prophethood

The question of the relationship between the revelation of Muhammad and the earlier revelations is crucial and somewhat complicated. Also polemical, this question has at times been collapsed into one extreme or another by both supporters and detractors of Muhammad. It ultimately comes down to the question of whether Islam is a reaffirmation of earlier revelations or whether it supersedes them. The tension has been preserved through the centuries, with Muslims of different persuasions gravitating now to this, now to that, perspective. The tension is not fundamentally different from how Christians have grappled with whether the statement in the Gospel of Matthew (5:17) that Christ "completes the Law" means that Jesus reaffirms the Jewish tradition or supersedes it. Here is what can be stated with certainty: the Qur'an certainly views itself as the latest revelation from the same One God who earlier sent guidance to humanity through prophets like Noah, Abraham, David, Solomon, Moses, and Jesus. Time and again we see passages in the Qur'an such as: "Verily, all of this has indeed been said in the earlier revelations—the revelations of Abraham and Moses" (Qur'an 87:18–19). In other words, what is significant about the revelation is not that it is new but that it reveals the truth that humanity needs to be reminded of—again and again. And again.

In fact, the cycle of revelation described in the Qur'an is seen as encompassing the whole of humanity. Muhammad himself is described in both the Qur'an and his biography as having been sent as a universal messenger:

And We sent you as a messenger to all of humanity. (Qur'an 34:28)

And,

When Muhammad the Messenger of God reached the age of forty, God sent him in compassion to humanity, as a messenger to all of humanity.[1]

The God who reveals the Qur'an is not a tribal god but rather the universal God of the whole humanity. At times the list of messengers in the Qur'an seems biblical in the most familiar way:

We have sent the inspiration to you,
as We sent it to Noah and the prophets after him.
We sent the inspiration to Abraham, Ishmael, Isaac, Jacob, and the
*   Tribes*

And to Jesus, Job, Jonah, Aaron, and Solomon.
And to David we gave the Psalms. (Qur'an 4:163)

This litany of biblical prophets is not an isolated example in the Qur'an. Aside from the narratives of individual prophets, we often find such lists that emphasize the commonality of all prophetic revelations:

Say ye: "We have faith in God, and in what has been revealed to us,
And what was revealed to Abraham, and Ishmael, and Isaac, and
*   Jacob, and the Tribes.*
And [to the scriptures] given to Moses and Jesus,
And that which was given to all the prophets from their Lord."
*   (Qur'an 2:136)*

Time and again the Qur'an emphasizes that since all the prophets bring the same divine message, we should not differentiate between them or favor one over another. Indeed, the faithful are commanded in the Qur'an to say: "We make no difference between one and another of them, we submit ourselves to God" (Qur'an 2:136). Some twenty-eight prophetic figures are named in the Qur'an specifically, a list that encompasses familiar figures like Adam, Noah, Abraham, David, Solomon, Moses, and Jesus. In fact, a key part of Islamic piety is to connect honorifics with each such figure. Adam is often called Safi Allah (the one purified and chosen by God), Noah is Naji Allah (the one saved by God), Abraham is Khalil Allah (the intimate friend of God), and Moses is Kalim Allah (the one with whom God spoke). Jesus receives special mention as Kalimat Allah (a Word from God) and Ruh Allah (a spirit from God). We saw at the end of the account of the heavenly ascension that Muhammad too receives his own honorifics as the Mustafa (purified and chosen by God), the Habib Allah (beloved of God), and Rasul Allah (messenger of God). A regular practice of Muslims is to send down blessings and salutations upon all the different prophets.

If God is the Lord of the whole universe, and if all of prophetic guidance is traced back to the same divine source, then the number of prophets would need to be drastically expanded beyond the familiar biblical scope. In addition to the figures named in the Qur'an, tradition puts the total number of prophets at 124,000[2]—a number equivalent to our notion of "zillion"—to indicate that God has sent a prophet to every community. According to the Qur'an, the scope of prophetic guidance is so vast that some of the prophets remain unnamed and unknown even to Muhammad:

> We did send messengers before you.
> Of them there are some whose story we have told you [Muhammad],
> and some whose story we have not told you. (Qur'an 40:78)

The mention of prophets sent by God who are nevertheless not explicitly named in the Qur'an allowed later Muslims to incorporate other theistic traditions (including Zoroastrianism in Iran and even some metaphysical forms of the Hindu traditions) into a Qur'anic worldview without too much difficulty. More recently, pluralistically oriented Muslims have pondered the possibility of venturing beyond an explicitly theistic realm and recognizing the teachings of Tibetan Buddhism as part of sacred guidance.[3]

Islam and the People of the Book

Like any other religious community, the early Muslims had to establish their own particular identity. That is to say, they could not simply be generic "Abrahamics." They needed to have their own particular distinctions that demarcated them from Jews, Christians, and other monotheistic communities. This type of demarcation is commonly found in the different traditions. The early Jewish tradition asserts a particular covenant that sets the People of Israel apart from the rest of God's creation, even favoring them above the rest of humanity. In some readings of the early Christian tradition, on the other hand, we see an effort (particularly through Paul) to distinguish the nascent Christian community from the surrounding Jewish and Hellenistic communities. The teachings of the Buddha likewise differentiated his path from those of the more severe forms of Hindu asceticism. The case of Islam is not drastically different, and in demarcating itself from earlier communities, particularly those that were theologically the most similar, Islam was following a common pattern in human religious history.

Significantly, however, the Qur'an makes no move to negate the earlier revelations. In fact, the Qur'an criticizes the Jewish and Christian communities around Muhammad for having become too exclusivist and for denying the truth of other revelations. The response of the Qur'an seems to have been to connect the example of Muhammad to that of Abraham, the archetypal prophet and monotheist:

> They say: "Become Jews or Christians if you wish to be guided."
> Say you: "No! I would rather be part of the tradition of Abraham,
>   the true one,
> who did not associate partners with God." (Qur'an 2:135)

In the previous chapters, we have seen that the teachings of the Prophet harkened back to Abraham's notion of primordial monotheism. In other verses, the Qur'an positions itself vis-à-vis the polemics of Jews and Christians toward one another:

> Jews say: "The Christians have nothing to stand on."
> Christians say: "Jews have nothing to stand on."
> Yet they both profess to study the same Book! (Qur'an 2:113)

In a typical Qur'anic pattern, the ultimate evaluation is relegated back to God:

But God will judge between them in their quarrel
on the Day of Judgment. (Qur'an 2:113)

Some of the angriest Qur'anic dismissals are leveled at claims that any one religious community can offer exclusive salvation to the neglect of others:

And they say: "None shall enter Paradise unless he be a Jew
Or unless he be a Christian."
Those are their vain desires.
Say: "Produce your proof if you are truthful."

In the worldview of the Qur'an, the gates of salvation are open to all religious communities and no one group—including Muslims—can claim exclusive salvation:

No, whoever submits his core being to God
and is good and beautiful shall have a reward with his Lord.
On such a soul shall be no fear,
no grief. (Qur'an 2:111–12)

In the Qur'anic worldview, "Islam" is not so much the name of a new religious tradition as it is the quality of submitting oneself to God wholeheartedly. The preceding verse, for example, mentions submitting one's "core being" (*wajh*, literally "face") to the Divine. The characteristic Qur'anic refrain for salvation is one "on whom shall be no fear, no grief." The door of salvation will remain open to the one who has submitted wholeheartedly to God and is good and beautiful (*muhsin*). To put it differently, for the most part in the Qur'an the word "Islam" is a verb, not a noun. Different individuals are talked about as having "Islam-ed"—that is, having submitted themselves wholeheartedly to God.

Another Qur'anic idea was a radical notion that would surface here and there in Islamic thought. Muslims, as much as other religious human beings, speak in terms of Absolute Truth. Yet from this perspective, articulated in the Qur'an and more fully teased out in the context of Islamic mysticism, Truth as such can be identified not with a religious tradition but only with God. The word Truth (*Haqq*) is in fact a name of God: when we come across a reference to Truth in Islamic texts, the referent is always God. This is how these Muslims read the Qur'anic verse about the Divine being revealed in three sites: in scripture, in the natural realm, and inside the very souls of humanity. As such, the study of scripture leads one to God. Scientific study of the natural realm can lead one to marvel at the majesty and intricacy of God's plan. And significantly for these readers of the Qur'an, understanding how our hearts and souls function, the very faculty of both mysticism and social ethics, is also connected to approaching the Divine. This is how these Muslims have read the Qur'anic verses:

> *We shall show them Our Signs* (ayat)
> *on the furthest horizons,*
> *and inside their own souls,*
> *until it becomes manifest to them that God is Haqq. (Qur'an 41:53)*

This is one of the ways in which the word "sign" (*aya*) functions in the Qur'an. The same word that is used for each verse of the Qur'an (*aya*) also means a sign or a symbol. A sign is something that points to a meaning beyond itself, and so does each verse of the Qur'an. Each verse can also be seen as an invitation to meditate and ponder. And yet the Signs of God are not only in scripture but also in the natural domain and inside humanity. This is a religious worldview in which reading scripture, meditation, study of the natural domain, and mysticism all go hand in hand to lead humanity back to the Divine.

From this perspective, Islam is a path that leads one to Truth, but it is not the Truth itself. Truth can only be equated with the Origin and the Destination—only with God. That which comes from God may be true, and Muslims undoubtedly hold the Qur'anic revelation and Islam to be true, but religion cannot be considered Truth in the same way that God is Truth. This too is part of the radical monotheism of Islam.

Yet not all Muslims would be pluralists; just as some Jews and some Christians have come to see their own tradition as the zenith of God's engagement with humanity, so have some Muslims. These Muslims tend to focus on other passages in the Qur'an—specifically those that use "Islam" not as the verb of surrendering to God but as a noun. Here it might be useful to distinguish between generic and specific usages of the terms "Islam" and "Muslim" in the context of the Qur'an.

For the most part, the Qur'an does not conceive of Judaism, Christianity, and Islam per se, but simply lays out the notion of One God and one guidance being sent through a multiplicity of messengers to address the multiplicity of humanity. So most of the uses of words that come from the root word "Islam" have to do, not with the revelation of the Prophet, but simply with submitting oneself wholeheartedly to God. It is in this vein that prophetic figures prior to Muhammad also identify themselves as "muslim" in the Qur'an. In the Qur'an, Abraham is identified as a pure one who submits wholeheartedly to God:

> *Abraham was neither Jewish nor Christian,*
> *but he was a pure monotheist* (hanif)
> *who submitted himself wholeheartedly to God* (muslim).
> *(Qur'an 3:67)*

Likewise, in the Qur'an, the young son of Jacob, Joseph, who is also considered a prophet, offers this prayer to God:

> *O my Lord!*
> *You have indeed bestowed on me power,*
> *and taught me the hidden meaning of events.*
> *O You the Creator of the heavens and earth!*
> *You are my protector in this world, and in the Hereafter*

Take my soul as one who submits wholeheartedly to you [muslim]
And unite me with the righteous ones. (Qur'an 12:101)

In engaging—and occasionally confronting—the People of the Book (*Ahl al-Kitab*, including Jews and Christians), Muslims are instructed to not engage in endless disputations but rather to follow a path that is lovely:

And dispute not with the People of the Book,
except in a way that is lovely,
unless it is with those who are oppressing you.

Say to them: we have faith in the revelation that has come to us,
and in that which has come down to you.
Our God and your God is One.
We submit wholeheartedly to him. (Qur'an 29:46)

Lastly, it is worth pointing out that in the context of the Qur'an, Jesus's disciples tell him that they will be his helpers (*ansar Allah*) in the path of God and that they have faith in God. Significantly, they ask Jesus to bear witness that they have "surrendered ourselves unto" God—literally become *muslim*^{un} to God—and they ask God to make them one with all those who bear witness to the Divine. So what does it mean if figures like Abraham, Joseph, and Jesus's disciples are identified as "muslim"? Surely they cannot in any ordinary historical sense be conceived of as having followed the practices of Muhammad, the seventh-century Arabian prophet. Although Arabic does not distinguish between terms in this way, we can make a distinction between "Muslim" as the identity of one who follows the Muhammadi tradition of Islam and "muslim" as that of one who submits wholeheartedly to God, regardless of which prophet he or she follows. Likewise, we can distinguish between "Islam" as the Muhammadi religious tradition and "islam" as a universal and primordial pattern of submitting oneself wholeheartedly to God. It is in this latter sense that the Qur'an refers to the prophetic figures who lived prior to Muhammad's age.

Yet any tradition—particularly an emerging tradition—eventually needs to set some boundaries. Flowing water needs the banks to be defined as a river. A few places in the Qur'an do mention "Islam" as something closer to our notion of a religious system—especially a famous verse that is often taken to have been the last verse ever revealed to Muhammad:

> *Today, those who are bent on denying the truth*
> *have lost all hope of [your ever forsaking] your religion:*
> *Do not, then, hold them in awe, but stand in awe of Me!*
>
> *Today have I perfected your religious law (din) for you,*
> *and have bestowed upon you the full measure of my blessings,*
> *and willed that self-surrender unto Me [islam] shall be your religion*
>   *(din). (Qur'an 5:3)*[4]

The word *din* comes closest to our notion of religion, although it implies a whole host of meanings, ranging from humanity's debt to God to what we think of as religion. Those who wish to see Islam as a completed (and even perfect) body read the notion of a whole system of laws, practices, and beliefs back to (and into) this verse, which, according to them, has already guaranteed humanity perfection. This reading of Islam, for example, has become popular among Muslims who experienced colonialism and Christian missionary activity and who responded by coming to believe that Islam supersedes earlier revelations. One "countermissionary" Muslim polemic against Christianity originated in South Asia and is now found in many other places as well. According to this interpretation, God has chosen Islam—here capitalized—as humanity's religion. Muslims today, however, vary in their interpretations of how these verses are related to the more pluralistic approaches quoted earlier. More inclusive Muslims make the same critique of the "countermissionary" interpretation as the

Qur'an seems to have made in the Prophet's time of the exclusivist Jewish and Christian communities that claimed the door of salvation was open only to them. Yet it remains the case that both pluralistic and exclusivist Muslims seek to justify their positions by resorting to the Qur'an, another indication of the authority of the scripture for Muslims and the fluidity of the meanings that can be extracted from it—and projected onto it.

The majority of the references to the People of the Book in the Qur'an are positive, emphasizing the commonality of revelation and guidance. Historically, this theological pluralism, sanctioned in the very verses of scripture, was of profound sociological importance for Muslims, since it allowed them to live in peace with those who did not share their faith—conducting trade with them, eating with them, even conducting that most crucial of human interactions, marriage, with them—because they were all People of the Book.

> *This day all things good and pure*
> *are made lawful unto you.*
> *The food of the People of the Book is lawful unto you,*
> *and yours lawful unto them.*
> *Lawful unto you in marriage*
> *are chaste women who are believers (Muslims),*
> *and chaste women from the People of the Book. (Qur'an 5:5)*

There would, of course, be restrictions and clarifications: male Muslims were generally free to marry non-Muslim women from the People of the Book, for instance, but the same courtesy was not extended to Muslim women marrying men from the People of the Book. This restriction is one that today many Muslim women, particularly in the West, are questioning.

Yet commonality and identity should not be confused. After all, if the Qur'an merely repeated what Christianity holds about Jesus, then Muslims would be called Christians. There are a few verses in the Qur'an about the People of the Book that have a definite polemical edge to them. The critique of Christians is theological, mainly in asserting that the nature of Christ is equal to that of God:

> *Christ, son of Mary, was not more than a messenger [of God].*
> *Many were the messengers that passed away before him.*
> *His mother was a woman of truth.*
> *They both had to eat their daily bread.*
> *See how God makes his Signs clear to them,*
> *Yet see in what ways they are deluded away from truth.*
>   *(Qur'an 5:75)*

and

> *They do blaspheme who say: "God is Christ the son of Mary."*
> *But Christ said: "O children of Israel!*
> *Worship God, who is my Lord and your Lord."*
> *Whoever associates deities with God,*
> *then God will forbid him entry to paradise,*
> *and Hellfire will be his abode. . . .*
> *They do blaspheme who say that God is one of three in a Trinity,*
> *For there is no deity except the One God.*
> *If they desist not from their words of blasphemy,*
> *Indeed a grievous penalty will befall the blasphemers among them.*
> *Why turn not to God and seek God's forgiveness?*
> *For God is most-forgiving, full of compassionate mercy.*
>   *(Qur'an 5:17)*

Many Christians also see the notion of God described here as "one of three in a Trinity" as referring to a heretical understanding that might be properly characterized, not as monotheistic, but rather as tritheistic. It is worth remembering that in Muhammad's age Arabia was filled with Christian movements that orthodoxy had deemed heretical.

This criticism in the Qur'an, combined with the ambiguous passages that seem to counter the claims of Jesus's crucifixion—or at least

one Jewish group's boast of having crucified Jesus—do present something of a theological impasse between Islam and Christianity. Here is
the opaque verse, directed against an unnamed Jewish group:

> *And so, [We punished them] for the breaking of their pledge, and*
> *their refusal to acknowledge God's messages, and their slaying of*
> *prophets against all right, and their boast: "Our hearts are al-*
> *ready full of knowledge."*
>
> *Nay, but God has sealed their hearts in result of their denial of the*
> *truth, and [now] they believe in but few things—and for their*
> *refusal to acknowledge the truth, and the awesome calumny*
> *which they utter against Mary and their boast, "Behold, we have*
> *slain the Christ Jesus, son of Mary, [who claimed to be] an apostle*
> *of God!"*
>
> *However, they did not slay him, and neither did they crucify him,*
> *but it only seemed to them [as if it had been] so; and verily, those*
> *who hold conflicting views thereon are indeed confused, having no*
> *[real] knowledge thereof, and following mere conjecture.*
>
> *For, of a certainty, they did not slay him: nay, God exalted him unto*
> *Himself, and God is indeed almighty, wise. (Qur'an 4:155–59)*

Knowing that Jesus's crucifixion took place at the hands of the Romans—and not Jews—the Qur'anic commentaries have interpreted this
verse, which is surely open to a great deal of debate and controversy, in
multiple ways. Some Muslims have taken the phrase "they did not slay
him" to mean that Jesus was in fact not crucified, whereas some have
taken the phrase "but it only seemed to them" to mean that a look-alike
was sacrificed in place of Christ. Perhaps the most charitable reading
is that the verses are addressed to the haughty claims of a particular
Jewish group rather than the historicity of the crucifixion itself.[5]

These verses do point to some theological demarcations between
Islam and Christianity, yet it is important to read them in light of the
long and detailed passages in the Qur'an whose attitude toward Christ—
and Mary—is strongly reverential. Muslims are fond of pointing out

that Mary receives much more extensive treatment in the Qur'an than she does in the New Testament. Long and beautiful passages in the Qur'an describe the Nativity of Jesus, and Mary is presented in the same glowing fashion as Muhammad—as a woman chosen above all other women of the cosmos. Mary is described as having been *Isti-faki*, while Muhammad is *Mustafa*—both words coming from the root whose meaning implies being purified and chosen.

> *And Lo! The angels said: "O Mary! Behold, God has elected thee and made thee pure, and raised thee above all the women of the world.*
> *"O Mary! Remain thou truly devout unto thy Sustainer, and prostrate thyself in worship, and bow down with those who bow down (before Him)." (Qur'an 3:42–43)*

The Annunciation of the coming Christ child, including the Virgin Birth, is celebrated in the Qur'an in the most reverential terms:

> *Lo! The angels said: "O Mary! Behold, God sends thee the glad tidings, through a word from Him, [of a son] who shall become known as the Christ Jesus, son of Mary, of great honor in this world and in the life to come, and shall be of those who are drawn near to God."*
> *(Qur'an 3:46)*

Mary expresses her astonishment—after all, she has had no sexual relations with any man up to that point: "O my Sustainer! How can I have a son when no man has ever touched me?" The response comes:

> *Thus it is: God creates what He wills. When He wills a thing to be, He but says unto it, "Be"—and it is. And He will impart unto thy son revelation, and wisdom, and the Torah, and the Gospel, and make him an apostle unto the children of Israel. (Qur'an 3:46–48)*

It is worth noting that at the beginning of this narrative the angels address Mary. Mary, on the other hand, addresses God directly and receives a response back from God. The fact that she communicates with God directly led some premodern Muslims (such as the followers of the Zahiri school) to recognize her as a prophet. Other Muslims insisted that maleness was a necessary qualification of prophethood. Here is another indication of the ways in which gender norms have shaped the ways in which Muslims read some of the most sublime verses of scripture.

Returning to the Qur'anic narrative, we see that after the birth of Christ some of his miracles are commemorated:

> *I have come unto you with a message from your Sustainer, I shall create for you out of clay, as it were, the shape of a bird, and then breathe into it, so that it flies by God's permission.*
> *And I shall heal the blind and the leper, and bring the dead back to life by God's permission. And I shall let you know what you may eat and what you should store up in your houses. Behold, in all this there is indeed a message for you, if you are truly faithful. (Qur'an 3:49)*

In these miracles—which are also attested to in some of the apocryphal gospels, such as the Infancy Gospel of Thomas—Jesus reenacts, by God's permission (the Qur'an never tires of emphasizing), the divine process of creation by taking a piece of clay and breathing into it. It is the breath/spirit that God has also breathed into humanity. Jesus's miracles include the familiar stories of healing and bringing back to life, which for Muslims was both literal (as in the Lazarus story) and metaphorical (bringing dead hearts to life). After all, the Qur'an repeatedly reminds humanity that the Earth was dead and God brought it back to life (Qur'an 41:39). In these types of narratives, yet again, we see Jesus both as a historical prophet and as what might be called a prophetic mode of consciousness, leading some mystics like Rumi to wonder who or what is the Jesus of our own soul, the pharaoh of our own hearts, and so on.[6]

Jesus ends his proclamation to the Children of Israel by stating:

> *I have come to confirm the truth of the Torah before me, and to make lawful unto you some of the things which were forbidden to you.*
> *And I have come unto you with a message from your Sustainer: remain, then, conscious of God, and pay heed unto me. Verily, God is my Sustainer as well as your Sustainer, so worship Him alone. This is a straight way. (Qur'an 3:50–51)*

The Qur'an and the People of the Book Today

The comments of Jesus in addressing his own community, the Children of Israel, provide us with a transition point to the Qur'an's complex treatment of the Jewish community. These questions, needless to say, have important consequences for contemporary Muslims and Jews.

In some ways, the tension between the Islamic and the Jewish traditions is vastly overstated, as both essentially function as a monotheistic tradition with a core of revelation, scripture, and a strong legal component. The Islamic tradition has put more emphasis on mysticism, which has reached a popularity among Muslims that rivals and occasionally equals interest in the Islamic legal tradition.[7] Yet theologically the two traditions function in very similar fashions. In fact, one could argue that many of the tensions between the two traditions are similar to those seen between siblings. For the overwhelming majority of their history, Muslims and Jews have lived side by side, if not always in mutual love then at least in coexistence. According to scholars, from the eighth to the tenth century somewhere between 85 and 90 percent of all Jews lived among Muslims.[8] Certainly Muslims have a far superior history of coexistence with

Jews than can be claimed by Christians, among whom a millennia-old tradition of anti-Semitism has often been tied to readings of Christian theology. Yet there are some very fundamental tensions between Muslims and Jews, both in the Qur'an and in episodes of Muhammad's life. These episodes have tended to be magnified in the twentieth-century context: the establishment of the state of Israel through the exile and marginalization of the indigenous Palestinian population has created an unprecedented level of sustained hostility between Muslims and Jews. As such, it is particularly urgent that the tensions in the Qur'anic narrative be handled in a thoughtful and dispassionate manner.

We have seen that some Muslims make a theological critique of the Christian view of the Trinity and of Christ's crucifixion. Yet paradoxically, in the life of the Prophet Muhammad, Christians were by and large viewed with favor—as shown, for instance in the appreciation for the intervention of the Abyssinian Christian king, Negus, in protecting the Muslim community. Some Jews, on the other hand, are the subject of ethical criticism in the Qur'an, which most often directs its polemics against those Jews who were members of clans and political groups in Medina that formed open or clandestine alliances against Muhammad and the nascent Muslim community. The Qur'an often charges the Jewish opponents with breaking the covenant and with arrogance, both themes as old as the Hebrew Bible, and both probably familiar to the Qur'an's contemporaries. In some passages of the Qur'an, some Jews are depicted as having boasted to Muhammad that they would escape divine retribution:

> "Hellfire will most certainly not touch us for more than a limited
> number of days."
> Say [to them]: "Have you taken a promise from God,
> for God never breaks His promise?
> Or is it that you say of God that which you know not."
> (Qur'an 2:80)

The other crime with which the Qur'an charges Jews is attributing to God that which was not originally part of the revelation given to them. At times the Qur'an describes this literally:

> *Woe, then, unto those who write down, with their own hands, something which they claim to be divine writ, and then they say: "This is from God," in order to acquire a trifling gain thereby.*
> *Woe, then, unto them for what their hands have written, and woe unto them for all that they may have gained. (Qur'an 2:78–79)*

At other times, the Qur'an speaks more metaphorically about such actions as ones that make religion hard for people, and it describes Jesus as having come back to the Children of Israel to facilitate matters of religion for them. Some Jews are also criticized for rejecting the message of the Qur'an even though it originates from the same God and confirms much of their own teaching:

> *And when there comes to them a scripture from God,*
> *confirming what is with them*
> *—even though from of old they had prayed for victory against those without faith—*
> *when there comes to them that which they should have recognized,*
> *they refuse to believe it. (Qur'an 2:89)*

Like many of the passages in the Bible that some Christians have used over the years to justify their animosity toward Jews, these types of verses are most dangerous when they are read outside of the historical context in which they were revealed. In Muhammad's own time, leaders of some—but probably not all—Jewish clans in Medina at various points conspired with the polytheists of Mecca to oppose Muhammad's fragile community. As a result, those Jewish clans were viewed with suspicion. We have seen examples of these tensions in the episodes of Muhammad's life dealing with Banu Nadir and Banu Qurayza.

Perhaps the corollary example about the need to read verses in their historical context will make the point in a slightly different fashion. When speaking in a contemporary setting with Christians, Muslims often privilege those verses that emphasize the commonality and affection between Muslims and Christians:

> *You will find that the closest to the [Muslim] faithful*
> *are those who say:*
> *"We are Christians."*
> *This is because among them are those devoted to learning,*
> *and those who have renounced worldliness,*
> *and they are not arrogant. (Qur'an 5:82)*

Yet in these same gatherings Muslims rarely cite the beginning words of that same verse:

> *You will find that*
> *the most hostile to the believers are Jews and the polytheists.*
> *You will find that the closest to the [Muslim] faithful*
> *are those who say:*
> *"We are Christians."*
> *This is because . . . (Qur'an 5:82)*

Contemporary Muslims often praise the second part of the verse, especially those in Western settings, where Muslims live in largely Christian (or post-Christian) contexts. It is as if these verses stand above time and place, pointing to an archetypal affection that Muslims and Christians are to have for one another. And yet, when confronted with the first part of the verse, Muslims often quickly retreat to the answer that "one must read things in their proper historical context." The truth of the matter is more complicated. To have an intellectually honest reading of any scripture—including the Qur'an—it is vital to handle consistently questions of historicity and context. Either all of these verses should be read in the light of their immediate historical context, or all of them should be read in a transhistorical fashion. Otherwise, how do we articulate a position that some verses correspond to direct historical precedents, while others express eternal truths? It is this picking and choosing that often leads, at best, to methodological inconsistency; intellectually and spiritually honest readings of scripture demand a more holistic and consistent approach. Given today's political realities, it seems particularly prudent that these types of verses not be taken as license to justify perpetual animosity between Muslims and Jews.

All of our scriptures contain these multiple possibilities. There are passages in both the Qur'an and the Bible that preach mutual respect and coexistence, and in both scriptures there are also passages that justify chauvinism and even violence. The question for us is how to approach any scripture in a way that is both historically informed and intellectually honest. This challenge is harder than most of the faithful are willing to admit—at least publicly.

In today's globalized world, no religious community lives in isolation. Muslims in particular live as neighbors to Jews and Christians in many settings, including both the places where all three groups have lived for over one thousand years (like the Middle East) and newer settings like Europe and North America. One challenge for Muslims is re-creating the sense of Muhammad as a *biblical* prophet, which, as we saw in the introduction, is present in sources like "Tales of the Prophets" by Kisa'i and the illuminated miniatures. A similar challenge is for Jews and Christians to come to terms with the fact that God's communication with humanity includes Abraham's descendants through both Isaac and Ishmael—which is to say Jews, Christians, and Muslims. The challenge for those who aspire to the God of Abraham is to recall that this God blessed all the offspring of Abraham.

The children of Abraham have no option but to get along and learn to live together. As Martin Luther King Jr. said: "Either we go up together or we go down together."[9] In today's world, this "going up together" is not merely a theological challenge, but a political issue of life and death—and just as importantly, a matter of dignity. For many Muslims, there is indeed something worse than death—a life deprived of dignity. It is past time for all the children of Abraham to live in dignity.

The children of Abraham have a mixed legacy of living together in dignity. Today they often find themselves at odds, yet it would be a mistake to imagine that they have always lived in tension with one another. Furthermore, it betrays a poverty of both imagination and compassion to say that the children of Abraham are somehow destined to live in a state of conflict and to enact a "clash of civilizations." The tensions of the twentieth and twenty-first centuries are in many ways historically unprecedented and more often than not are related to the traumas and aftershocks of colonialism.

One way to avoid fixating on modern tensions between Muslims, Jews, and Christians is to adopt a larger historical perspective. It is worth noting for most of the past 1,400 years, the most important clashes involving Muslims have not been against Jews or Christians but rather against fellow Muslims. If the *Umma* as the mother-community of faith remains the ideal for all those who commemorate Muhammad, in reality Muslims have fallen short of that reality just as frequently as other members of humanity have failed their own faith traditions. Like members of other religious traditions, Muslims too have given in to infighting and schisms. In the next chapter, we begin an examination of these internal conflicts by exploring the split between the Sunni and Shi'i followers of Muhammad, two groups whose attachment to Muhammad has led them to take distinct and at times divergent paths.

CHAPTER FIVE

Life After the Prophet, Death After Hossein

LESS THAN FIFTY YEARS AFTER the death of the Prophet Muhammad, many of the surviving members of his family found themselves captives of the Umayyads, the ruling powers of the Muslim state. Their captivity came after a gruesome battle in the year 680 CE on the hot plains of Karbala in Iraq, where a few dozen members of the Prophet's family and their supporters were first surrounded by an army much larger in size. This army—which massacred the family of the Prophet and trampled over their corpses—belonged not to a foreign invading power but to the ruling Muslim powers. Most of the men in the Prophet's family had already been killed, and now a band of women, children, and a few young men were being dragged through the Iraqi desert, marching from the plains of Karbala to Kufa. If the procession was humiliating for them, it was horrific for those who saw it. This was a procession unlike any that Muslim society had ever witnessed. According to one of the major sources for the early history of Islam, the respected tenth-century historian Tabari, the Umayyad soldiers had hoisted the severed heads of seventy-two of the family members of the Prophet Muhammad on lances. Violating Islamic rules about the mutilation of bodies, the soldiers were publicly parading the raised severed heads, and the few survivors, through the cities of Kufa before making their way to the seat of the empire in Damascus.

In Kufa the few surviving members of the family of the Prophet stood before Ibn Ziyad, who ruled there by the authority of the Umayyad Caliph Yazid. In a shocking scene that was almost unbelievable to most of those present, Ibn Ziyad was presented with the captives and a tray, which was positioned in front of him. On the tray was the severed, bloodied head of the grandson of the Prophet Muhammad, Hossein—the same Hossein whose mother was Fatima, Muhammad's daughter, and whose father was Ali, Muhammad's cousin and the first male convert. Imam Hossein had been killed by order of the rulers of Muslim society and his head was now being presented as a trophy.

When the bloodied head of Imam Hossein was brought to Ibn Ziyad's court, the cruel tyrant took his cane and mockingly struck the lips of the severed head of Hossein, as if to taunt the fallen grandson of the Prophet. An old man in the crowd, named Zayd, the son of Arqam, who had been a longtime follower of the Prophet Muhammad, was unable to control himself any longer. He stepped forth and, breaking all courtly decorum, shouted at the ruler:

> *Remove your cane from these lips!*
> *By God,*
> *on these lips have I seen the lips of the Prophet of God,*
> *kissing them.*[1]

How did something like this happen? How did the Muslim community go from lovingly gathering around Muhammad to witnessing the killing of his precious grandchildren in less than two generations? These questions are at the very heart of the eventual schism between those who came to be known as the Shi'i and the Sunni factions of Islam.

There have been some events in world history whose significance far outstripped their mere historicity. A first-century Palestinian Jew, the son of a carpenter, is hung between two thieves at the behest of Roman authorities, and today over one billion Christians see the crucifixion of Jesus Christ as the ultimate symbol of God's deliverance of humanity from sin. Six centuries before Christ, an Indian prince sat under a tree, vowing not to move until he had transcended the cycles of birth and rebirth. Today hundreds of millions of Buddhists look at the enlightenment of Siddhartha Gautama Buddha as the very model of how to rise above attachment and ignorance. The significance of these events blossomed beyond what actually happened in the narrow historical sense and became manifest when seen through the faithful eyes of those who came later and based their lives—and some their deaths—on these events.

The martyrdom of Imam Hossein was such an event. At face value, his death was just one among those of the seventy-two people massacred at the behest of a corrupt and violent ruler. It would be neither the first nor the last time the blood of innocents was shed on this Earth. And yet, for many Muslims, particularly those who call themselves the Shi'a, the martyrdom of Imam Hossein was no mere bloody battle, or even massacre, on the remote Karbala plains of seventh-century Iraq, but a cosmic event. All such events—the crucifixion of Christ, the awakening of the Buddha, the martyrdom of Hossein—become symbols of something fundamental about the nature of the universe. Looking at the symbolism of Christ, the Buddha, and Imam Hossein, we are reminded, respectively, that there is sin and it must be redeemed, that there is attachment/suffering and it must be transcended, and that there is injustice and humanity has the cosmic responsibility to rise up against it. In all of these cases, what happened historically is also projected against all time and space. Christians do not "look back" at the crucifixion of Jesus, but see that act of redemption as shaping their lives here and now. For Buddhists, the key is not understanding how the Indian prince became awakened, but rather how we are to be enlightened. And for Shi'i Muslims, the question is not what Hossein did on the tenth day (*Ashura*) of the Islamic month of Muharram of the year 680 CE on the plains of Karbala in Iraq, but rather what *we* are doing today.

The cosmic significance of these events illustrates the power of religious imagination, which makes every place a sacred place and every day a sacred time. An Iranian intellectual of the middle of the twentieth century said it best:

> *Every day is Ashura,*
> *Every place is Karbala.*[2]

Much of Shi'ism is about memory and commemoration—about the need to remember those who came before, how they lived, and how they died. The ethos of Shi'ism is about more than sentimental remembrance: it Shi'i is about the cosmic urge to *not forget*—to not forget Hossein, to not forget the possibility of rising up, and to not forget the possibility of living a heroic life.

The Split Between the Sunni and Shi'i Factions

In the rest of this chapter, we retrace events from the death of the Prophet Muhammad in the year 632 CE to the martyrdom of Imam Hossein in 680 CE and document the fracturing of the community of Muhammad into the Sunni and Shi'i factions. These fissures did not form immediately, but they always harkened back to the early tensions. The differences between Sunnis and Shi'a should not be overestimated: they believe in the same God, have the same cycle of prophets, read the same Qur'an, and perform the same religious rituals. Theologically there is often as much internal variation among the various Sunni (and Shi'i) schools as there is between the dominant Sunni and Shi'i schools. And yet the events of the two generations from Muhammad to Hossein would prove so foundational that they have come to color the very ways in which the followers of Muhammad remember the Prophet, the age of the Prophet, and the legacy of the Prophet. So let us explore some of the ways in which these early episodes shaped the memory of Muhammad.

Remembrance of the Prophet is not merely intellectual or emotional, but woven into every imaginable ritual element as well. All Muslims are to pray five times a day toward Mecca. During prayer, they alternately stand, bow down, and prostrate themselves by placing their foreheads on the ground. The forehead in many religious traditions symbolizes the highest of human faculties, and in lowering it to the ground we remind ourselves of the dust from which we come. Were it not for the Breath of God that is breathed into each and every one of us, we would be nothing but dust. And yet for Shi'a Muslims, the prayer is also imbued with Hossein's martyrdom. Rather than placing their heads directly on the ground, they often prostrate themselves on a dried piece of clay that has been fashioned into a rectangle or oval. The clay comes from the dust of the plains of Karbala, the place where Hossein was martyred. As the Shi'a say, this dust has been made fragrant by his blood.

All Muslims long to make the pilgrimage (*Hajj*) to Mecca. In addition, many Muslims, Sunni and Shi'a alike, participate in ritual visits to local shrines. This practice, commonly referred to as *Ziyarat*, recognizes the sacredness of indigenous sites apart from Mecca. Some of these sites are shared by all Muslims—like Medina, since it is the burial place of the Prophet Muhammad. Many tend to venerate the burial places of Sufi masters, such as Konya in Turkey, which contains the tomb of Mawlana Jalal al-Din (known in the West as Rumi), and Ajmer in India, which is the home of the shrine of Khwaja Mu'in al-Din Chishti. Shi'a tend to visit the shrines of the *Ahl al-bayt* (the Family of the Prophet), in particular those associated with the imams. Most of these are located in Iraq (Najaf, Karbala, Kazimiyya, and Samara) and Saudi Arabia (Medina). One of them is in the city of Mashhad in Iran. Like the prayers, pilgrimage is a practice shared by Sunni and Shi'a Muslims, but each community has a distinctive version of it.

Like the larger Sunni calendar, the Shi'i religious calendar includes all of the Islamic rituals, such as pilgrimage and fasting. In addition, it contains the dates of the birthdays, deaths, and martyrdoms of each of the imams, and even some of the extended family members of the Prophet. There are close to fifty such commemorations, meaning that one never goes for more than about a week without being reminded of another saintly personality who lived a luminous life, endured in the face of oppression and tyranny, and, in far too many cases, paid for that resistance with his or her life. Such a spiritually populated cosmos (and calendar) is quite familiar to Christians coming from the Catholic and Orthodox traditions, even though it strikes many Sunni Muslims (and Protestants) as cluttered.

Much of the contention was related, ironically, to different claims on the Prophet. A twentieth-century metaphysician has perhaps said it best. Those who later on became the Sunnis loved the Prophet so much that they could not imagine any other group coming close to his authority. So they demarcated the example of Muhammad from that of others and invested the bulk of the authority in the sayings of the Prophet (the hadith narratives). In fact, the learning and transmission of the sayings of Muhammad became one of the paramount religious practices in Sunni Islam. Those who would later on become the Shi'a loved the Prophet so much that they could not imagine living without those who reminded them of their beloved Prophet. So they came to see the legacy of the Prophet has having been preserved primarily in the imams, the physical and spiritual descendants of Muhammad. One of the last sayings of Muhammad was that he had left his community with "two weighty (that is to say, precious)" gifts behind. And yet the Sunnis and the Shi'a remember these two gifts slightly differently: both groups remember the Qur'an as scripture, but the Sunnis take the example of Muhammad (the *Sunna*, where the word *Sunni* comes from) as guide and commentary on the Qur'an, whereas the Shi'a take the Family of the Prophet as their guide and living commentary.

Even this definition of their differences is not entirely as cut and dry as it might seem at first. The Shi'a also transmit the hadith (sayings) of the Prophet. Rather than transmitting them through the companions of the Prophet, however, as the Sunnis tend to do, the Shi'a transmit them through the Family of the Prophet (*Ahl al-bayt*). In other words, the Shi'a seek to connect themselves to the grace of the Prophet through the Family of the Prophet. In the Sunni spiritual cosmos, it is often the mystics (Sufis) who perform a similar task of transmitting the spiritual grace and power (*baraka*) of the Prophet Muhammad.

To complicate matters a bit more, there is a great deal of attachment and devotion to the Family of the Prophet even among the Sunnis: in Sunni-majority Turkey, the martyrdom of Imam Hossein is commemorated with great tenderness every year, and one of the holiest shrines in overwhelmingly Sunni Cairo is devoted to Imam Hossein—and reportedly contains the blessed head of Hossein that the devious ruler Yazid had ordered to be carried to his court in Damascus. A tragic demonstration of competing Sunni and Shi'i devotion to the Family of the Prophet occurs in Pakistan almost every year. Far too often during the month of Muharram, when both Sunni and Shi'a processions take to the street to commemorate the martyrdom of Imam Hossein, they compete to see who can mourn more and express greater remorse for Hossein's martyrdom and often end up clashing. One last example of how devotion to the Family of the Prophet has been shared by Sunnis and Shi'a will suffice here: many of the first commemorations of Hossein's martyrdom, including the famed *Garden of Martyrs*, were in fact written by Sunni scholars.

In spite of these important and real commonalities between the Sunni and the Shi'i, in time each of their narratives has hardened a bit. In particular, the two sides bitterly contest the events surrounding the passing away of the Prophet Muhammad, and each has constructed its own sacred narrative. The early communities had their own loyalties as well, and there are conflicting narratives that can be easily traced back to the partisan parties at that early phase. It is almost pointless to fall into the trap of "the quest for the historical," however, and more important to document how each faction recollects those painful and turbulent days between Muhammad and Hossein.

The Death of the Prophet

It is natural at times to project the way that history has played out back onto the earlier phases and attempt to see later trends as inevitable. Yet part of the task of a historian is to allow for multiple possibilities and indeed indulge the murkiness. It is a mistake to take the ways in which the later Sunni and Shi'i traditions hardened into a polemical embrace and project that history back onto the life of the Prophet. Indeed, even at the time of the Prophet we find all gathered around him the many companions who would later line up on different sides (even on battlefields). In the time of the Prophet Muhammad, it was easy enough to resolve differences, since guidance in this charismatic community was based on God's revelation and the virtuous example of Muhammad. But how did charismatic communities survive the passing of a charismatic figure like the Prophet?

It would have been difficult in any case for the followers of Muhammad to prepare themselves for his death, an event they referred to as the "closing of that gate of mercy." They would often recall that the Qur'an called Muhammad "a mercy to all the universes" (Qur'an 21:107). In many times and places, human beings have been more affected by the tangible people of God than by the present though invisible God. Thus, even some of those who had been closest to Muhammad, like Umar (who would become the second successor to the Prophet in the Sunni tradition), refused to believe that one such as Muhammad could have died and believed instead that Muhammad must have only gone up to be with God, as Moses had gone to be with God on Mount Sinai, and would return after forty days. It was only when Abu Bakr (the father of Muhammad's wife A'isha, and the first successor to Muhammad in the Sunni tradition) went in to see the Prophet for himself that he could see that, like all mortals, Muhammad too had passed away. Abu Bakr kissed the face of the Prophet and said: "You are dearer than my father and mother. You have tasted the death which God had decreed." Then Abu Bakr gently hushed Umar and gathered the community around him. He offered praises to God and then said:

O People!
Whosoever wishes to worship Muhammad,
verily Muhammad has passed away.
But whosoever wishes to worship God,
verily God is Living, Immortal.³

Muhammad's daughter, Fatima, and his grandchildren,
Hasan and Hossein, mourning the passing of the Prophet.
Courtesy of the Topkapi Palace Museum.

Abu Bakr then recited for the people the following verse from the Qur'an, a verse that seems to have been intended to prepare the community for life after Muhammad:

Muhammad is not but a messenger,
many were the messengers that passed away before him.

If he died or were slain, will you turn back on your heels?
If any did turn back on his heels, not the least harm will he do to
　　God;
But God will swiftly reward those who are grateful. (Qur'an 3:144)

And yet even those close to the Prophet said that, until that very moment, they had never imagined that these verses would refer to Muhammad's actual death. Even the messengers of God have to end their earthly existence. Perhaps at times like this the best that can be done is to remind oneself of the Eternal, Ever-Living God of Muhammad, God of Abraham, God of Jesus, and God of Moses.

If the sending down of each prophet is seen in Islam as an opening of a gate of mercy, then the death of each prophet is also accompanied by grief. One of those who wept after Muhammad's passing, Umm Ayman, said it best: "Not for him do I weep. Know I not that he hath gone to that which is better for him than this world? But I weep for the tidings of Heavens which have been cut off from us."[4]

The Selection of Abu Bakr as the First Sunni Caliph

When the Prophet passed away in Medina in the year 632 CE, his family members—including his daughter Fatima and her husband Ali, Muhammad's cousin and the first male Muslim convert—began the task of preparing his body for burial. While Ali, Fatima, and a few other intimate companions of Muhammad stayed behind in the Prophet's house, many of the other followers, particularly the Helpers (*Ansar*) from Medina, along with a handful of senior Meccan followers like Abu Bakr and Umar, met in a rushed session at the nearby Saqifa of Bani Sa'ida to discuss the affairs of the community. After all, Muhammad had been not only the spiritual center of authority but in a very real sense the political ruler of the Muslim community in Medina. This overlapping model of politics and religion was, of course, the common societal pattern prior to the Enlightenment in the West, and it is very much the model of biblical prophets in the Hebrew Bible and the New Testament as well as in the Qur'an. In a real sense, the nascent Muslim community was confronted with the vital challenge of keeping the message going after the Messenger was gone.

Many of the companions—though significantly, not Ali—met in this assembly. Following a time-honored Arab tribal custom to honor the elders of a tribe, the assembly (after intense debates) turned to Abu Bakr, who had been one of Muhammad's dearest and oldest friends and followers. Abu Bakr had been among the first converts after Ali, and he was the father of A'isha, one of Muhammad's wives. In fact, all of those who would be termed the "Four Rightly Guided Caliphs" in Sunni Islam had a marital connection to Muhammad, either having married one of Muhammad's daughters or having married their own daughter to him. All of these close companions of the Prophet, though of vastly different temperaments and spiritual gifts, were respected members of the community. Abu Bakr had been the companion who accompanied Muhammad in the Hijra, the migration from Mecca to Medina, and he was alluded to as the "second of the two" (Qur'an 9:40).[5] In many ways, he was seen as an elder of the community (*shaykh*), and he was also designated as a representative or deputy of the Prophet. Those in the council—which, again, did not include Ali—swore their allegiance to Abu Bakr, and he was recognized as the political ruler of the Muslim community and the successor to the Prophet.

The choice of Abu Bakr was not inevitable, nor was it made without great controversy. At the very least, there were important tensions among the Quraysh members from Mecca who wanted to keep rule in their own tribe, and the Ansar (Helpers) of Muhammad from Medina, who might have seen their own allegiance to the now-departed Prophet as more personal. In many ways, Abu Bakr was the acceptable compromise choice in the Saqifa meeting. Given the ad hoc nature of the gathering and how quickly it was called after the unexpected death of the Prophet, many of the close companions who had migrated from Mecca were not present. Perhaps more significantly—and problematically from a long-term perspective—was the fact that Ali and other crucial companions and family members of the Prophet did not attend the meeting. There were important tensions between Abu Bakr and the Family of the Prophet, in particular Fatima. These tensions were exacerbated when Abu Bakr refused to allow Fatima to receive the inheritance she believed she was due from her father the Prophet. It seems that in refusing the Family of the Prophet physical inheritance, Abu Bakr was also stating a claim that the spiritual legacy of the Prophet could not be passed on to the physical family of the Prophet. This episode would be especially remembered as a point of contention by the later Shi'i tradition, which saw in it a tangible example of the usurpation of the rights of the Family of the Prophet by Abu Bakr. At the heart of this debate between Abu Bakr and the Family of the Prophet was the very issue of whether the spiritual legacy of the Prophet would be linked to family that claimed genealogical descent from Muhammad.

When Ali was informed that Abu Bakr had been chosen as Caliph, he initially refused to accept that choice. Ali, who clearly viewed himself as the rightful heir to the Prophet, stated to Abu Bakr:

> *What has prevented us from pledging allegiance to you, Abu Bakr, was neither denial of your excellence, nor consideration of you as unworthy of any bounty which God has conveyed to you.*
> *Rather we held that we had a right in "this matter" which you have arbitrarily seized from us.*[6]

Although eventually forced to recognize Abu Bakr, Ali kept aloof from the Caliph for the rest of his life. The full manifestation of this tension would become clear much later. In the meantime, Abu Bakr ruled for only two years, during which time he strove to keep the majority of the community together and prevent the fracturing of the community that had gathered around Muhammad's charismatic authority. To emphasize continuity with the Prophet, Abu Bakr chose the title Khalifa Rasul Allah (the Successor to the Messenger of God). It is this term, Khalifa, that became anglicized as Caliph.

Abu Bakr's main challenge was dealing with the Bedouin tribes that, with Muhammad's passing, were attempting to break away from the Muslim society. Some even claimed their own prophets, who might have been seeking to duplicate Muhammad's success. Dealing with the competing prophets, such as the revolt of Maslamah (whose name Muslim sources usually record in the mockingly diminutive form Musaylimah, or "Little Maslamah"), and dealing with the internal rivalries among Muslims (such as that between the Muslims indigenous to Medina and the Muslims who had arrived from Mecca) were among the urgent tasks facing Abu Bakr and the young Muslim community. The extent of this challenge was articulated by A'isha, who, as Abu Bakr's daughter, could naturally be expected to cast her father in the most favorable light:

> *When the messenger died, the Arabs apostatized, and Christianity and Judaism raised their heads and disaffection appeared.*
> *The Muslims became as sheep exposed to rain on a winter's night through the loss of their prophet until God united them under Abu Bakr.*[7]

There was also a crucial change in the conception of Islam at this time. During the time of the Prophet Muhammad, the Qur'an had instructed Muslims that Islam was simply the latest revelation of the message that God had been revealing to humanity all along, and ultimately the decision to accept or not accept it was up to each individual and each community. With the death of the Prophet, Abu Bakr and the nascent Muslim community in Medina also came to think of loyalty to the Muslim community itself as a part of the faith. In fact, the wars they undertook under the competing movements came to be characterized as the *Ridda* wars, meaning wars of apostasy. In other words, the Bedouin tribes that were breaking away from the Medina Muslim community after the death of Muhammad were seen by Abu Bakr and many other Muslims as in fact having apostatized—that is, as having rejected the Islamic faith after initially embracing it. To be a Muslim would henceforth mean loyalty not just to the faith but also, in ways that would always be contested and negotiated, to the community.

The Designation of Umar as the Second Sunni Caliph

At the end of his two-year reign as Caliph, Abu Bakr designated Umar as his successor. For Sunni Muslims, then, Umar serves as the second of the Caliphs. From the Sunni perspective, Umar was a pious and worthy companion of the Prophet and Abu Bakr was acting within his right to follow the method of designation that ensured the greatest efficiency in the transfer of power. For the Shi'a, however, the designation of Umar represents the second time Muhammad's closest companion, Ali, was bypassed. From the Shi'a perspective, the event at Ghadir Khumm, when the Prophet declared "whosoever I was his master, Ali is his master," served to designate Ali as Muhammad's rightful heir. Furthermore, Shi'a Muslims would object that, from the Sunni point of view, the whole premise of the Banu Sa'ida session that had led to Abu Bakr's designation in the first place had been that Muhammad left no specific instructions for who the successor should be. If Muhammad did not select a successor, the Shi'a would argue, then how could Abu Bakr do so? Most of the Shi'a came to see the choice of Abu Bakr—and even more so of Umar—as illegitimate.

Umar had the personality of a pious if hotheaded convert. The narratives of the life of Muhammad are replete with accounts of outsiders who come to Muhammad and mock the Prophet. Umar would often turn angry at such encounters and would ask the Prophet for permission to cut off the head of the offender. Muhammad would gently ask Umar to sit down and then would continue to reason patiently with the one who had just offended him. Quite often, the offender would come to embrace Islam and become part of the community. In spite of the character flaw of being quick-tempered, Umar was seen as a scrupulous soul whose faith and piety were sincere.

Umar ruled for ten years, during which time Islam successfully expanded into the Persian and Byzantine Empires. Some of the important administrative work of the emerging Islamic Empire—such as the organization of the Muslim army, the designation of the bold leadership of Khalid, the son of al-Walid, to lead that army, and the transformation of the Medinan community into a successful empire—were among the significant developments that took place during Umar's reign. Umar was not seen as a religious authority in his own right, but mainly as the Commander of the Faithful (*Amir al-mu'minin*), a title that denoted his military and political responsibilities. By the end of Umar's reign, the Arabian Peninsula was under Muslim dominion. In addition, important urban centers like Damascus and Jerusalem had been brought under Muslim rule. All Persian-dominated areas in present-day Iraq were also conquered. Many of the precedents for military conquest and the distribution of goods acquired during the wars of expansion were established during Umar's reign from 634 to 644.

The Selection of Uthman as the Third Sunni Caliph and the Reemergence of the Umayyad Clan

Umar met with a tragic end when he was assassinated at the hands of a Persian slave in 644. As he lay mortally wounded, Umar ordered that six of the leading companions of Muhammad meet in a tent and choose the next Caliph from among themselves. Umar had always been known as a stern figure, even harsh, and that temperament was displayed in his model for choosing the next Caliph. He specifically instructed that should any of the six members of the selection committee refuse to participate, or if any refused to not recognize the eventual choice, they were to be immediately slain! The two clear candidates were Ali and another early companion of Muhammad named Uthman, the son of Affan, from the Umayyad clan.

The model proposed by Umar was different from the previous models followed for the selection of Abu Bakr and his own selection, but it did include Ali, with a caveat: he and Uthman were each asked to declare their loyalty not only to the Qur'an and to the example of the Prophet (which they both readily did) but also to the precedents set by Abu Bakr and Umar. Uthman agreed, whereas Ali steadfastly refused. He did not and had not recognized Abu Bakr and Umar as legitimate, and he would not agree to support their precedents if they came into conflict with his own conscience. The other companions offered the caliphate to Uthman, who gladly agreed to serve as the third Caliph (in the reckoning of the later Sunni tradition).

Uthman had been a close follower of Muhammad and one of the first male converts. The later tradition remembers this close relationship by noting that Uthman married first one daughter of Muhammad (Ruqayyah) and then, after she died, another (Umm Kulthum). Because of this unprecedented honor of being twice Muhammad's son-in-law, Uthman is occasionally called "he of the two lights," with each light referring to a daughter of the Prophet. He was also known to be pious personally. One of the delegation that went to Abyssinia, he was also an astute businessman who owned a great deal of property and had an intimate knowledge of trade networks.

It was this same business connection, however, coming out of his own family background, that would cost Uthman and earn him criticism much later. Uthman was generally seen as a weaker character than the previous caliphs, and he was repeatedly accused of nepotism. This charge deserves closer scrutiny. Uthman was descended from the Banu Umayya tribe (the children of Umayya). The leader of this tribe had been Abu Sufyan, who was one of the leaders of the pagan Meccans who persecuted the Prophet Muhammad and who converted late, and only halfheartedly, at the conquest of Mecca. In fact, it was Muhammad's generosity that spared his former enemy. Abu Sufyan's son, Mu'awiya, had become one of Muhammad's followers, and the Sunni tradition remembers him as one of the scribes of the Qur'an.

The Banu Umayya were usually seen as a mercantile group, with business interests throughout the Arabian Peninsula and beyond. The earliest Muslim community had been a meritocracy: in the words of the Qur'an, the only distinction in the eyes of God came from a person's piety and God-consciousness (*taqwa*). The aristocratic merchants of the Banu Umayya, however, never entirely bought into the radical egalitarianism of the early community around Muhammad. Whether it was nepotism or a belief that his mercantile tribesmen had the bureaucratic experience necessary to serve as officials, Uthman designated many of them as governors for the new Muslim cities and garrisons. This earned him the displeasure of those who gravitated toward Ali, many of whom had converted owing to the Islamic message of egalitarianism and social justice. Also displeased were many of the Ansar families of Medina, who saw the only recently converted pagan aristocracy yet again gaining the upper hand.

Perhaps the most illustrious example of a close companion of the Prophet who vigorously objected to the nepotism of Uthman was the famed Abu Dharr al-Ghifari. Abu Dharr was an early convert, perhaps the fourth or fifth person to have taken up Muhammad's message. He came from a very humble background and had little patience for the aristocracy of the Banu Umayya. In many ways he epitomized those attracted to the social justice teachings of Islam.[8] In particular, he objected when Uthman would lavish extravagant sums of money obtained from conquest booty on his own family members and supporters: according to some sources, Uthman gave 500,000 coins to one follower (Marwan, son of al-Hakam), 300,000 to another (al-Harith, the son of al-Hakam), and 100,000 to yet another (Zayd b. Thabit). In particular, Abu Dharr spoke up in the presence of the Caliph, quoting those verses from the Qur'an that warn those who hoard wealth. Siding with his own family members, Uthman banished Abu Dharr to Syria. In Damascus, Abu Dharr proceeded to criticize Uthman's family member Mu'awiya, who was building the opulent palace of al-Khadra for himself. Mu'awiya asked Uthman to have Abu Dharr extradited back to Medina, and this time Uthman ordered the courageous and pietistic Abu Dharr to be permanently exiled into the desert (in the province of al-Rabadha), where he died in the year 652. Thus, we see that some thirty years after the death of the Prophet Muhammad, old tribal customs and nepotism had come to dominate caliphal politics; there would always be the Abu Dharrs of the Muslim umma, however, who would speak truth to power, even at the risk of banishment for life.[9] This tension between social justice and empire would be an enduring feature of the Islamic experience. The legacy of Abu Dharr has been resurrected at times and in places as wide-ranging as the twentieth-century Iranian revolution, anti-apartheid activism in South Africa, and the peace and social justice movements in North America.

Much of the later Sunni tradition, too embarrassed by this part of caliphal history to acknowledge Abu Dharr's banishment, portrays it falsely as a voluntary exile. Furthermore, the mainstream of the Sunni tradition credits Uthman with finalizing the task of gathering up the manuscripts of the Qur'an, and in fact the edition of the Qur'an used today by all Muslims is usually termed the Uthmani Version. Still, his corruption and nepotism led many to revolt against him, and in the end it was one of the revolting groups that assassinated Uthman. Like Umar before him, another Caliph of Islam was murdered. It would not be the last time one group of Muslims killed another.

What followed was the first genuine civil war within the Muslim community. This time has been termed the *fitna*, a term that means strife, trial, and tribulation. Although the later Sunni tradition likes to see the early period after the time of the Prophet as a golden age of sorts—the most perfect of periods after the time of the Prophet itself— the actual historical record is much messier. Many of the dear companions of the Prophet who, during his lifetime, had stood shoulder to shoulder now took up arms against one another after the passing away of the Prophet. Some aspects of the Sunni tradition attempt to whitewash the tensions in this period among the key companions. A classic example is that of inventing prophetic traditions that promise paradise to ten key followers of Muhammad, even when some of these ten (such as Ali, Talha, and Zubayr) took up arms against one another!

These tensions even extended to the Prophet's own family. For example, after the murder of Uthman, the Prophet's wife A'isha (daughter of Abu Bakr) led an army into battle against Ali. Some of this might have had to do with the past rivalry between A'isha and Fatima—the Prophet's daughter and Ali's wife—to secure the attention and favors of the Prophet. A'isha even enlisted the aid of some senior companions of the Prophet, who along with her took up arms against Ali. Ali emerged victorious in battle and chivalrously had A'isha escorted back. Yet the legacy of the beloved ones of Muhammad taking up arms against one another would remain. A modern scholar of early Islam, Mahmoud Ayoub, has perhaps put it best: "Because the battle was fought at all, the whole of the Muslim umma lost."[10]

The Selection of Ali as the Fourth Sunni Caliph and the First Shi'i Imam

After the murder of Uthman, the community turned to the individual who was now most recognized as the worthiest successor to the Prophet, Ali. Doubtless, he and his followers—who dubbed themselves the Shi'a of Ali ("the faction that supports Ali")—believed that he had been the Prophet's intended successor all along. Sadly, Ali would not get an opportunity to implement his vision for Muslim society, because he had to deal with the aftermath of Uthman's murder. Uthman's fellow tribesmen were quite literally waiving Uthman's bloody shirt, demanding vengeance.

The main tension after the murder of Uthman was between the followers of Ali and the followers of Mu'awiya, who, like Uthman, was from the Banu Umayya tribe. Mu'awiya claimed the right to avenge Uthman following the Arab—though pre-Islamic—blood rites. Ali refused, and further conflicts ensued. Making matters more complicated was yet another schism in the community: many of the most pious members of the community, particularly those who had memorized the Qur'an and were masters of its recitation, seceded from the camps of both Ali and Mu'awiya and formed a third group called the Khawarij. They insisted on a total meritocracy based not on descent from the noble clans of the Quraysh (as Mu'awiya insisted) or the Family of the Prophet (as the Shi'a of Ali insisted), but rather simply on piety. A failed arbitration session ensued in which Ali and the Khawarij failed to come to a resolution. The terms of this arbitration are instructive for Muslims today: the Khawarij claimed that they would submit to no authority other than the Qur'an. Ali famously responded that the Qur'an was silent and could speak only when it was interpreted by human beings. This insight, from the very foundational period of Islam by the one closest to the Prophet, is of paramount importance for Muslims today, who often seek to legitimize their own position by "text-proofing" (citing scripture selectively, and often out of context) while hiding or denying their own philosophical and ideological perspective.

Like Umar and Uthman before him, Ali too would meet a violent end. In the holy month of Ramadan in the year 661 CE, Ali was in Kufa (in Iraq) to perform the morning prayers. Shouting, "Judgment belongs to God, O Ali, and not to you," one of the Khawarij named Ibn Muljam attacked and mortally wounded Ali while he was in the midst of prayer. The Shi'i tradition recalls that when the assassin struck Ali with a poisoned sword, Ali exclaimed: "By the God of Ka'ba, I have triumphed!"

Sources document that Ali, the model of chivalry in Islam, prevented the crowd from taking revenge on the assassin by torturing or inflicting pain on him and that he even made sure Ibn Muljam was fed the same food and water that Ali himself—the Caliph of Islam—was receiving in his dying days, including half of his own bowl of milk. When Ali died two days later, his shrine in Najaf (in present-day Iraq) became a major Islamic pilgrimage site.

It is to be expected that the Shi'a would, of course, venerate Ali as the forefather of the later imams. Yet it might come as a surprise to know that Ali is also a role model for many who come from a Sunni background. After the Prophet Muhammad, perhaps no other Muslim figure has been the subject of so much idealization. Ali has come to embody the brave knight, the perfect chivalrous soul, the just ruler, and the quintessential mystic. He is remembered as the young man who courageously lay down in Muhammad's bed to serve as a decoy when the Prophet went on the Hijra to Medina even though he knew that the assassins who were after Muhammad would be descending on him. The combination of his valor, piety, knowledge, and closeness to the example of the Prophet led future generations to idealize him. Perhaps the greatest twentieth-century scholar of early Shi'ism, Wilferd Madelung, states: "In the memory of later generations Ali became the ideal Commander of the Faithful."[11] Both Sunni and Shi'i sources record that close companions of the Prophet, such as Abu Dharr—the champion of justice who criticized Umayyad nepotism— would weep upon seeing Ali and state: "By God, whenever I see you, I remember the Prophet."[12] Ali was a walking memory of the Prophet for the Muslim community.

One of Ali's legacies was a magnificent collection of sermons and aphorisms known as the *Nahj al-Balagha* ("Peak of Eloquence"). For Shi'i Muslims in particular, this collection is second in importance only to the Qur'an; because they trust Ali to be a more faithful reminder of the Prophet's teachings than the Sunni hadith collections, they refer to the *Nahj al-Balagha* perhaps even more than the collections of sayings of the Prophet Muhammad. In the *Nahj al-Balagha*, Ali reveals himself as a great and eloquent master of the Arabic language, as well as a spiritual sage whose teachings are designed to be implemented in daily life:

- Mix with people in such a way that if you die, they weep for you, and if you live, they yearn to be with you.

- If you conquer your enemy, forgive him, and be grateful to God for the power and blessing.
- No wealth is more beneficial than wisdom, and no loneliness is more frightening than self-love. Nothing is nobler than piety, and no inheritance is better than beautiful manners.[13]

As with many spiritual traditions, Ali counseled his followers to speak little and to remember that the heart of a wise human being is the treasure chest of secrets.[14] Speech, when not accompanied by deep thought and reflection, is for Ali like a wild animal that leads one to damnation and ruin.[15] No doubt reflecting on his own experience of living for twenty-five years through the period of infighting among Muslims, Ali says: "In times of unrest, be like a suckling calf, which has no back to be ridden and no udder to be milked."[16]

Muslims in this early phase expressed their spirituality not through otherworldly miracles, but through wonder at the everyday awesomeness of creation, a trait that was in fact quite resonant with the Qur'anic description of the natural cosmos as being a "sign" (*aya*) of God. Ali glories in God's masterpiece, the human being, when he states: "I marvel at the creation of humanity: The human sees through a clear veil (the eye), speaks through a piece of meat, hears through a bone and a cartilage, and breathes through a narrow opening."

Ali as the Model of Muslim Chivalry

Ali became the object of the intense devotion of pious Muslims in large part because of the model of behavior he provided during his life and in his death. Many of those who are mystically inclined have focused on the wealth of traditions attributed to the Prophet in which Muhammad declared himself the "city of knowledge" and Ali its gate. For example, every Sufi group traces itself back to the Prophet Muhammad through a special genealogy known as the *silsila*, a chain through which the grace of the Prophet is transmitted to the community.[17] Even in Muslim iconography, the famous two-pronged sword that Ali used in battle, known as Dhu 'l-fiqar, became iconic. It has been depicted in countless miniatures, and small representations of it are occasionally worn as amulets.

Perhaps no story depicts Muslim devotion to Ali better than that of the thirteenth-century Muslim saint Mawlana Jalal al-Din Rumi. Recall that Rumi was decidedly a Sunni, yet his Sunni loyalty did not prevent him from deeply admiring Ali and other members of the Family of the Prophet. To put it differently, love and devotion to the Family of the Prophet have historically been shared among most Muslims and have not been considered the exclusive monopoly of Shi'i Muslims.

Rumi did not have to do much embellishing on Ali's already legendary courage on the battlefield. The Prophet and his followers were engaged in the heated Battle of Khandaq (the Trench) against the pagans of Mecca. As was the Arab custom, prior to the battle each side chose its bravest champion to engage in a one-on-one duel. The pagans sent forth a giant warrior, a mountain of a man. He asked for a worthy adversary, yet his sheer size caused the hearts of even the bravest Muslim champions to tremble. The pagan champion, named Amr, the son of Abdu Wudd, began taunting the Muslims, saying: "Where is your garden of which you say that those you lose in battle will enter it? Can't you send a man to fight me?" Ali, still a teenager, volunteered. The Prophet, mindful of Ali's youth, asked him to sit down. Three times the champion asked for an adversary by saying: "I've become hoarse from shouting. Isn't there one among the lot of you who'll answer my challenge? I've stood here like a fighting champion while the so-called brave are cowards."

Each time none but Ali volunteered. At last the Prophet relented, and Ali stepped forth to confront the mighty warrior, saying:

Don't be in a hurry. No weakling has come to answer your challenge. A man of resolution and foresight. Truth is the refuge of the successful.

A great duel ensued, full of hand-to-hand combat. In the midst of the cloud of dust, all that the two sides could see were two mighty champions wrestling and struggling against one another. At long last they heard the cry, "God is great," and saw Ali lift up the mighty pagan, throw him to the ground, and conquer him. Up to this point in the narrative, the story is attested to in the famed biography of Muhammad written by Ibn Ishaq in the eighth century.[18]

Rumi offers his own ingenious take on this narrative. According to Rumi's masterpiece the *Masnavi*, Ali sat on Amr's chest to slay the defeated warrior. The pagan champion, flustered and humiliated, spat on Ali's face. At this point, Rumi says:

Learn how to act sincerely from Ali
God's lion, free from all impurity:

During a battle, he subdued a foe
Then drew his sword to deal the final blow.

That man spat in Ali's pure face, the pride
Of every saint and prophet far and wide

The moon prostrates itself before this face
At which he spat—this act was a disgrace!

Ali put down his saber straight away
And, though he was on top, he stopped the fray.

The fighter was astonished by this act,
That he showed mercy though he'd been attacked.

Ali came to be seen as the model of chivalry not simply because of his sheer power and strength. As Rumi says, if the measure of a human being were simply power, then elephants would be more human than humans! Rather, the model of humanity is to strive in the Path of God, yet to empty oneself of selfish desires so that one can be imbued with godly qualities. Ali's model is not one of pacifism per se, yet it is one in which even fighting is striving in the Path of God. When the champion spat on Ali's face, Ali—luminous though still human—became angry. Had he proceeded to slay the champion, he would have been acting, not out of God's command, but merely out of his own anger. Rumi picks up on this point, having Ali say:

> *He said, "I use my sword the way God's planned*
> *Not for my body but by God's command;*
>
> *I am God's lion, not the one of passion—*
> *My actions testify to my religion: . . .*
>
> *I've moved the baggage of my self away,*
> *"All but God's nonexistent," I now say.*

In a clever pun in Persian (a language that Rumi spoke but Ali did not!), Rumi has Ali contrast his own internal strength as a mountain (*Kuh*) with a straw (*Kah*) to say that a person who is "blown" into this or that action by every passing whim is not a mountain of a man but like a straw caught up in the winds of the ego:

> *A mountain of forbearance and deep calm*
> *The fiercest winds can't blow away or harm;*
>
> *That which is swept by wind is trash, no more,*
> *And there are many winds like this in store!*
> *The wind of rage and that of greed and lust*
> *Blow those who don't pray at the time they must!*
>
> *I am a mountain, God's my solid base,*
> *Like straw I'm blown just by thought of His face;*

My longing changes once His wind has blown,
My captain is the love of Him alone.

In the style so typical of Muslim spirituality, the conclusion of the story is one of spiritual liberation, where the once-pagan mighty warrior is invited into a life of love and faith.

"Rage can't enslave me," said Ali, "I am free,
There naught here but God's attributes—come see!

Enter! God's grace has liberated you!
His mercy comes before His anger too!

Come in! Now you've fled danger that you've known
You're like a jewel that was once a stone.

You've fled the thorn of unbelief and doom
So in the rose-bed of God you will bloom!

In medieval cosmology, jewels were in fact "precious stones" that had been illuminated. When light—the light of God reflected through saintly beings—fell on them, even those (or those with hearts of) stones would be illuminated into jeweled hearts. Ever the mystic, Rumi has Ali obliterate the boundaries of I and Thou by recognizing that the defeated warrior and Ali are in fact one in faith. So Ali even addresses the fallen warrior as "Ali," since duality has disappeared and One remains:

Illustrious one, I'm you and you are I,
Ali, how could I cause Ali to die!

The conclusion of the narrative is an invitation to grace and mercy, qualities that must be combined with power and strength to make a genuine champion of Islamic chivalry:

Enter! The door is open for you now—
You spat but I gave favors anyhow;

I grant such gifts to those who torture me
And bow my head down in humility,
Imagine what I give men who are loyal—
Treasures and kingdoms that are all eternal![19]

Here, as in so many places in Islamic literature, the lines between outright history and devotion are blurred. What matters to Muslims is not the exact geographic location and atomic time of the battle, but the spiritual lessons to be learned from these events. To put it differently, whether one speaks of Muhammad or Ali or Hossein, Zaynab or Fatima, what matters to Muslims is not the historicity of the events but the ways in which these episodes can be used to map out spiritual lessons for living a luminous life.

This story from Rumi's *Masnavi*, doubtless one of the most famous stories of all the books of Islamic literatures, has been told and retold countless times by both Sunni and Shi'i Muslims. Nor was his voice the last to commemorate Ali in such a pietistic fashion. Moving from Rumi's thirteenth-century context of Iran and Turkey to twenty-first-century Pakistan, we see another Sunni figure, the larger-than-life Pakistani vocalist Nusrat Fateh Ali Khan, who likewise engaged in poetic and musical praise of Ali. Nusrat was a Qawwal, a singer of mystical songs that originated in the mystical context of Sufi Islam. These songs were first sung in gatherings of Sufis as a way of moving souls to ecstasy in sessions filled with chanting and prayer, music and poetry. Many of the Qawwali sessions in South Asia begin by reciting the *Qal Tarana*, the famous song composed by the famed Indian Persian-speaking poet, Amir Khusraw. The song commemorates the transmission of spiritual grace from the Prophet Muhammad to Ali by recalling:

Man kontu mawlahu, fa 'ali mawlahu.
(For whomever I was his master, Ali is his master.)

Here we note a parallel between the Shi'i and Sufi traditions, which both operate from the idea that mystical knowledge was transmitted from the Prophet to Ali, and then from Ali to his heirs. In the Shi'i case the heirs are his biological heirs (the Shi'i imams), and in the Sufi case the heirs are the Sufi masters. What should we make of this overlap? It is not a case of Sufis being quasi-Shi'a, or Shi'a in disguise. Yet again, it is a reminder that Islamic life is not usually black-and-white but rather takes on the full spectrum of color. People's lives, cultures, ideas, and sensitivities are more fluid and waterlike than rocklike: they are in constant motion. Unlike the charts that literally color some parts of the Islamic world "Shi'a" (Iran, parts of Lebanon, East Africa, Iraq, and segments of Bahrain and Pakistan) and the rest "Sunni," in fact Muslim customs are overlapping and diffuse across the majority of the parts of the world where Muslims live. The Sunni and Shi'i legacies of Islam would have their own particularity, yet they would always exist side by side within the fold of Muhammad's community.

From Ali to Hossein

As significant as devotion to Ali is for both Sunnis and the Shi'a, the story of Shi'ism does not end with him. In fact, the martyrdom of Ali, as tragic as it was, does not color the spiritual cosmos of the Shi'a in quite the same way that Hossein's martyrdom does.

Even prior to Ali's death, Mu'awiya had moved to consolidate the base of his power. He came to exert his authority over Egypt and much of what is today the Arab Middle East. He had chosen as the seat of his power the Syrian city of Damascus. The shift from Medina to Damascus was symbolically central. Medina had been, and would forever remain, the City of the Prophet. Those who looked to Medina would always be reminded of the legacy of the Prophet and those whose authority was inextricably tied up with the memory of the

Prophet. For Mu'awiya, and particularly his descendants, the move to Damascus symbolized a break (or at least transition away) from the legacy of Medina and the establishment of an empire whose ruler's authority would be primarily militaristic and political. Whereas rulers like Ali, Abu Bakr, and Umar could always claim a close connection to the Prophet and authority based on their piety, in time many of the Umayyad rulers in Damascus came to be derided as drunk fornicators who lived (and drank) more like Byzantine Caesars than like Muslim exemplars. Islam was now also the formative vision through which an empire expressed itself. It would forever remain a spiritual path for those seeking to find their way back to God, but in addition it became a complex ethical, legal, and aesthetic network bringing together humanity, a broad and internally nuanced civilization, and the blueprint for an empire—simultaneously heir to the legacies of Rome and Persia. Many Muslims recognized that this inheritance of power came at a high cost, as all great power does.

Mu'awiya's rule in particular was not directly based on teachings of Islam, though it tapped into those mores for support. Above all else it was based on the complex network of military and financial power gained as Muslim armies expanded into the lucrative Iraq and Syria regions. Voices of dissent could be ruthlessly quashed, and in fact often were. Particularly susceptible to this fate were many of the ardent partisans of Ali (the Shi'a) whose appeal was primarily based on piety and social justice. Mu'awiya ordered many of them exiled or killed. A dramatic case was that of the martyr Hujr, the son of 'Adi, and a dozen other ardent supporters of Ali. Mu'awiya offered Hujr a chance to save his own life if he would publicly curse Ali, to which the courageous prisoner responded: "By God, we will never do this." Hujr and his companions were summarily beheaded after that. As already mentioned, it was also Mu'awiya who sent Abu Dharr, the early companion of the Prophet, into exile.

One of the consequences of these changes in the nature of Islamic rule was that over time very few in the Muslim community would continue to look at the Caliphs as the paragons of moral excellence and piety. In fact, when Ali was seeking to rally support among the Muslims of Kufa against Mu'awiya, he had warned them that unless they chose rulers based on their piety and precedence in faith, they would be ruled over by kinglike figures who resembled the rulers of Byzantium and Persia. Here, in Ali's invitation, was the promise of the model of society that had been envisioned by Islam, even if somewhat derailed under the Umayyads and some later rulers: a society in which the ruler was not only a king but a spiritual exemplar. Here and there, even under the Umayyads, there were pious exceptions (like the Caliph Umar, the son of Abd al-Aziz), but the paradigm had changed. Henceforth, the Caliphs were rulers, kings, and, at best, forces to lead the Islamic Empire and keep the community together. When Caliphs were described as *Amir al-mu'minin* (Commander of the Faithful), the word *Amir* (commander) had a very political and even military connotation. For spiritual excellence and piety, Muslims would turn increasingly to scholars, saints, and the Family of the Prophet. The idealization of the caliphate for many Muslims in the age of postcolonialism (in the twentieth century) is not something that many Muslims historically would have shared in. The caliphate might have served as a useful symbol of political unity, but it quickly lost its luster as the moral center of the *umma*.

When Mu'awiya consolidated his power base, he had to deal with the Family of the Prophet. They presented the most serious challenge to his authority, especially Hasan, Ali's elder son. Hasan did not recognize Mu'awiya as a legitimate Caliph and is said to have written to Mu'awiya in the following terms:

> But now what a great astonishment and shock it is to see that you, O Mu'awiya, are attempting to accede to a thing which you do not deserve. You do not possess any known merit in religion, nor have you any trace in Islam which has ever been praised.
>
> On the contrary, you are the son of the leader of the opposition party from among the parties; and you are the son of the greatest

*enemy of the Prophet from among Quraysh. . . . So give up your
persistence in falsehood and enter into my homage.*[20]

In his reply, Mu'awiya asserted that he preferred himself as Caliph
because he believed that he would serve the interest of the community
better, he was older than Hasan, and he had more experience in government administration. Mu'awiya concluded: "It would therefore be
better for you not to insist on what you have asked me; if you enter
into obedience to me now, you will accede to caliphate after me."[21]
Interestingly enough, Mu'awiya did not assert his own piety, religious
knowledge, or practice over Hasan. He based his decision on being
a better politician and ruler than Hasan, a point that was probably
valid; he was certainly inferior to the grandson of the Prophet, however, in religious matters.

Hasan was unable to raise enough support to mount a serious challenge and eventually was forced to abdicate the caliphate to Mu'awiya
temporarily. Here the Sunni and Shi'i narratives differ substantially.
The Sunni (and Sunni-sympathetic) narratives generally emphasize
that Hasan abdicated the caliphate for a significant sum of money
from the Iraq treasury, plus promises that his father (Ali) would not be
cursed. Many Shi'i sources dispute this reading, since it casts Hasan as
essentially having sold out (or leased, more properly) the prerogative
of leading the Muslim umma. In the Shi'i versions, the terms of the
agreement were that the caliphate would be returned to Hasan after
Mu'awiya's death, that Mu'awiya would not appoint anyone as Caliph
after himself, and that he would rule according to the Qur'an and the
example of the Prophet.

As expected, few of these terms were honored. Hasan died a mysterious death that many of the Shi'i sources attribute to poisoning.
The caliphate was never returned to the Family of the Prophet, and
Mu'awiya instead appointed his own son, Yazid, as the next Caliph. It
was the designation of Yazid as the Caliph—the first time the designation of the caliphate had proceeded in a dynastic fashion—that led
many Muslims to rise up in revolt against Yazid and the Umayyads.

The majority of this support came from those who remained loyal to the Family of the Prophet, in particular Ali's son—and Muhammad's grandson—Hossein. This support was centered in Iraq, where Ali had based his operations. Many of these supporters remembered Hossein as the light of Muhammad's eye—the grandchild he doted on with great fondness and affection. The son of Ali and Fatima (Muhammad's daughter), Hossein could claim the most exclusive descent from the Prophet, and he had impeccable credentials in terms of his religious knowledge and practice. In the year 680, somewhere between twelve thousand and eighteen thousand people in the city of Kufa signed a petition asking Hossein to leave Medina to come to them to lead them as their Caliph. Incidentally, this marks one of the largest demonstrations of "public election" in the early Muslim community.

Hossein replied:

From Hossein, the son of Ali, to the believers and the Muslims. . . .

You must be clear about the fact that the Imam is only one who follows the Book of God, makes justice and honesty his conduct and behavior, judges with truth, and devotes himself to the service of God. Peace.[22]

This letter is significant because it demonstrates that Hossein saw the task of an imam as a religious one, concerned with affairs of justice and the necessity of serving the faithful with honesty. In another letter to the Shi'a of Basra, Hossein warned the folks there that the example of the Prophet Muhammad had already become obliterated and that innovations in the religion were actively being spread. This letter as well, found in prominent Sunni historical sources like Tabari, attests that to the Shi'a the *Sunna* (example) of the Prophet Muhammad was not somehow magically or passively transmitted from generation to generation, but had to be realized and protected from falsehood.

Hossein departed from the safety of Medina and headed toward Kufa. At the same time, the Umayyad ruler Yazid appointed his strong-man, named 'Ubayd Allah, the son of Ziyad, the governor of Kufa. 'Ubayd Allah delivered a terrifying speech in which he threatened the citizens of Kufa with instant death should they persist in their support for Hossein. To set an example, he detained Hossein's messenger and beheaded him. 'Ubayd Allah further announced that anyone suspected of support for Hossein would be hung without a trial and their homes would be burned.

'Ubayd Allah dispatched a large army led by a general named Hurr, the son of Yazid (not the same as the Caliph), to intercept Hossein. When Hurr caught up with Hossein, it was in the middle of a hot day in the Iraq desert, and Hurr's army was exhausted and thirsty. Ever the chivalrous son of his father Ali, Hossein ordered his army to share their water with the army that had been sent to curtail them. Hossein personally served water to soldiers of the op-posing camp. As an indication of their respect for Hossein, even the Umayyad army prayed behind Hossein for their communal prayers (*salat*).

In the first few days of the Islamic month of Muharram, in the sixty-first year after the Prophet's migration to Medina (680 CE), Hossein and his followers arrived at the famed plains of Karbala. Faithful Shi'a commemorate every stage of the pathos-filled days and nights there in a way that resembles the passion plays of medieval Catholicism. Like every genuine heroic figure, Hossein attempted to save those around him. On the night of *Ashura* (the tenth of Muhar-ram), he gave a speech to his family members and companions in which he said:

> *I know of no worthier companions than mine. I think tomorrow our end will come. . . . I ask you all to leave me alone and to go away to safety. I free you from your responsibilities for me, and I do not hold you back.*[23]

Needless to say, most of his supporters and family members persisted in what they knew was certain death. They spent the night in prayer, reciting Qur'an and engaging in *dhikr* (remembrance of Allah). The next morning Hossein prepared himself for battle by wearing the mantle of the Prophet. He offered the following prayer to God:

> *O God, you are my only Trust in every calamity; you are my only hope in every hardship;*

> *You are the only promise in the anxiety and distress in which hearts become weak and human action becomes slight, in which one is deserted and forsaken by his own friends, and in which the enemies take malicious pleasure and rejoice at his misfortunes.*

> *O God, I submit myself to You.*[24]

The enemy began taunting Hossein and his followers for rushing headlong into hellfire. Hossein asked his followers to not respond, and not to shoot their arrows, so that history would record that it was not their side that initiated the conflict. Hossein's followers— thirty-two horsemen and forty on foot—were vastly outnumbered by a force that had five hundred archers alone and hundreds more on foot and on horseback. Hossein's supporters shielded Hossein and the Family of the Prophet, and so long as a single one of the supporters remained, no harm came to the Prophet's family. Hossein's sister, the heroic Zaynab (we will revisit her at the end of this chapter), saved Hossein's son Ali from certain death. Around noontime, Hossein prayed the *zuhr* prayer and then offered the prayer that Muslims pray in situations of immense calamity and disaster. One by one, the Umayyad army killed the family members, ranging from Hossein's half-brother to Hossein's infant child. Hossein himself charged the army, which surrounded him on all sides. At long last he fell to the ground. Hossein's nephew had rushed out to protect his fallen uncle by stretching his arms over him, and the soldiers cut off the young boy's arms. In full view of the tent of the women and children of the Family of the Prophet, the soldiers cut off Hossein's head. As one last insult, the horsemen trampled over the body of the grandson of the Messenger of God. His blessed head was cut off, put on top of a lance, and brought as a trophy, first to the governor and then to the drunkard Yazid, who looked, dressed, and lived more like a king than the Commander of the Faithful. The soldiers did not bother burying the bodies on the field. That task fell to a tribe that came by two days later and buried the bodies of Hossein and his followers in Karbala. That burial site in Karbala became a major pilgrimage site for Shi'a Muslims.

Hossein was gone, but his memory remained. And much of the Shi'i tradition henceforth would be concerned with the commemoration of this event, in multiple ways. As already mentioned, it is not just the Shi'a who remember Hossein. For another example of Sunni devotion to Hossein, we can visit a famous poem that is popular in Muslim South Asia and attributed to an Indian Sufi of the thirteenth century, Khwaja Mu'in al-Din Chishti. While many of the Shi'i rituals are noted for their mournful note, this poem, a favorite of many Qawwali singers (including the previously mentioned Nusrat Fateh Ali Khan), is almost jubilant in its delight, not at Hossein's martyrdom, but rather at his refusal to submit to tyranny:

> *Shah ast Hossein o paadeshah ast Hossein*
> *Deen ast Hossein o Deen-panaah ast Hossein*
> *Sar daad o nadaad dast bar dast-e yazid*
> *Haqqa ke bina-ye "la ilah" ast Hossein.*
> *(Hossein is the king, Hossein is the emperor.*
> *Hossein is the religion,*
> *He is the protector of the faith*
> *He preferred to have his head severed than to lend a hand to Yazid.*
> *By God! Hossein is the foundation of "There is no god [but the One*
>   *God].")*

So here is another indication of how the webs of Islamic remembrance work: the grandson of the Prophet Muhammad rose up from Medina, only to fall on the plains of Arab Karbala in Iraq. His memory was kept alive by a thirteenth-century South Asian Sufi who wrote a poem in Persian. The poem was recited in the late twentieth century by a Punjabi-speaking Pakistani Qawwal (Nusrat Fateh Ali Khan), whose music was popularized first by Peter Gabriel and who is adored all over South Asia—and the West.

Remembrance of Hossein

The Shi'i tradition remembers Hossein as a spiritual and tender soul who often called out to God in beautiful prayers. Some of the loveliest came when he stood on the plains of Arafat, during the pilgrimage season to Mecca. Those who saw him remarked that tears would readily flow down his blessed face, as if his eyes were made out of containers of water. Indeed, it is far too rarely remembered that the same medieval Muslim model of manliness for chivalry (*futuwwah*) and courage in battle also included tenderness to the point of shedding tears at the recitation of prayers or poetry. One of the tender prayers recalls his gratitude toward God:

> *Thou watched over me in the cradle*
> *as an infant boy,*
> *provided me with food,*
> *wholesome milk,*
> *and turned the hearts of the nurse-maids toward me.*
> *Thou entrusted my upbringing to compassionate mothers,*
> *Guarded me from the calamities brought by the jinn*
> *And kept me secure from excess and lack. . . .*
> *O Merciful! O Compassionate!*[25]

This prayer recalls the connection that Hossein felt to the women who had nurtured him so lovingly, in particular his mother, Fatima, who had been the darling of Muhammad's life. Passages like this one have always been treasured in particular by Muslim women who see in the martyrdom of Hossein the injustice inflicted upon their own beloved sons and the tyranny that they themselves have had to endure. In fact, devotion toward Hossein, his mother Fatima, and his brave sister Zaynab have always been key components of female Shi'i piety. Particularly memorable is the example of Hossein's sister, Zaynab. Sayyida (Lady) Zaynab, as she is remembered in the Shi'i tradition, became yet another of the paragons of speaking truth to the power, who confront prejudice and tyranny even when powerless. When she came face-to-face with the tyrant Yazid, she said:

> *Do you know what you have done!?! You have killed the best household of the Prophet; and you have chopped off the roots and branches of the tree of the garden of his mission.*[26]

She proceeded to condemn and curse Yazid. It is important to note the recognition in the Shi'i tradition that all that is needed for evil to succeed is for the good to do nothing. So Zaynab also criticizes the people of Kufa, who failed to rise up:

> *O people of Kufa, you deceptive, fraudulent, lying and treacherous people; by God, you have made false promises, and turned your hypocritical faces toward my brother, and sent him deceptive letters . . . and conspired to destroy the household of the Prophet (may God's Peace and Blessing be upon him and his family). . . .*
> *[You] have chosen to give the worst of worldly people authority and power over the best of people, and instead of defending the truth and justice, you simply stood by at a distance, as spectators; now you dare to share hypocritical tears on our behalf!?!*[27]

In conveying Zaynab's criticism of the people of Kufa, the Shi'i tradition is actually chastising today's Kufa—that is, the good-hearted but weak-willed Muslims of today and every day who fail to rise up against today's Yazids. Zaynab's task, a powerful reminder of female heroism in Islam, was not only saving Hossein's offspring—the young boy Ali, who was suffering from an ailment—but performing the equally arduous work of keeping Hossein's memory alive. Indeed, she reportedly said to Yazid in Damascus: "You will never take from us our memory."[28]

This commemoration is key to Shi'ism. Like so many great dramas, this narrative is not just a way of remembering something that happened in the past but the key to understanding our own dramas. Facets of this cosmic drama—the struggle between the Hossein of justice and the Yazid of tyranny—was resurrected in the twentieth-century Iranian context when Ayatollah Khomeini recast it to explain Iranian struggles against Western-supported monarchy. In Khomeini's retelling, he and his supporters represented the faction of Imam Hossein and the secular Shah of Iran, backed by the United States, represented Yazid. These recastings are not much for nuance and subtlety. Instead, they make powerful, almost visceral, identifications between current social and political forces and spiritual archetypes. As such, they are not just a way of casting a drama but a call to action.

This identification of one's own situation with past spiritual episodes has often been repeated in recent years, including in the very lands of Iraq where Hossein's martyrdom took place. The women of Iraq, for example, came to connect their suffering at the hands of the genocidal dictator Saddam Hossein to Imam Hossein's suffering in Karbala: "History is repeating itself. We are oppressed by Saddam as Hossein was oppressed by Yazid."[29] The particular identification of many Iraqi women with the heroic example of Lady Zaynab offers a remarkable way in which memories of suffering and courage are woven together, stretching forward from Hossein's time to our own age today.

Where Was/Is God in Karbala?

To remain relevant, religious traditions have to come to terms with the perennial questions that confront humanity—not just the ones about love, beauty, and life, but also the ones about the existence of evil, affliction, and unearned suffering. This is the common— though no less daunting—question of "why do bad things happen to good people." A hurricane comes, and homes are destroyed. Children starve in a famine. A tsunami befalls Asia, and hundreds of thousands perish. Families live in refugee camps or under occupation for generations, with no end to their misery in sight. Genocides take place, and the world stands by. Where is God in all of this? This question tests the very limits of human understanding, and no person of compassion can or should seek to rush to a quick answer. There is a need to pause and reflect on the enormity of the suffering, at all levels. Where is God when bad things happen? For the Shi'a in particular, it is vital to answer this question with respect to the horrific events of Karbala.

It is often like this with unearned suffering. Christian icons like Martin Luther King Jr. have often linked their personal and communal suffering to that of Jesus Christ by reminding their flocks that nothing shall be more redemptive than unearned suffering.[30] The early Shi'a also had to confront this question: How could a just and compassionate God watch the slaughter of the beloved grandson and family members of the Prophet? How could the same God that sent the Prophet Muhammad as a mercy to all of Creation stand by when the followers of that same Prophet raised the severed heads of the Prophet's family members? Where was God in all of this?

The Shi'a ultimately decided that God was present, but humanity was not. In careful theological treatises, like the *I'tiqadat al-Imamiyya* ("A Shi'ite Creed"), great tenth-century Shi'i theologians like Shaykh al-Saduq grappled with these questions. Such theological struggles were, of course, entirely common to the medieval tradition of Aquinas and Augustine, Maimonides and others. A rigorous Shi'i theologian, Shaykh al-Saduq carefully delineated what God wills and desires, the boundaries of human responsibility, and God's foreknowledge of all matters. In this Shi'a theology, God had the power to save Imam Hossein, as he had done previously with Abraham. (In the Qur'anic narrative, when the pagans threw Abraham into a fire, God commanded the fire to be cool for Abraham, sparing him.) In other words, the Shi'a theologian wanted to affirm God's foreknowledge, absolve God of the sin of Imam Hossein's murder, and put the responsibility squarely on human shoulders.

> But we say that God desired that the sin of the sinners should be contradistinguished from the obedience of those that obey. . . .
> And we hold that God's wish was that the murder of Hossein should be a sin against Him and the opposite of obedience.[31]

Indeed, part of the ethical teaching of Shi'ism is to confront humanity with its failure to stand up: the failure to stand up not just for the historical Hossein but for all the Hosseins of the world. Here Shi'ism becomes an invitation to respond to the silent cries of all the dispossessed and the marginalized of the world. One of the early responses in the Shi'i tradition to the tragedy in Karbala was a "repentance" movement known as the Tawwabun. As many as three thousand of these penitents rose up in the same city of Kufa that had initially asked for and received Hossein's help and then, in cowardly fashion, failed to show up to support him. Something about Hossein's sacrifice shook them out of their state of moral and cosmic lethargy. That is ultimately one of the measures of the success of a tragic figure like Hossein, who understood the power of a soul force confronting the brute power of a cold military. The realm of the spirit has the ability to move those who have become cowards, and in Hossein's case this moral power reaches out across the centuries. As one Shi'i author has stated, it is impossible to know the full extent of the impact of Hossein's rebellion, precisely because he did rebel. Had he not, we might have seen the full-blown transformation of Islam into an Arab monarchy completely cut off from the grace of the Prophet.

So let us reflect on the divergent ways in which Sunni and Shi'i Muslims have come to make sense of the transition from the passing away of Muhammad to Hossein's rebellion, which was simultaneously a political failure and a spiritual success.

The Idealization of the "Righteous Forefathers" in Sunni Islam

The turbulent transition from the period of the Prophet Muhammad to the succession disputes and the martyrdom of Hossein left a huge imprint on the views of different Muslims throughout history on the relationship between time and the realm of the spirit. In much of the Sunni tradition, a notion eventually developed that with the passage of time the spiritual state of the cosmos gradually devolves. The most perfect of days were deemed to be those of the Prophet and the age of revelation, then the age of the *al-Salaf al-Salih*, the Righteous Forefathers, and then the age of those who came after, the Followers. Even this model was modified slightly to allow for a *mujaddid* (renewer) figure who will rise once every century to reinvigorate the faith, but the notion of moral and spiritual decline did persist in some parts. A critical part of this notion of decline was a romanticization and idealization of the early period, particularly of the first four Caliphs, who were idealized as the "Rightly Guided Ones" (*al-rashidun*). Muslims could not realistically seek to re-create the age of the Prophet, since there would never again be anyone like him who would receive revelation directly from God. Yet the age of the first four Caliphs held promise as a paradigm for the post-prophetic age in which the Muslim community—allegedly—lived in accordance with the teachings of God and the Prophet.

It would be much harder for the Shi'a to participate retrospectively in the idealization of "the Righteous Forefathers," with the exception of Ali. After all, the same period of the *al-Salaf al-Salih* and the subsequent generation of the Followers is the one in which Ali was disenfranchised from the position of leadership that according to the Shi'a was his and his alone, and even more importantly, so many of the family members of the Prophet were massacred at this time. To put it differently, the historical differences between the Shi'i and Sunni perspectives are not just about who should have been the leader of the Muslim umma or what the roles and responsibilities of this figure should have been, but about the very worldview of each tradition. These differences and the particularities of each tradition are of paramount importance as Muslims today seek to take dialogue between Sunnis and Shi'a as seriously as they have taken interfaith dialogue. Today we see many Muslims, in what is surely a meritorious enterprise, speaking in ecumenical voices with the intention of bringing together the Sunni and Shi'i perspectives. At the same time, it is vital that mutual respect and coexistence not be a license for eradicating real historical grievances and particularities. This is particularly important for the Shi'a: as the minority tradition, they must maintain their identity in the face of a larger and dominant Sunni tradition.

Is the Schism Within Islam Permanent?

Having reviewed the turbulent two generations after the time of Muhammad that saw the formative events that would lead to the formulation of distinct Sunni and Shi'i Islamic identities, let us come back once more to the issue of how Muslims make sense of the rise of these sectarian divisions in Islam after Muhammad and the death of Hossein.

Unlike the Christian tradition, which saw the splintering off of the Protestant tradition from the existing Catholic (and Orthodox) tradition, or for that matter the Jewish tradition, which saw the emergence of the Reformed and Conservative traditions out of the Orthodox, in

Islam the Sunni and Shi'i traditions emerged simultaneously. In other words, in spite of the frequent association of "orthodox" with Sunni interpretations of Islam, it is a mistake to identify Islamic orthodoxy in an exclusive fashion with either the Sunni or the Shi'i tradition. There are, of course, exclusive voices within both camps that like to claim all of orthodoxy for themselves and see the other as outside the fold. Yet, from a historical perspective, it is important to acknowledge that both the fully formed Sunni tradition and the fully formed Shi'i tradition emerged more or less simultaneously. Both reached back into the revelatory grace of the Qur'an and the spiritual being of the Prophet. Although one may privilege the sayings-legacy of the Prophet and the other the family-legacy of the Prophet, both traditions represent orthodox understandings of Islam that, if properly followed, can, and in fact do, lead humanity back to the Divine. And that, whether within Islam or any other theistic tradition, is and has always been the task of religion—to be a path leading us back to our celestial home, the home that is at once our Origin and Destination.

Both the later Sunni and Shi'i traditions contain profound internal diversity, and surely one can find strands of each that stand closer to one another than to other perspectives within each school. And yet each provides an important fundamental perspective. Like much else within Islam, their differences are perhaps not a matter of absolute right or wrong, or of one school containing all of the truth, but rather a reminder that the reality of existence is too grand to be entirely contained by one perspective or one school of thought. One is reminded here of the story, so dear to Muslims (and Indians, and Buddhists, and others), of the elephant wandering into the city of the blind. The citizens of the town came up to the creature, trying to identify it by feeling it. Each person felt a portion of the elephant and tried to match what they felt to what they knew. The one who felt the belly thought that the creature was rough like a wool carpet, the one who felt the husk thought it was smooth, the one who felt the tail imagined it as a snake, and the one who grabbed the legs thought of a massive pillar.

In reality, the totality transcended what any one perspective could grasp. All the experiences of the elephant were valid, but none alone provided a complete picture.

And so it is with Islam, where the totality transcends the main emphasis in each tradition. The Sunni tradition emphasizes the notions of public order and the rule of law. Rebellion as such is always looked upon with some suspicion, as lawlessness can so easily descend into chaos and disorder, which, in turn, is often seen as paving the ground for heresy. Also, Sunnis fundamentally believe that history, particularly sacred history, more or less unfolds according to God's will. Here or there it may be a mystery, but something so fundamental as the succession to the last Messenger of God is deemed too dear and precious as to have gone entirely askew.

In the Shi'i tradition, on the other hand, the emphasis is fundamentally on justice and the cosmic need to stand up for justice, even if it is necessary to do so against one's own coreligionists, one's own community. In this tradition, there is something redemptive about the very process of rising up against injustice, even if one does not achieve immediate success. The Qur'an reminds Muslims that the Truth has come, and falsehood is indeed doomed to vanish. All traditions with an emancipatory message come to oppose injustice and tyranny, even when they do not hold any political power. The very act of resistance is redemptive. As those who have struggled against injustice have reminded us, "no lie can last forever." South Asian Shi'a Muslims have beautifully summarized the significance of Imam Hossein's martyrdom:

> *The slaughter of Hossein is in reality the death of Yazid.*
> *Islam is revitalized after every Karbala.*

For these Muslims, Karbala is not a onetime historical event but a spiritual event that echoes here and now. Likewise, Islam is not a constant stream but one that spiritually ebbs and flows and is in need of occasional revitalization. Both Sunni and Shi'i Muslims have tried to tap into powerful regenerative forces to revitalize Islam in every generation. The Sunni Muslims have done so by keeping up the legacy of the Prophet as faithfully conveyed through the companions of Muhammad. For the Shi'i Muslims, the effort has been above all to keep alive the memory of Muhammad by connecting themselves to the Prophet through the Family of the Prophet.

In the next chapter, we explore some of the ways in which devotion to the Prophet has allowed Muslims to continue to attach themselves to Muhammadi grace.

CHAPTER SIX

Echoes of Muhammadi Grace

THE CLASSIC LOVE STORY OF Islam—one that preceded *Romeo and Juliet* and has been emulated and retold over an even larger historic, geographic, and linguistic range than Shakespeare's masterpiece—is known as the Tale of Layla and Majnun. This tale has been imagined in sources ranging from Persian and Arabic to Turkish and Urdu, from Bangladesh to Morocco, over the last one thousand years. Most Westerners know the name Layla through Eric Clapton's 1970 masterpiece of the same name.[1] The song, with its haunting opening guitar riff, was inspired by that loftiest of poetic muses, unrequited love—a heroin-afflicted Clapton played the part of Majnun, and Layla was embodied by George Harrison's wife, Patti Boyd.

Muhammad, Eric Clapton, and the Tale of Layla and Majnun

More than one thousand years earlier, however, the Tale of Layla and Majnun was already the stuff of legends in Persian, Arabic, and other Islamic languages. The archetypal lover of this narrative composed so many love poems for his beloved that he earned the nickname "Love-Crazed" (*Majnun*). According to one particularly charming story told by the Persian poet Sa'di, the ruling Caliph heard these love poems and, sight unseen, fell in love with Layla. The Caliph figured, naturally, that anyone who inspired such lovely and love-infused poems must have been a celestial beauty, one of God's own angels. The Caliph commanded that all the women from Layla's tribe be brought to his court, along with Majnun. The Caliph eagerly looked through all the women to see which one stood out from all the rest, matching the descriptions of the poems. But in his eyes, none of the women resonated with the surpassing beauty described in Majnun's poetry. Baffled, the Caliph turned to Majnun, who, surmising what the Caliph was puzzled over, offered: "To see the beauty of Layla, you have to look through the eyes of Majnun."

And so it is with the Prophet Muhammad.

Just as we are told that we can only see Layla through the eyes of Majnun, we can only perceive the full importance of Muhammad by looking through the eyes of the tradition of Islamic piety, learning, and spiritual practice that grew up around the memory of the Prophet. It matters little if some, like the Caliph who was blind to Layla's beauty, fail to grasp the importance of Muhammad initially. What matters from a historical perspective is that for the past 1,400 years most Muslims have had a devotional connection to the Prophet. If we are to understand the civilization that grew up around Muhammad's revelation and teachings, we need to take seriously the love-filled glances of Majnun—that is, the devotional attachment of the community to the Prophet.

Muslims' perceptions of the Prophet have remained no more static over the centuries than have Christians' estimations of Christ or the Buddhists' engagement with Gautama Buddha. This is particularly the case for modern Muslims, who have in many ways become quite Protestant in terms of their religious sentiments. Many modern(ist) Muslims, like the moderns of all religious varieties, have come to accept the siren calls of all the new gods of science, Reason and Rationality, the Market, and the Nation, that have flattened the cosmos, both spiritually and metaphysically. Many modern Muslims have come to view Muhammad in juxtaposition to Christians' under-standing of Christ. If Christ is said to be divine, a miracle-worker, a healer, and the Logos, then many modern(ist) Muslims have em-phatically come to adopt the mantra of "Muhammad was a man, just a man." From this point of view, any mention of miracles, cosmic sig-nificance, or mystical powers associated with Muhammad are down-played or dismissed. At the risk of poetic exaggeration, we can say that the modernist Muslim estimation of the role of the Prophet is not much more elevated than that of a UPS delivery man, dropping off the divine revelation of the Qur'an at the doorstep of humanity, maybe pausing long enough to obtain a signature to ensure that the item has been received, and then departing, never to be seen again.

How different Layla looked through the eyes of Majnun, and how different is this characterization of Muhammad from the views of Muhammad throughout Islamic history as the Prophet of Mercy (*Nabi al-Rahma*), the model of intercession before God (*sahib al-shafa'a*), the Light of God, the one for whose sake the universe was created, and even in some understandings the Firstborn of Creation. Both the devotional and the modernist understandings turn to the Qur'an, albeit different verses of the Qur'an, to support their respective positions.

If there is one verse of the Qur'an that has shaped the historical grace-filled understanding of the Prophet, it is the verse in which God addresses Muhammad: "We sent you as a mercy to all the universes" (Qur'an 21:107). Modernist Muslims also cite a particular verse of the Qur'an repeatedly—the one in which the Prophet is instructed to say *Ana basharun mithlukum* ("I am a creature just like you"). In the premodern tradition, a pietistic response to the recitation of this verse was to say: *Bal, kal yaqut bayn al-hijar* ("Yes, but like a ruby is among stones"). In medieval mineralogy, jewels were indeed precious stones, but even more, they were illuminated stones. The being of the Prophet was understood as such a jewel that had been illuminated through the light of God and alchemically transformed from an ordi-nary stone into a precious stone. This understanding and the cosmic significance of the Prophet are stated explicitly in some of the *hadith qudsi* (sacred statements of Muhammad) that were the favorites of the mystics of Islam. In them God conveys to Muhammad: "Were it not for you (*law laka*), I would not have created the Heavens and the Earth." These statements became so well known that in poetry it would become sufficient to merely state "were it not for you" to recall the notion of the whole universe being created out of God's love for the Prophet. In prose passages, the notion is elaborated upon more fully. The thirteenth-century mystic Rumi stated:

> *It is obvious that Muhammad was the origin, for God said to him, "Were it not for you, I would not have created the heavens." Whatever exists—such as nobility, humility, authority, and high station—all are gifts from him, shadows of him, inasmuch as they were manifested through Muhammad.*[2]

Aside from being the cause of creation, other hadith qudsi identify the Light of Muhammad (*Nur Muhammad*) as a primordial manifestation, one that has been embodied in every prophet from Adam to Muhammad himself. Many statements pointed to this cosmic aspect of Muhammad that preceded his manifestation as the earthly Arabian prophet of the seventh century. One such hadith qudsi states: "I was a prophet while Adam was still between water and clay." These verses resemble some of the biblical statements of Jesus (for example, "Before Abraham was, I am" [John 8:58]). Aside from arguments about his temporality, such teachings were often used to describe this cosmic aspect of Muhammad as the perfect mirror through which divine qualities were reflected onto this terrestrial realm. Such teachings were perfected through the teachings of the thirteenth-century Andalusian mystic Ibn 'Arabi, whose metaphysical teachings became widespread across all the lands of Islam. Muhammad's mirroring of divine qualities provided the basis for the notion that a human being becomes complete by serving as the embodiment of divine qualities, becoming a true human being (*Insan al-Kamil*).

Ibn 'Arabi's writings, which were in Arabic, were soon incorporated into other key Islamic languages, such as Persian, Urdu, and Turkish. A famed Central Asian poet of the fifteenth century, Jami, incorporated Ibn 'Arabi's ideas into exquisite poetry. Many of these poems continue to be sung in devotional contexts in India and Pakistan, Afghanistan, Iran, and elsewhere. The poem cited here is transcribed from a recording entitled *Wa Salla Allahu 'Ala Nurin* ("May God Bless That Light"). Poems like this from Jami and others are recited in the devotional context known in South Asian circles as *Na't*: the recitation of poetry in honor of the Prophet. Here again is a sign of the widespread networks of Islamic civilization: the praise of an Arabian prophet, understood to be the light of God by an Arabic-speaking mystic from Andalusia, is put to poetry in Persian by a Central Asian poet of the fifteenth century, recited in the twentieth century by an Urdu-speaking Na't-reciter of South Asia, Qari Wahid Zaffar Qasim, and listened to today by Urdu-speaking Muslims in Chicago.[3] Heartland America is now a part of the spiritual and literary landscape that echoes Muhammad.

Here is a perfect illustration of a translinguistic, cross-regional performance of devotion to the Prophet, carried across Arabic,

Wa salla Allāhu alā nur-in	*(May God bless that Light*
kazu shod nur-ehā peydā.	*From whom all the lights came into*
	manifestation.)
Zamin as hob-e u sāken	*(The Earth stood still,*
falak dar 'eshq-e o sheydā.	*The Heavens went into a trance*
	out of his love.)
Muhammad, Ahmad o Mahmud	*(The Creator praised him by the*
veyrā khāleqash besotud	*names Muhammad, Ahmad,*
kazo shod bud har mojud, azo shod	*and Mahmud.*
didehā binā.	*Whatever is, came to be through him.*
	The sights came to see, through him.)

Agar nām-e Muhammad rā nayā-
  varde shafiʿ Adam
na Adam yāfteh tawbah
na Nuh az gharq najjaynā.

(If they hadn't brought up
the name of Muhammad as intercessor,
Adam would not have found repentance,
nor would We have "saved Noah from
  drowning.")

Do chashm-e nargesinash rā ke
  "mā zāghal basar" khānan
do zolf-e ambarinash rā ke "va
  layl-e idhā yaghshā."

(His two Narcissus-like eyes,
those that "they did not waver" [from
  beholding the face of his Lord];
His tresses, fragrant like the musk,
"like the night, wrapping around the
  day.")

Ze serr-e sine-ash Jāmi che miporsi
ze meʿraj-ash che midāni
ke "subhāna ladhi asrā."

(O Jami, what do you ask of the
  secrets in his heart?
You wish to know of his Ascension?
"Blessed be the One who took
  [Muhammad] by the night.")

Persian, and Urdu. Notions from a thirteenth-century mystic (Ibn ʿArabi) relating to the Prophet as the light through which all the lights are created is wed to Muhammad as the intercessor not just for his own community but even for the previous prophets, like Noah and Adam. The love of Muhammad is described as making the heavens and the earth ecstatic, and he is the source through which all of creation is brought into existence. These cosmic interpretations are wrapped around verses of the Qur'an, such as "Blessed be the One who took [Muhammad] by the night" (17:1) and Qur'an 53:17, in which Muhammad's eyes "did not waver" from beholding God. Naturally, all of these verses come from the Qur'anic passages dealing with Muhammad's heavenly ascension. And as we shall see shortly, if Muhammad is blessed, all of him is held to be blessed. His ascension is blessed, the revelation given to him is blessed, his manners are blessed, and even his eyes ("like Narcissus," never wavering from beholding the Divine) and his tresses are blessed. The description of Muhammad, in body and spirit, forms the context of an artistic genre that we now explore in further detail.

Blessed Manners, Blessed Body, Blessed Memory

Muslims have had a rich engagement with the memory of Muhammad. On the one hand, Muhammad stands apart from the founders of many other religious traditions in that he emerged fully in the spotlight of history. The community around him was so devoted to preserving his memory that we know more details about Muhammad's personal life, etiquette, and social relations than we do about any other major premodern spiritual figure. Already before the end of the ninth century—that is, less than three hundred years after the death of the Prophet—Muslim scholars like Tirmidhi had written treatises like the *Shama'il* to commemorate every detail regarding Muhammad. The title *Shama'il* refers to "portraits" of the Prophet, not in images but in beautiful descriptions of his being. The chapters of the *Shama'il*—which is still read today—deal with every conceivable facet of the Prophet's body, behavior, worship, and ethics, from his overall nature to how he combed his hair, walked and sat, and laughed and joked, to his worship and devotion.[4] Some details are particularly touching: Muslims delight in learning that Muhammad never yawned, because he always found what God did in every small detail to be a source of fresh wonder.

It might seem strange, or inconsequential, to record details about a religious figure like the fact that he left the collar of his shirt open, or that he possessed only one robe, one shirt, one sheet, and one pair of shoes. Yet for the Muslim who is enamored of the Prophet, every detail about his life is blessed, and the cultivation of these details is a sanctifying experience. The chapter headings refer to every detail as "blessed" (*mubarak*): blessed hair, blessed ring, blessed laughter, and so forth. For both the writer and the readers of the *Shama'il*, every detail of Muhammad's being drips with *baraka*, divine grace. Thus, the commemoration of Muhammad becomes a blessed process for the entire community.

It is natural enough to be intrigued by the ethics of a religious figure: the *Shama'il* records that Muhammad never avenged personal insults but sought vengeance only for transgressions against God. In the Battle of Uhud, one of his enemies threw a stone that struck Muhammad's face. As the narrative states, his teeth "were martyred" and blood covered his blessed face. Some of his companions, angered at the attack on Muhammad, beseeched him to curse the man who had thrown the stone, but Muhammad only said: "O God, guide my people, for they do not know." This behavior, naturally, is deemed worthy of imitation and emulation. And Muslims in Western societies recall this narrative knowing that it will be met with the approval of a Christian audience raised to think of Christ's example of turning the other cheek as the epitome of religious ethics.

More surprising to some will be the fact that even Muhammad's seemingly mundane behavior is recorded and emulated. After all, if one has to base one's behavior on something, or someone, why not the Prophet? The notions of emulation and idealization are not lost on our contemporary sensibilities. In our own age, we have simply adopted a new cast of prophets, many of them from the sports, pop culture, and celebrity realms. One can see a WWJD (WHAT WOULD JESUS DO?) bracelet on someone's arm right next to one commemorating Lance Armstrong's heroic struggle against cancer. In the 1990s, a whole generation of American youth (including the present author) was mesmerized by a catchy little jingle by Gatorade, beseeching the listener to emulate a certain bald (er, shaven) athlete wearing the number 23 from Chicago with an unearthly ability to make us believe that he—and we—could fly. Here is that memorable 1992 Gatorade paean to the saint of pop culture, Michael Jordan:

Sometimes I dream
That he is me
You've got to see that's how I dream to be.

I dream I move, I dream I groove
Like Mike
If I could Be Like Mike
Like Mike

Oh, if I could be like Mike
Be like Mike, be like Mike

. . .

I wanna be, I wanna be
Like Mike
Oh, if I could be like Mike.[5]

If one has to be "like" someone, the devotional aspect of Islam asks: why not seek to emulate the one whom God has described in the Qur'an (33:21) as "a lovely example" (*uswatun hasana*) for humanity? The example is not exclusive to Muhammad, as the same phrase is also used for Abraham. This model (*uswa*) is a type of beautiful that is good and lovely (*hasana*). *Hasana* comes from the same etymological root (H-S-N) as *Ihsan*, the term for what Muhammad identified as the highest rank of faith—the level at which we behave as if we see God at all times and, if we do not, where we recall that God nevertheless sees us. Muhammad's grandson Hossein (whose name comes from the same H-S-N root) records Muhammad's behavior as follows:

I asked my father [Ali] about the conduct of the Messenger of God, may God bless him and send him peace in his assemblies. My father replied:

"The Messenger of God, may God bless him and send him peace, was always happy and easy mannered. There was always a smile and a sign of happiness on his blessed face. He was soft-natured and when the people needed his approval, he easily gave consent. He did not speak in a harsh tone nor was he stony-hearted. He did not scream while speaking, nor was he rude or spoke indecently. He did not seek others' faults. He never overpraised anything nor exceeded in joking, nor was he a miser.

He kept away from undesirable language and did not make as if he did not hear anything. If he did not agree with the next person's wish he did not make that person feel disheartened, nor did he promise anything to that person. He completely kept himself away from three things: from arguments, pride and senseless utterances."[6]

In examining such narratives, it is easy to see how they identify Muhammad as a virtuous model to be emulated. For example, in the following the Qur'an connects Muhammad's model of behavior (*Sunna*) to the love of God:

Say: If you love God, then follow me.
God will love you and forgive you your sins.
God is Forgiving, Merciful. (Qur'an 3:31–32)

The narrative transmitted through Hossein and Ali, like so many other such narratives, tells the faithful how to follow Muhammad. It is one thing to tell people to knock on Heaven's door so that it shall be opened. It is another thing entirely to point out to them where the door is and show them how to knock.[7] These narratives provide the moral, legal, ethical, and spiritual method of knocking on Heaven's door. Muhammad, who was himself nothing less than a gate of mercy to the heavens, was adored by his followers to the extent that he said he had to tease them and joke with them so that they would not be in such awe of him. Indeed, the Qur'an describes that relationship in these words: "The Prophet is closer to the faithful than their own souls." For many in the community of Muhammad, it is now as it was then.

Remembering the Prophet Through the Arts

The Prophet has been commemorated in many ways down through the centuries. One of the most tangible ways has been through a well-known artistic tradition called the *Hilya* (or *Hilye*, in Turkish). The word *Hilya* simply means adornment, and the practice has been a beautiful way to adorn the memory of the Prophet. In the Ottoman tradition that flourished in Turkey and southeastern Europe, it became customary to depict in a richly illuminated manuscript an edified description of Muhammad, detailing his body and his manners. There are slightly different versions of what would be inscribed there. One version reports a tradition from Ali:

> *He was the most generous of men in his heart, the most truthful of them in speech, the mildest of them in temper, and the noblest of them in descent. Anyone who saw him immediately felt awe, and anyone who partook of his knowledge loved him. The one who described him says he has never seen anyone like him, either before or after him.*
>
> *May God bless him and grant him peace. God, bless and grant peace to Muhammad, your servant, your Prophet and your messenger, the illiterate Prophet, and to his family and companions, and grant them peace.*[8]

What stands out in these types of accounts, which are calligraphically written down in the center of the Hilya's medallions, is the praise for both Muhammad's physical form and his qualities. They also invite the reader (or viewer) to connect to the Prophet by sending traditional prayers of blessings upon him.

A slightly different version of the reports about Muhammad often found at the center of Hilyas comes from Umm Ma'bad, a Bedouin woman the Prophet met during his journey to Medina. She offers even more details of the beauty of the Prophet's form:

> *I saw a man, pure and clean, with a handsome face and a fine figure. He was not marred by a skinny body, nor was he overly small in the head and neck. He was graceful and elegant, with intensely black eyes and thick eyelashes. There was a huskiness in his voice, and his neck was long. His beard was thick, and his eyebrows were finely arched and joined together.*
>
> *When silent, he was grave and dignified, and when he spoke, glory rose up and overcame him. He was from afar the most beautiful of men and the most glorious, and close up he was the sweetest and the loveliest. He was sweet of speech and articulate, but not petty or trifling. His speech was a string of cascading pearls, measured so that none despaired of its length and no eye challenged him because of brevity.*[9]

The examples of the Hilya reproduced here are particularly refined. The description of the Prophet fills up the central medallion. Written in larger script across the Hilya is a verse from the Qur'an that praises the Prophet's noble nature, "We only sent you as a mercy for all of the universe" (Qur'an 21:107), which appears in both of the Hilyas seen here, one from a Turkish collection and another from an American Muslim artist. Sometimes another verse of the Qur'an is used, recording God's praise of the Prophet: "Truly, you are great in character" (Qur'an 68:4).

This Ottoman Hilya bears the familiar Qur'anic verse proclaiming
Muhammad as "a mercy to all the worlds." From the
Sakip Sabanci Museum, Istanbul, Turkey.

These verses recapitulate what Carl Ernst has beautifully described as "the Muhammad of grace"—the understanding of the Prophet that has always been at the center of Muslim piety. The verses serve an important function in allowing the faithful to imagine both the physical beauty and the noble qualities of the Prophet without having to resort to physical depictions. When the Danish cartoon controversies broke out in 2005, many pundits—and some Muslims—stated that Muslims have never physically depicted the Prophet. That is actually not the case: Muslims in India, Afghanistan, Persia, and Turkey did have a courtly tradition of depicting the various prophets, including Muhammad, in miniatures, as can be seen in this example.

Ottoman miniature depicting Muhammad praying by the Ka'ba.
Courtesy of the Topkapi Palace Museum.

However, the Hilya as a genre spread beyond the courtly context and became featured in mosques, shrines, and other religious buildings precisely because it did not include a physical image. Emulating Muhammad when he triumphantly reentered Mecca and cleansed the Ka'ba of idols, Muslims have tended to prohibit graven images in places of worship. Moreover, one might say that all of the most important of the Islamic arts—recitation of the Qur'an, calligraphy, poetry—involve language. After all, did God not reveal Himself to this world through the Word that was the Qur'an? The Hilya is almost always depicted in gorgeous calligraphic writing and thus combines the aesthetic with the devotional—yet another feature of Islamic spirituality, in which form and function remain perpetually comingled.

Hadith Scholarship as Legacy

If there is no monotheism without God, there is also no Islam without Muhammad. The full legacy of Muhammad is in a sense the Islamic civilization. Every facet of the civilization—intellectual, spiritual, political, artistic, and social—bears a memory of Muhammad and the revelation entrusted to the Prophet. At times the memory is explicit, but more often it is implicit, as illustrated by an analogy. Medieval Muslims, mindful of the need to not privilege one prophet over another, were fond of comparing the various prophets to different flowers in a garden, with Muhammad being roselike. Various accounts of Muslim piety recall echoes of Muhammad's beauty in the rose. It is even said that all roses used to be white, but that when celestial roses saw Muhammad's beauty during his ascension, they blushed in the Prophet's presence—hence pink and red roses. Some might adorn their homes with fresh-cut roses or give roses to their loved ones. Roses might be dried and placed as potpourri around a home. Their essence might be worn as a perfume. Paintings of a rose could be placed around a house. A ruler's sarcophagus might contain depictions of roses in marble. Rose essences might be added to food when cooking; indeed, almost all Persian and Indo-Persian sweets contain a hint of rose. A poet might use the imagery of a rose in a poem. All are roses, and all are traces of that original flower that represents the perfection of love, harmony, and beauty.

And so it is with Muhammad's legacy in the Islamic civilization. Like the rose, he stands both at the center and all through the civilization that grew around the teachings he brought to humanity. At times the memory of Muhammad is explicit. The Qur'an identifies Muhammad's beautiful model of behavior as the loveliest of examples (*uswatun hasana*). This ideal model was eventually codified as the Way of Muhammad, or his *Sunna*. There would always be multiple sources for the Sunna, and being able to flesh out the Sunna of Muhammad by transmitting the authenticated statements traced back to him (hadith reports) became a key feature of Islamic learning. In the Qur'an itself, Muhammad's authority is closely linked to that of God: "Obey God and the Messenger, that you may receive mercy" (Qur'an 3:132) and "If you differ in anything among yourselves, refer it to God and His Messenger if you have faith in God and the Here-after. That is best, and the loveliest of references" (Qur'an 4:59).

During Muhammad's life, religious questions and requests for elucidation were referred to him personally. After his death, it was natural that the community would look back on his example as the best of examples to follow. Being mindful that there were multi-ple claims to representing Muhammad's teachings, a key concern of the community became establishing, with the greatest degree of certainty, the actual teachings of Muhammad. One of the central ways of doing so was to ascertain the veracity of the hadith reports. Through a combination of sincere devotion to Muhammad, the tendency to attribute every aphorism to him, and sectarian tenden-cies to praise different companions of the Prophet at the expense of others, perhaps over 600,000 hadith reports came into circulation in the centuries after Muhammad's passing. The hadith therefore circulated for many decades orally before they were written down in canonical collections.[10] Obviously, not all of these various re-ports were authentic. The majority of them had similar or identical contents and differed only in the way they were traced back to Muhammad. Recognizing the need to distinguish those traditions that could be authenticated from those that could not, Muslim scholars developed a meticulous scholarly tradition of evaluating the reliability of the various reports.

Each hadith report consisted of two parts: the actual content of the text (*matn*) and the chain of transmission (*isnad*). The task of the *isnad* was to provide, ideally, an uninterrupted chain between the present generation and that of the Prophet. The science of hadith verification focused to a large extent on proving the veracity and reliability of dif-ferent transmitters and documenting whether the same text could be traced back to Muhammad through various chains of transmissions. The more a statement could be traced back to the Prophet through multiple chains of reliable transmitters, the greater the likelihood that it was authentic (*sahih*).

Hadith criticism, a combination of intellectual detective work and a variety of textual criticism dealing with oral material, became one of the more crucial Islamic intellectual sciences. Scholars of hadith criticism soon began to sift through all the existing hadith reports to compile collections consisting only of hadith rated as sahih. In the Sunni tradition, the collections of the scholars Bukhari (d. 870) and Muslim, the son of al-Hajjaj (d. 875), came to be considered especially authoritative. Each of the two collections includes about four thousand hadith reports. Bukhari waded through about 600,000 traditions to arrive at his collection, an indication of both the vast number of reports traced back to Muhammad and the rigor of classical hadith scholars, who accepted only 1 to 2 percent of the hadith in circulation as reliable. Slightly less significant were other hadith collections, including one by the same Tirmidhi who authored the *Shama'il*. Shi'a Muslims use parallel collections that often contain similar statements traced to the Prophet through the Family of the Prophet.

The proliferation of isnad chains and the need to authenticate all of them was a significant challenge in the effort to codify the memory of Muhammad. The fact that so many reports were in circulation is one proof of how many different individuals traced opinions back to Muhammad. The two hadith compilations of Muslim and Bukhari relied on about 2,400 hadith transmitters who met their very strict criteria. There were thousands of individuals who were deemed worthy when they met the strict criteria of reliability; spread across the young Islamic civilization, they narrated, transmitted, and taught the reports of Muhammad. Like many other Islamic intellectual pursuits, hadith criticism also necessitated travel throughout the vast lands of Islam to study with the greatest hadith experts in the world. And as with other Islamic disciplines, one did not study a subject but rather learned from a living master.

As significant as the hadith have been, they have not been the only memory of Muhammad. Like the rose that lends its fragrance in multiple ways, Muhammad's imprint has also been left on Islamic societies in more subtle ways. If what eventually became the Sunni tradition recalls Muhammad as having stated that he would leave "the Book of God and My Sunna" for the community, those who became known as the Shi'a recall Muhammad as having said that he would leave behind "the Book of God and my family." In other words, for Shi'a Muslims, the Family of the Prophet is not separate from the memory of the Prophet. Who would know the Prophet better than his own family?

The mystics of Islam, the Sufis, likewise traced many of their own experiences back to the example of the Prophet. We have already seen that the Mi'raj, the heavenly ascension of Muhammad, served as the paradigm of spiritual experiences for mystically inclined Muslims. While the Sufis, like all Muslims, trace their lineage back to the Prophet, in a way their connection to the Prophet is more existential. Like all Muslims, they cite hadith, but they prefer many of the hadith qudsi that emphasize the cosmic role of the Prophet. The Sufis have often been criticized by other scholars of Islam for not relying on stricter criteria of hadith scholarship, but the Sufis have often retorted that their knowledge comes from a less mediated source. As always, the memory of Muhammad has had multiple echoes, and quite often these echoes have been internally contentious. Yet until the arrival of modernity, these various approaches resided more or less side by side, available as options to people of different spiritual and intellectual temperaments.

One of the common features of all parts of the Islamic civilization has been devotion to the Prophet, which has been expressed in many ways across the centuries. We now turn to an exploration of some of these various ways of echoing Muhammad.

Devotion to Muhammad

Muslims' declaration of faith does not stop at *la ilaha illah Allah* ("there is only one deity"), but goes on to address how that deity relates to humanity: *wa Muhammad Rasul Allah* ("and Muhammad is a messenger of God"). This *wa* ("and") is seen as a crucial linkage between the two declarations of faith. Faith in God leads to faith in the Prophet of God. The Muslim community was devoted to the Prophet during his life, and this devotion did not stop with the return of the Prophet to his maker. Devotion to the Prophet Muhammad became one of the characteristic features of Islamic piety through the centuries. A few examples might suffice.

Many of the prayers we examine here had their origins in various North African regions, but in a typically Islamic way they gained popularity across the world wherever Muslims kept alive the memory of Muhammad. One of the best examples of a litany in praise of the Prophet is the famed Prayer of Ibn Mashish, a thirteenth-century Moroccan saint whose litany continues to be recited even in our own day.

> *O my God, bless him from whom derive the secrets and from whom gush forth the lights, and in whom rise up the realities, and into whom descended the sciences of Adam, so that he has made powerless all creatures, and so that understandings are diminished in his regard, and no one among us, neither predecessor nor successor, can grasp him.*
>
> *The gardens of the spiritual world (*malakût*) are adorned with the flower of his beauty, and the pools of the world of omnipotence (*al-jabarût*) overflow with the outpouring of his lights. There exists nothing that is not linked to them, even as it was said: Were there no mediator, everything that depends on him would disappear! [Bless him, O my God,] by a blessing such as returns to him through You from You, according to his due.*

After offering the blessing of Muhammad, Ibn Mashish addresses God and recalls the intimacy Muhammad shares with the Divine:

O my God, he is Your integral secret, that demonstrates You, and Your supreme veil, raised up before You. Carry me on his way, surrounded by Your aid, toward Your presence.

O First, O Last, O Outward, O Inward, hear my petition, even as You heard the petition of Your Servant Zacharia; succor me through You unto You, support me through You unto You, unite me with You, and come in between me and other-than-You: Allâh, Allâh, Allâh! Verily He who has imposed on you the Qur'ân for a law, will bring you back to the promised end (Qur'an 28:85).

In a typically Islamic way, Ibn Mashish's prayer links together verses of the Qur'an and praise of previous prophetic figures with the adoration of Muhammad. The goal is to be led along the path taken by Muhammad back to God, so that there remains nothing between God and humanity, nothing that is other-than-God.

Our Lord, grant us mercy from Your presence, and shape for us right conduct in our plight (Qur'an 18:10). Verily God and His angels bless the Prophet; O you who believe, bless him and wish him peace (Qur'an 33:56).

May the graces (salawât) of God, His peace, His salutations, His mercy and His blessings (barakât) be on our Lord Muhammad, Your servant, Your prophet and Your messenger, the un-lettered prophet, and on his family and on his companions, [graces] as numerous as the even and the odd and as the perfect and blessed words of our Lord.

Glorified be your Lord, the Lord of Glory, beyond what they attribute unto Him, and peace be on the Messengers. Praise be to God, the Lord of the worlds (Qur'an 37:180–82).[11]

Many of the most popular devotional prayers have been Arabic. What one can call devotional Arabic is easily understood by many Muslims around the world owing to its heavy incorporation of Qur'anic phrases. Many such devotional works became widely distributed among both Arabic and non-Arabic Muslims. One of the signs of the ways in which different parts of the Islamic world remain connected is in the popularity of the prayer manuals written by two of Ibn Mashish's spiritual descendants, Busiri (d. 1298) and Jazuli (d. 1465). The devotional works of both authors would become known in North Africa, East Africa, Turkey, the Arab lands of the Middle East, Iran, Central Asia, Afghanistan, what is today Pakistan and India, Malaysia and Indonesia, and beyond.

Busiri's poem in praise of the Prophet circulated throughout the world even more widely than Ibn Mashish's short poem. Busiri was a Sufi from Egypt who wrote a few poems in honor of the Prophet; none is more famous today than *al-Kawakib al-durriya fi madh khayr al-bariyya* ("Celestial Lights in the Praise of the Best of Creation"). This poem is more commonly known simply as the *Burda* (cloak, mantle). According to Muslim lore, Busiri had suffered a stroke, and in his misery he turned to the Prophet's presence and prayed for healing.

> *I began to contemplate writing a poem in the qasida form, and soon after, I did so as a way of interceding by it with the Messenger of God to God, the Exalted, hoping that he might heal me.*
>
> *I was repeating it often, singing it, calling upon God through it, and seeking intercession with it. During that time, while sleeping, I saw the Prophet, upon him and his family be prayers and peace. He wiped over my face with his blessed hand and thrust upon me his cloak.*[12]

To cast a mantle upon a person is simultaneously to bless that person and invest him or her with authority. In other words, the composition and recitation of the *Burda* is linked to the Mantle (*burda*) of the Prophet, the Mantle is linked to the Prophet, and the Prophet is linked to God. The appearance of the Prophet in Busiri's dream-vision (*ru'ya* in Arabic, *Roya* in Persian) is also a reminder of an important part of the piety tradition in Islam: it is said that the form of the Prophet is the one form that Satan cannot assume in dream life. Fully consistent with a premodern view shared not just by Muslims but indeed by all of humanity, the blessing (*baraka*) of the poem extended not just to its meaning and sound but to every artifact associated with it. As such, the *Burda* were used as amulets or written on the walls of mosques, shrines, and private homes.

Displaying the global reach of Islam, the *Burda* was translated (and expanded) into Persian, Urdu, Turkish, Panjabi, Pashto, Swahili, English, Malay, and Shila-Berber.[13] Recently the American Muslim leader Hamza Yusuf has produced a magnificent English translation of the *Burda* that contains a thorough introduction, commentary, and recitation of the beloved poem. America now is part of the global community that praises the Prophet through the seven-hundred-year-old *Burda* poem. In other words, Islamic piety in America is not emerging from a blank slate, but rather, in this new homeland of Muslims, the traditional notions of praise that have proven efficacious throughout the centuries in different contexts are being modified and translated. English is now joining the ranks of the other languages through which Muslims have expressed their religiosity and spiritual yearning.

The words of the *Burda* unmistakably speak of a Prophet who is an intercessor: "He is the beloved in whom we have hope of intercession from every calamity." Muhammad is identified as *sayyid al-kawnayn* ("the master of the two realms"—generally understood to refer to that of the human and the nonhuman). His beauty is compared to the sun and the moon and to natural phenomena:

> *Like a flower in tenderness and like the full moon in glory,*
> *Like the ocean in generosity and like time in grand intentions.*[14]

Mention has already been made of the legendary power of the *Burda*, and how people loved to surround themselves with the healing power of the blessed and blessing poem. Nor should it be assumed that such faith in its healing power was a superstition confined to the "lower classes": Muslim scholars in Egypt, recognizing its efficacy, asked for gorgeous copies of the *Burda*. Perhaps no Muslim empire attained to greater glory than the Ottomans, who reigned supreme from their magnificent capital of Istanbul. When the Ottomans controlled the Arabian region of Hejaz (which contains both Mecca and Medina), they patronized the inscription of the *Burda* poem along the walls of the Mosque of the Prophet in Medina. Furthermore, when the Ottomans established the Topkapi Palace in Istanbul as the symbol of their power, they often received visitors and dignitaries in the Privy Chamber, which was decorated with beautiful blue Iznik tiles bearing inscriptions from the Qur'an—and the *Burda* of Busiri recalling the miracles of the Prophet.[15] The choice of the poem was especially appropriate for the Ottomans, who also possessed what they believed to be relics of the Prophet, including his mantle, his sword, and his standard. These items, referred to as "the Sacred Trusts," would be brought out in public on extremely special occasions to emphasize the Ottomans' close connection to the Prophet, their orthodoxy, and thus their claim to religious legitimacy.

The relics of the Prophet were brought to Istanbul after they were obtained by the Ottomans in their conquest of Egypt in 1517. Scholars have questioned the historicity of the relics—that is, whether they could have belonged to the historical personage Muhammad. What seems beyond doubt, however, is the tender care and attention that the Ottomans paid to these items. In other words, even if the sword and the mantle did not belong to the Prophet, the Ottomans' faith surely did. If the poem describing the Prophet's mantle was so esteemed, how did the Ottomans treat the very Mantle of the Prophet? Once a year they brought out the Mantle, washed it, and dried it over incense. The water it was washed in was presented in small bottles to people as spiritual gifts, and some was kept in the palace for its healing power, to heal the sick there. Other items associated with the Prophet also received reverential treatment. The Seal of the Prophet, which Muhammad was said to have used to seal his correspondence with other leaders, was kept in a crystal vase, inside an ebony box near the Ottoman throne. This seal was reverentially taken out of the box, the vase was kissed tenderly, and the seal was washed. After washing, it too was dried over burning incense. Even the walls of the throne room, which contained these relics, were washed in the holy month of Ramadan with sponges dipped in rose water, yet again dried with the smoke of incense. Not even the dust of these walls was discarded but instead was carefully taken to a holy well.[16] These seem like the rituals of a different world, and yet this was the same Ottoman Islamic civilization that led the world for a long time in religious pluralism and the pursuit of wisdom.

The throne room in the Privy complex of Topkapi Palace, adorned by the Burda poem in praise of the Prophet. © *1992 MIT Press.*

Rivaling the *Burda* in fame and historical spread was another collection of blessings on the Prophet called the *Dala'il al-Khayrat* ("The
Proof of Blessings").

Illustrated 1722 Ottoman manuscript of Dala'il al-Khayrat, *depicting*
Mecca and Medina. Image courtesy of Special Collections, Bridwell Library,
Perkins School of Theology, Southern Methodist University.

The *Dala'il al-Khayrat* is a series of litanies, one for each day of
the week. For the most part, they consist of the petitioner asking God
to send blessing on the Prophet as many times as there are grains of
sand on the earth, as many times as there are drops of rain, as many
times as there are those who remember him, as many times as there
are those who forget him, as many times as there are stars in the sky,
and so on. The legacy of Muhammad and the family of Muhammad
is always linked with that of Abraham:

O God, send blessings upon Muhammad and the family of
   Muhammad
as you sent blessings on Abraham and the family of Abraham.

Many of the nights of prayer conclude with:

O God, let us live according to the way of Muhammad.
Let us die following his religion
Place us among those who receive his intercession
And resurrect us in his company,
and let us be fed from the pool of mercy he sits at.

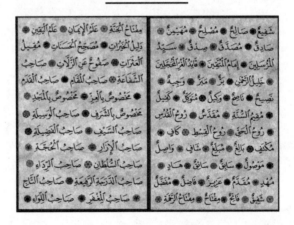

Copy of the Dala'il al-Khayrat. *Pages shown describe the Prophet as the*
"key of Mercy," the "key to Paradise," and the Possessor of the power of
Intercession before God. Courtesy of http://www.dalail.co.uk/

Aside from spreading from one geographical region to another
and from one language to another, texts like the *Burda* and the *Dala'il*
al-Khayrat are now also part of the cyber-worship community of
Muslims. Magnificent websites now make the full text of the *Dala'il*
available in multiple languages, along with instructions for its recita-

tions. The Internet, though much maligned for its lack of accuracy and overpopulation with distractions, is also a way in which Muslims, like other human beings, reach out to one another to establish a sense of community. One sophisticated website based in England, called Dala'il al-Khayrat (http://dalail.co.uk), carries hypertext images of the *Dala'il*, illuminated manuscripts, and full translations. Here is one of the site's images:

Illuminated Dala'il al-Khayrat. *Courtesy of http://www.dalail.co.uk/*

Remembering and Contesting the Prophet Today

Muhammad's legacy can be seen on YouTube today as Muslims use ubiquitous digital media to commemorate the Prophet. Hundreds of videos uploaded on YouTube feature recitations of the *Burda* and the *Dala'il al-Khayrat* from all over the world. Some are exclusively in Arabic, and many are in multilanguage formats. Some feature only men, some both men and women. Some are clearly homemade videos from devotional contexts, others are every bit as sophisticated as an MTV music video.[17] There are also Facebook accounts through which lovers of the Prophet can receive daily notes about the Prophet or hagiographic accounts of how people's lives have been transformed through contact with the Prophet.

Nevertheless, the *Burda* and *Dala'il* are part of the contentious terrain of modern Islam, where all is contested. One would not imagine that something as simple and Qur'an-sanctioned as sending blessings and salutations on the Prophet would be a source of contention among Muslims today. Yet, since medieval times, Muslims have slowly been changing their conceptions of the Prophet, because their conceptions of God, humanity, reality, politics, gender, and everything else have also been changing. In medieval times, almost all Muslims would have unanimously agreed that the Prophet is a cosmic being whose intercession is to be hoped for, a channel of mercy and grace to this world. In the modern period, however, the cosmic and mystical aspects of the Prophet have been downplayed in order to emphasize the role of Muhammad as a community leader and social engineer. Indeed, it is Muhammad as "nation-builder" who is the icon of many modern Muslim biographies. It is no accident that these works have shown up at the same time Muslims have increasingly found themselves under the tyrannical yoke of European colonialism. The more Muslims become nationless, the more they look to Muhammad as a nation-builder. Yet something perverse has also taken place here: the global and spiritual conception of the *umma*—the mother-community of all the faithful—has anachronistically morphed into that of a modern nation-state.

Many Enlightenment-era thinkers (including Thomas Jefferson) minimized the emphasis on Christ's miracles. Modern Muslims who have also internalized the assumptions of the Enlightenment likewise downplay the miracles of Muhammad, as well as mystical concepts like the Light of Muhammad (*Nur Muhammad*). For modernists, if religion must retreat from the public arena, then Muhammad's model too must be redefined as one limited to the ethical and personal realms. Another attack on the cosmic Muhammad and the devotional Muhammadi life has come from Islamists, those twentieth- and twenty-first-century Muslims who want to see Islam projected onto the political landscape. They approach the Prophet from yet another direction, one that emphasizes Muhammad's political skills and social leadership. Some twentieth-century political figures went even further in identifying the teachings of Muhammad with the dominant ideologies of the day: Michel Aflaq, the Christian founder of the Baath Party, saw Muhammad as "the summary of the Arab spirit." Gamal 'Abd Nasser, the Egyptian socialist, called Muhammad the "imam of socialism." And some leftist thinkers of Egypt even described Muhammad as "a kind of Marx before Marx."[18]

It would not, of course, end there.

The Wahhabi movement rose in the eighteenth century in what is today Saudi Arabia as a puritanical (or self-styled "reform") movement. Wahhabis target many of the devotional practices of Islam, particularly those related to prayers and blessings upon the Prophet, as at best superstition and at worst actual polytheism (*shirk*). Today Saudi authorities prohibit or discourage worshipers from reciting blessings upon the Prophet from the *Dala'il al-Khayrat* in the Mosque of the Prophet in Medina. Under the influence of Wahhabi clerics, Saudi authorities have also erased all but the last line of the *Burda* poem in praise of the Prophet that had been inscribed on the walls of the Mosque of the Prophet during the Ottoman reign. The line that remains, however, is quite telling, considering that it survived the fanaticism of the Wahhabis:

He is the beloved whose intercession is hoped for
As arms against a host of relentless calamities.[19]

Had the Wahhabis had their way in 1812, it would not have been merely the *Burda* that was effaced but the entire Mosque of the Prophet. Out of the puritanical desire to make sure that no one confused devotion to Muhammad with worship of the God of Muhammad, the Wahhabis systematically destroyed many holy sites associated with the Prophet in Medina and Mecca. In Mecca they destroyed the domes that stood over the homes historically associated with the birthplaces of the Prophet Muhammad, Khadija, and Imam Ali. The Wahhabis also destroyed some of the historical cemeteries in Mecca, such as that of al-Ma'ala. In Medina the gravestones and structures of many of the companions of the Prophet, some of Muhammad's wives, and several imams from the Family of the Prophet in the historical cemetery Jannat al-Baqi (the Paradise of the Eternal One) were destroyed. The Wahhabis also contemplated—and even began—the destruction of the Mosque of the Prophet in Medina. Through what some have seen as providential grace, they were prevented from putting this calamity in motion when several of the Wahhabis who attempted to climb the dome of the Mosque of the Prophet fell to their deaths.[20]

Tensions over these echoes of Muhammad remain: the Wahhabi and revivalist assault on the devotional practices has not gone unanswered. Part of the revival of Islam among North Americans has been precisely focused on devotion to the particular person and example (*Sunna*) of the Prophet. One contemporary Muslim figure has thus responded to the critiques of devotional texts like the *Dala'il al-Khayrat*:

> In the post-caliphal period of the present day, Imam Jazuli's masterpiece has been eclipsed by the despiritualization of Islam by "reformers" who have affected all but the most traditional of Muslims. As the Moroccan hadith scholar 'Abdullah al-Talidi wrote of the Dala'il al-Khayrat:
>
> "Millions of Muslims from East to West tried it and found its good, its baraka, and its benefit for centuries and over generations, and witnessed its unbelievable spiritual blessings and light. Muslims avidly recited it, alone and in groups, in homes and mosques, utterly spending themselves in the Blessings on the Most Beloved and

praising him—until Wahhabi ideas came to spread among them,
suborning them and creating confused fears based on the opinions of
Ibn Taymiya and the reviver of his path Muhammad ibn 'Abd al-
Wahhab of Najd.

After this, Muslims slackened from reciting the Dala'il al-
Khayrat, *falling away from the Blessings upon the Prophet*
(Allah bless him and give him peace) in particular, and from
the remembrance of Allah in general" (al-Mutrib fi awliya' al-
Maghrib, 143–44).[21]

Such is the condition of the echoes of Muhammad today: there is
no unsullied and uninterrupted tradition per se, but rather a discursive mingling of tradition, critique, and countercritique. In looking
at the Muslim devotional connection to the Prophet, the Wahhabi
and modernist assaults on these practices, and the neotraditionalist
defense of them, one theme does emerge. Whether the concern is to
remain devoted to the Muhammad of grace or to "purge Islam" of
influences believed to have crept in from outside and to "reform" it,
different Muslims continue to see themselves as Muhammadi. Muhammad remains immutable.

We will let the South Asian poet and philosopher Iqbal have the
last word. Iqbal offers a hauntingly beautiful image to describe the
relationship between the Prophet and the Umma, the global Muslim
community:

Love of the Prophet runs like blood in the veins of his community.[22]

With that reminder, we conclude our story of the community
that is kept alive by faith in God, but also by love of the Prophet.
The Muhammadi community (*ummat-i Muhammad*) is alive to the
extent that it continues to embody the qualities of Muhammad.
When it loses its connection to Muhammad and is no longer alive
through the love of the Prophet, the umma will be spiritually dead.
Even through the many triumphs and great turmoil the umma has

experienced, that time has not come. If we are to take Muslim poets at their word, if we believe that Muhammad was a rose in the celestial garden of beauty, then the fragrance of Muhammad can still be detected in the hundreds of millions of simple Muslims whose ordinary lives are perfumed by the memory and presence of the Prophet.

CONCLUSION

You can deny God,
but you cannot deny the Prophet![1]

THESE AUDACIOUS WORDS BELONG TO Muhammad Iqbal, the same famed South Asian poet and visionary we met at the end of chapter 6. Iqbal's *Javid-nama*, which features this boast, is a poetic masterpiece that describes his own spiritual experience of ascending to heaven, as it were, in the footsteps of Muhammad. Leaving aside for a moment the poetic license that great works of literature are entitled to, it is worth pondering the point that Iqbal is making. In the contemporary world, the rhythms of modernity and secularization have led many to live apart from any meaningful connection to the sacred realm. For many, God has become an option, and worship a luxury. Denying God—or more generously speaking, neglecting the Divine—seems to be a viable position for many. Iqbal's perspective resonates with the majority of those human beings who have followed in Muhammad's footsteps and keep the memory of Muhammad alive. One can choose to live—temporarily, as the Qur'an hauntingly reminds us—in neglect of God. One can ignore God (temporarily), but for Muslims one cannot deny Muhammad's beauty and greatness.

Iqbal's words are particularly shocking to many non-Muslims (and a few modern Muslims!). Of all the founders of the major religious traditions—at least the ones that have an identifiable "founder"—Muhammad is simultaneously the least understood and the most mistrusted by many non-Muslims. Most non-Muslims would be hard-pressed to produce any teaching of Muhammad that might resemble spiritual advice. An easy way to document this is to stroll down to a local bookstore and check out the religion section. You are likely to find titles from the Christian, Jewish, Hindu, Buddhist, and Zen (not to mention New Age, Wiccan, and so on) perspectives that offer spiritual guidance for daily life. But can you find a single title directed at a broad audience that presents the teachings of Muhammad in a similar fashion? There is, for example, a *Chicken Soup for the Jewish Soul* and a *Chicken Soup for the Christian Soul*. There is no corresponding *Chicken Soup for the Muslim Soul*.

In fact, the ongoing polemic against Islam—asserting its propensity toward violence, denigration of women's rights, inability to endure modernity and live peacefully with non-Muslims, and unwillingness to recognize the rights of religious minorities—continues to set the parameters for discussions of Islam and Muhammad. To put it differently, the "Islam" section of most bookstores today is nothing less than a jihad, terrorism, and women's oppression shelf. Without defending or too quickly dismissing these allegations, it is worth noting that the dominant Western approach to the Prophet does not engage with what might be termed Muhammad's spiritual teachings. If we are to understand the Islamic civilization that rightly sees itself as being shaped by the revelation given to Muhammad, it behooves us to engage the multiple ways in which Muslims have come to cultivate the memory of Muhammad. What, after all, has been inspiring Muslims to keep alive the memory of Muhammad and the teachings of Muhammad? If Muhammad delivered God's call to them, the Muslim community's response to that same call represents the echoes of that revelation and delivery. In this book, we have attempted both to trace the narrative of Muhammad's life and teachings and listen to the echoes of Muhammad as remembered by Muslims over the past 1,400 years.

What Would Muhammad Do?

In the closing decades of the twentieth century, many young Christians in North America could be seen wearing bracelets that bore the initials WWJD—WHAT WOULD JESUS DO? It was a simple though remarkably effective pietistic—and commercial—success. The claim was as simple as it was irresistible: that the best ethical guidance for every faithful Christian is to put on Jesus's sandals and contemplate how he would treat the person one was encountering or how he would behave in one's situation. This represented a modern adaptation of a far older tradition, that of *imitation dei* (the "imitation of God"). In the Jewish tradition, there had been "You shall be holy: for I the LORD your God am holy" (Leviticus 19:2). In the Christian tradition, there had been "Therefore you are to be perfect, as your heavenly Father is perfect" (Matthew 5:48). At times this imitation of divine manners also became embodied in representatives who walked the Earth, in the following of Christ, and, in the Catholic tradition, in the saints.

The approach of seeking to embody the loftiest ethics by imitating the most luminous souls is not unique to Christianity. For more than a millennia before WWJD showed up on bracelets, billions of human beings participated in a similar ethical and legal self-questioning: WWMD–WHAT WOULD MUHAMMAD DO?

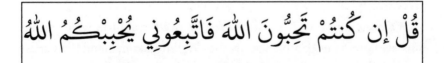

Say: "if you love God, follow me, and God will love you" (Qur'an 3:31).

Imagine a civilization where aspiring to Muhammadi ethics (*akhlaq-e Muhammadi*) is considered the noblest ethical norm. Imagine intellectual traditions charged with the task of tracing a lofty pattern of behavior—indeed, the ideal model of human conduct—all the way back to Muhammad. This community and its intellectual traditions have in fact existed in the Islamic civilization as it has sought to embody the *Sunna*, the Way of the Prophet of Islam. Although the word *Sunna* today is understood to mean the way in which Muhammad conducted himself, like many other Islamic words, it originally had a more immediate and existential meaning: "the trodden path in a desert." Words and phrases like "the path" were all the more immediate in an arid context where following a trodden path in a desert could mean the difference between being led to a cool, refreshing, and life-giving oasis and getting lost among ever-shifting and treacherous sand dunes and possibly dying a miserable death from thirst. To this day, the language of "the path" has a life-giving and immediate resonance for Muslims.

In fact, a text devoted to celebrating the memory of Muhammad in the twelfth century makes this exact analogy. Entitled "The Healing" (*al-Shifa'*), this volume states that the celebrated phrase "Straight Path" (*al-sirat al-mustaqim*) that shows up in the opening chapter of the Qur'an is none other than Muhammad himself. In other words, for the author of *al-Shifa'*, when Muslims beseech God to "guide us to and keep us on the Straight Path," they are asking to be guided to Muhammad. Muhammad is the cool oasis of faith and serenity on the journey back to the Divine Beloved. This is the goal of the community of Muhammad: to be led to Muhammad, and from Muhammad to God.

One saying of Muhammad, much beloved by Muslims, is that he was sent to bring completion to the "nobility of manners" (*bu'ithtu li-utammim makarim al-akhlaq*). The word for "nobility" (*makarim*) in Islamic discourse has to do with generosity, as well as remaining ever-mindful of God. In other words, the goal for this model of ethics is to connect one's dealings with other human beings with the existential awareness that we are, at all moments, in the very Presence of God. How would we act if at all times we were mindful of being with God?

This is the model of spiritual excellence and beauty (*ihsan*) embodied by Muhammad that is referred to in the Qur'an as a "lovely example" (*uswatun hasana*):

> *You have indeed in the Messenger of God a Lovely Example,*
> *for anyone whose hope is in God and the Last Day,*
> *and who engages in the frequent remembrance of God.*
>   *(Qur'an 33:21)*

Here is one of the keys for understanding the Muslims' connections to the Prophet. Muhammad does not merely drop the Qur'an on the front door of humanity. He lives the Qur'an, he embodies the Qur'an, and as his wife said, his nature *is* the Qur'an. Muslims do not connect to Muhammad simply to learn disembodied hadith statements; they look to him to embody the very meaning of the connection with God. This is why for Muslims the key spiritual and intellectual guide to answering every legal and ethical dilemma has always been to ask: what would Muhammad do?

Yet Muhammad himself prophesied that his community would not find the answer to every new challenge spelled out in the pages of the Qur'an or in his sayings. Part of Muhammad's mission was to provide his community with the tools they would need to encounter every fresh challenge in situations from China to Africa, Malaysia to America. The well-commemorated episode that identifies this account is Muhammad's interaction with his companion Mu'adh ibn Jabal, who was being sent to lead another province as its new governor. In their last conversation, Muhammad asked Mu'adh how he would deal with the new challenges that would surely come his way. Mu'adh answered that he would first look into the Qur'an for guidance. Muhammad asked his close companion what he would do if he did not find the answer there. Mu'adh pondered further, then stated that he would look at the example of the Prophet himself—he would wonder what Muhammad would do. The Prophet pressed on a bit further, asking one last time what Mu'adh would do if asking this question revealed no specific instruction. Reflecting one last time, Mu'adh offered that then he would exert his own independent reasoning to come up with a fresh solution to the new dilemma. Finally satisfied, Muhammad sent his companion forth to lead his community.

This episode has been important for Muslims throughout the centuries because, as Muslims expanded from being the citizens of a small Arab community centered on Muhammad to a cosmopolitan community living on every continent, they would perpetually be forced to deal with new cultures, challenging situations, fresh dilemmas, and exciting opportunities. The question of "what would Muhammad do?" was never intended to be a fossilized and fully codified system, but rather a way of preparing the community of Muhammad to live in a global and perpetually changing world. It is this creative reimagining of what Muhammad would do that has in part allowed Islam to expand and become indigenous in so many cultural contexts.

The Memory of Muhammad for Those Who Never Saw Him

Texts like the Shama'il, which we encountered in chapter 6, attest to the affection, respect, and intimacy between Muhammad and his companions in this endearing description: "When Muhammad spoke, those present bowed their heads in such a manner, as if birds were sitting on their heads. They did not shift about, as birds will fly away on the slightest move."[2] Aside from being wonderfully evocative, the rich symbolism of the image is revealed when it is recalled that in many religious traditions, including Islam, birds almost always symbolize the spirit. When his companions bowed their heads before Muhammad, spirit-birds descended upon them. If Muhammad's words, behavior, and deeds commanded such affection from people in his immediate circle, his memory did the same through the centuries for those who never saw the Prophet with their own eyes yet who kept their hearts focused on his memory and on the memory of the One to whom Muhammad guided them. The tender devotional text called the *Dala'il al-Khayrat* calls out to God on behalf of those whose eyes were never graced by the sight of Muhammad:

> *O God, as I had faith in our master Muhammad,*
> *though I never saw him in this life,*
> *do not withhold from me a vision of him in Paradise.*

For the faithful followers of Muhammad, the memory of Muhammad is not simply a matter of passing down something through the generations. Remembering Muhammad is an act of participation, recollection, and reception that brings the teachings of the Prophet and an aspect of his very being into the here and now for those with insight into the Prophet in spite of never having seen him.

What Would Muhammad Do Today?

One of the intriguing realities of contemporary Islam is that most Muslim speakers and movements claim to be following in the footsteps of Muhammad. Every Muslim wants to embody the Sunna, the paradigm of Muhammadi behavior. The question is, which is the correct understanding of this paradigm? Or to put it differently, what would Muhammad do today?

This volume has tried to suggest a few answers to that lofty question. For most of the past few years, the majority of Muslims have had to spend far too much time discussing what Islam is *not* about: Islam is *not* about extremism, Islam is *not* about terrorism, and Islam does *not* sanction the oppression of women. Somewhere along the way far too many have lost the opportunity to talk about what Islam *does* stand for, what it *should* stand for, and, with God's grace, what it *will* stand for. That question is irrevocably connected to the memory of Muhammad.

By analogy we could ask, if and when Christ returns to Earth (God willing, as Muslims would add), what would we expect him to say? Which of his sayings would we expect to hear as the core of his message? Would it be the exclusivist voice that says, "No one shall come to the Father except through me" (John 14:6)? Or would we see a Christ who proclaims care for the poor and the downtrodden and the redemption of human suffering as his ultimate calling:

Preach the Gospel to the poor,
heal the brokenhearted,
set the captives free,
offer sight to the blind
and liberate those who are oppressed. (Luke 4:18)

Both statements are attributed to Christ, but they undoubtedly leave vastly different impressions. Not surprisingly, they create divergent memories of Jesus for the community of Christ: one of exclusivist claim to truth, and one of redemption and hope. And so it is with Muhammad and those who keep alive the memories of Muhammad. Show me your relationship to Muhammad, and I will show you what kind of Muslim you are. Are you a Muslim who sees yourself as following the "verse of the sword" above all else, or do you follow the Prophet who was sent as a source of mercy and compassion, not just for this world but for all the universes that exist? For that is the literal meaning of the Qur'anic phrase used for the Prophet, *rahmatan lil 'alamin*—a mercy to all the universes (Qur'an 21:107).

Where do Muslims stand today vis-à-vis Muhammad? Muslims in the post-9/11 era often cite the verse from the Qur'an that identifies the Muslim community as *ummatan wasatan*, meaning "the middle community," or the mediating community:

Thus have We made of you a middle community
  that ye might be witnesses over the nations
and the Messenger a witness over yourselves. (Qur'an 2:143)

This verse is nowadays taken by many Muslims to mean that Muslims should be drawn to the "middle path," avoiding extremes—that is, being moderates. Historically, many Qur'anic commentators have interpreted this verse to mean that the Muslim community is to be characterized by the quality of justice in its dealings with humanity—that the community of Muhammad is to be a just community. However, one leading tenth-century Qur'anic commentator, Imam Tabari, many of whose interpretations we have encountered throughout this book, offers an ingenious reading: if Muslims are the "middle community," it is because they stand between the world and Muhammad. In other words, the task for Muslims is to deliver Muhammad's message to the world, as Muhammad stood between the Muslims and the Divine.

If Muslims are to be worthy of the name "Muhammad's people," if the adjective "Muhammadi" is to be meaningful, then it is incumbent on Muslims to embody the qualities of mercy and justice that Muhammad so perfectly embodied. If "Muslim" is not to be simply a historic designation or civilizational marker but a spiritual indicator of aspiring to the ethics of Muhammad, then it is vital to live by the "lovely example" that Muhammad set (Qur'an 33:21).

Earlier we encountered a wonderful poem in praise of the Prophet Muhammad, the *Burda*, written by al-Busiri. Al-Busiri's own spiritual guide, Abu 'l-Abbas al-Mursi, reportedly said, "By God, were the Messenger of God concealed from me for a twinkling of the eye, I would not count myself among the Muslims."[3] For Muslims like this, Muhammad was not merely a historical figure in the past but a present reality that illuminated their spiritual lives here and now. If Muslims become hidden from the reality of Muhammad, the light of Muhammad, and the manners of Muhammad, then they deserve not to be counted among the People of Muhammad. To be counted among the People of Muhammad is not a matter of genetic or civilizational inheritance, but a spiritual responsibility and honor that every generation has to rise up to meet.

Aspects of this connection to an ever-present prophetic spirit even show up in the daily rituals of Muslims. The series of salutations offered by Shi'i Muslims at the end of their prayers are representative of Muslim daily prayer:

> *Al-salamu alayka ayyuha al-nabiyyu wa rahmatu Allah wa*
> *barakatuhu*
> *Al-salamu alayna wa 'ala 'ibad Allahi al-salihin*
> *Al-salamu alaykum wa rahmatu Allah wa barakatuhu.*
> *(O Prophet: Peace be upon you, and the mercy of God, and His*
> *blessings,*
> *Peace be upon us, righteous servants of God,*
> *Peace be upon you, and the mercy of God, and His blessings.)*

Muslim scholars over the centuries have offered many explanations of this prayer. For example, some have pondered whether the group greeting in the last line refers to an assembly of angels that gather for the prayers of the faithful. Perhaps the most intriguing and at times controversial debates have been about the first verse: what does it mean to offer a direct blessing and salutations to the Prophet at the end of the ritual of prayers? At least for some Muslims, this is yet another indication that the Prophet is present with them during prayers. Does the Qur'an not mention the Prophet standing as a witness to his community?

> *O Prophet!*
> *Surely we have sent you as a witness;*
> *as a bringer of glad tidings;*

and as a warner;
as one who calls to the way of God,
by His command;
and as a luminous light. (Qur'an 33:45–46)

One of the followers of Muhammad remarked that the day Muhammad entered Medina, the whole town became illuminated. The day Muhammad passed away, the town was engulfed in darkness.[4] Whether we choose to understand these types of narratives literally or symbolically (or both!), they point to the underlying centrality of the Prophet for Muslims.

It is by keeping alive the memory of Muhammad that the light of Muhammad endures with the people of Muhammad. The Islamic faith has always been based on a two-part declaration of faith: that there is but One absolute, universal, and compassionate God for all of creation (*la ilaha illah Allah*), and that Muhammad is a messenger of God. It is not merely enough to attest that there is a God. One also has to state how the One God relates to humanity. For Muslims, divine self-revelation (the Qur'an) comes through Muhammad, and his very life became the first commentary on the Qur'an ("And Muhammad is His messenger"—*Wa Muhammad Rasul Allah*).

This is why, in the Qur'an, God and the angels bless Muhammad. The people of Muhammad have done no less.

God and His angels bless the Prophet
O you who have faith, shower him with blessings and salutations.
　　(Qur'an 33:56)

For Muslims, if God is at the center of existence, it is Muhammad who marks the path to that center. Muhammad remains indispensable.

Acknowledgments

SOME YEARS AGO, I participated in a religious dialogue gathering at Princeton. Each participant was asked to identify the primary audience for their writing. While most identified their faith communities, it was clear to me that my primary audience has been and remains my children. I have spent my life surrounded by medieval and modern texts in Arabic, Persian, and Turkish, works in languages that my children often affectionately call "squiggly lines." I have spent my adult life figuring out how to make the wisdom and spirituality of these texts intelligible to my own children, and their children. If they have meaning to my children, I hope that they will have meaning to your children as well. The transmission of these teachings is not just a matter of translating from one language to another. It is often a more subtle task of translating across centuries, continents, cultures, and worldviews. So yes, my precious Jacob, the beautiful young man that you are, my devastatingly gorgeous Roya of the indomitable will, my sweet and lovable Amir of the tender heart, and my beautiful Layla of amazing eyes, this book is above all for you. These are the memories of Muhammad that I want to pass on to you, and make meaningful to you, and your as-of-yet-unborn children insha'Allah (God willing). Farshid jan, Farnaz jan, Farzad jan, Maman and Baba jan, thank you for sharing your memories of Muhammad with me.

That leads me to my life partner, my soul mate, and my collaborator in all that is good and beautiful: my radiant wife Holly. In reading through the sources on Prophet Muhammad's life, I came across a tender description where he praised his wife Khadija: *God has never blessed me with anyone better than her. She had faith in me when all others disbelieved; she held me truthful when others called me a liar; she sheltered me when others abandoned me; she comforted me when others shunned me.* Reading those words touched me to my core, because they reminded me of the Khadija in my life, my wife Holly. Holly, my love, thank you for being my Khadija, my rock, my source of support, and my inspiration. As a Muslim I take my monotheism seriously, but you have let me see why the volumes of Persian poetry that I love (a bit more than you do) describe the beloved as an idol, even a goddess. I do adore you. God has never blessed me with anything or anyone better than you.

I am indebted to Canguzel Zulfikar for helping to obtain the rich Ottoman and Persian miniatures in this book, as I am to Aylin Atikler Yurdacan and Ali Sir Yardim. Kadriye Özbiyik and Esra Müyessçroglu of the Topkapi Palace Museum, and Ayşe Aldemir Kilercik of Sabanci Museum, were particularly helpful. I am grateful to Majed Sultan, Nushmia Khan, Andrea Schuler, and Nagihan Haliloglu for graciously sharing their photographs with me.

My heartfelt gratitude goes to Carolyn Holland, who patiently worked with me on the production of this volume. I am also grateful to my agent, Giles Anderson, for finding an ideal home for this book.

I am especially grateful to Eric Brandt, my friend and editor at HarperCollins. We were planning a popular book that would trace the history of Islam from Muhammad to bin Laden. Eric, thank you for not giving up on this project (or our friendship) when this book insisted on being written first. And we will, God willing, write that history book together next.

I am grateful to Timur Yuskaev for having read the manuscript carefully. Ilyse Morgenstein Fuerst applied her own impeccable combination of wit, humor, insight, and grammar policing to the manuscript. Bruce Lawrence and Carl Ernst, thank you as always for the gift of your conversation and guidance.

Lastly, I wish to thank the inspiration behind this volume, Hazrat Peyghambar Muhammad Mustapha (S).

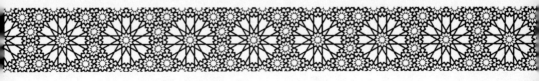

ART CREDITS

GRATEFUL ACKNOWLEDGMENTS ARE MADE for permission to reproduce the many illustrations contained here. The frontispiece illustration shows Muhammad accompanied by Gabriel, on his Heavenly Ascension (Mi'raj); a fine Ottoman miniature which shows Muhammad's face uncovered. Courtesy of the Topkapi Palace Museum. The three images on pages 21, 22, and 108 are from the *Qisas al-Anbiya*, as published by Rachel Milstein, Karin Rührdanz, and Barbara Schmitz in *Stories of the Prophets: Illustrated Manuscripts of Qisas Al-Anbiya'*, (Costa Mesa, CA: Mazda Publishers, 1999). The illustration on page 171 is reproduced from *Bustan of Sa'di; The Mi'raj or The Night Flight of Muhammad on his Steed Buraq* (3v). Safavid period, ca. 1525–35. Islamic, Attributed to: present-day Uzbekistan, Bukhara. Colors, ink and gold on paper, 7½ × 5 in. (19 × 12.7 cm). Purchase, Louis V. Bell Fund and The Vincent Astor Foundation Gift, 1974 (1974.294.2). Photo: Schecter Lee. Image copyright © The Metropolitan Museum of Art, New York, NY, U.S.A. The illustration on page 177 is from *The Miraj-Nama*, Persian, fifteenth century. Courtesy of Bibliotheque Nationale, Paris. RC-A-94848. The illustration on page 179 is from Nezami's *Khamsa*, produced in Tabriz, Iran, 1539–43. ©The British Library Board. All Rights Reserved (BL Or. MS 2265, f. 195). The illustration on page 286 is reproduced from *Architecture, Ceremonial, and Power: The Topkapi Palace in the Fifteenth and Sixteenth Centuries* by Gülru Necipoglu, figure 84, page 148, © 1992 MIT Press, by permission of The MIT Press. The image on page 287 is reproduced from *Dala'il al-Khayrat wa Shawariq al-Anwar fi Dhikr al-Salat 'ala al-Nabi al-Mukhtar.* by Muhammad ibn Sulayman al-Jazuli. Illuminated manuscript on paper. [Ottoman Empire], 1134 AH [1722]. Image courtesy of Special Collections, Bridwell Library, Perkins School of Theology, Southern Methodist University.

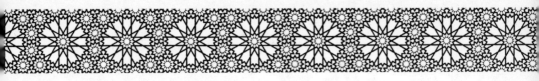

NOTES

Introduction: The "Muhammad Problem"

1. "Remarks by President Obama to the Turkish Parliament," April 6, 2009, available at: http://www.whitehouse.gov/the_press_office/Remarks-By-President-Obama-To-The-Turkish-Parliament/.

2. "Franklin Graham Conducts Services at Pentagon," CNN. com, April 18, 2003, available at: http://www.cnn.com/2003/ALLPOLITICS/04/18/graham.pentagon/ (accessed May 4, 2008). The same Franklin Graham was asked to preside over the 2003 Good Friday services at the Pentagon.

3. Alan Johnson and James Nash, "Huckabee, McCain Keep Rivalry in Motion," *Columbus Dispatch*, February 27, 2008.

4. "McCain's Spiritual Guide," YouTube.com, available at: http://www.youtube.com/watch?v=WXZbIGJrDkg (accessed May 12, 2008). It is striking to note that Barack Obama received weeks of scrutiny about the comments of the Reverend Jeremiah Wright, remarks that Obama repeatedly dismissed, yet McCain was never asked to explain his affiliation with preachers of hateful speech such as Hagee and Parsley, his efforts to seek the endorsements of these Christian preachers, or his

references to them as his "spiritual guides." McCain felt that it was important to distance himself from Hagee's anti-Catholic statements, but he remained silent about Hagee's and Parsley's anti-Muslim statements.

5. Dan Harris, "Evangelical Christians Take Aim at Islam," ABC-News.com, November 18, 2008, available at: http://abcnews.go.com/WNT/Beliefs/story?id=130008&page=1.

6. Mary Jayne McKay, "Zion's Christian Soldiers," *60 Minutes*, June 8, 2003, available at: http://www.cbsnews.com/stories/2002/10/03/60minutes/main524268.shtml. The interview was featured on *60 Minutes* on October 6, 2002. It is particularly telling that the focus of the show was actually Christian evangelicals' support of Israel: the program was titled "Zion's Christian Soldiers." Falwell later apologized, not for having said what he did, but for having hurt the feelings of "lawful Muslims." See Mary Jayne McKay, "Falwell Sorry for Bashing Muhammad," *60 Minutes*, October 14, 2002, available at: http://www.cbsnews.com/stories/2002/10/11/60minutes/main525316.shtml.

7. Some of these include Martin Lings, *Muhammad*; Karen Armstrong, *A Biography of the Prophet*; Tariq Ramadan, *In the Footsteps of the Prophet*.

8. Some salient examples include the fearmongering tactics of Daniel Pipes and David Horowitz, among others.

9. The classic study is Norman Daniel, *Islam and the West: The Making of an Image*.

10. See Princeton Dante Project, available at: http://etcweb.princeton.edu/dante/pdp/.

11. This evaluation of Islam as a "rational faith" was often an implicit criticism of Christianity's mysticism and alleged opposition to rationality. In other words, praise of Islam was actually criticism of Christianity and an implicit prioritization of rationality over revelation as a means of access to truth.

12. Cited by Juan Cole, "Muhammad Was a Terrorist?" George Mason University, History News Network, October 7, 2002, available at: http://hnn.us/articles/1018.html (accessed June 10, 2009).

13. Quoted in Paul Leicester Ford, *The Many-Sided Franklin* (New York: Century, 1899), 159.

14. *The Writings of George Washington: Life of Washington* (Harper and Brothers, 1852), vol. 1, 257, available at: http://books.google.com/books?id=VcJEAAAAIAAJ&pg=PA275&dq=If+th ey+are+good+workmen,+they+may+be+from+Asia,+Africa+or +Europe (accessed June 10, 2009).

15. For a history of Jefferson's encounter with the Qur'an, see Kevin J. Hayes, "How Thomas Jefferson Read the Qur'an," *Early American Literature* 39, no. 2 (2004).

16. *The Writings of Thomas Jefferson* (Washington, D.C.: Thomas Jefferson Memorial Association, 1904), 67.

17. The White House, Office of the Press Secretary, "Remarks by the President on a New Beginning," Cairo, Egypt, June 4, 2009, available at: http://www.whitehouse.gov/the_press_officeRemarks-by-the-President-at-Cairo-University-6-04-09 (accessed June 10, 2009).

18. The White House, "Remarks by the President on a New Beginning."

19. The White House, "Remarks by the President on a New Beginning."

20. Most often these shifting targets do not imply that past prejudices have eroded but only that they are multiplying. So, for example, the greater likelihood in today's public discourse that Hispanic immigrants and Muslims will be demonized does not mean that anti-Semitism toward Jews or prejudice against blacks has been eradicated.

21. This image comes from the Persian ethical treatise *Rose Garden* (*Golestan*) by the Shaykh Muslih al-Din Sa'di.

22. Flemming Rose, "Why I Published Those Cartoons," *Washington Post*, February 17, 2006, available at: http://www.washington post.com/wp-dyn/content/article/2006/02/17/AR200602170 2499.html (accessed June 10, 2009).

23. Gwladys Fouché, "Danish Paper Rejected Jesus Cartoons," *Guardian*, February 6, 2006, available at: http://www.guardian.co .uk/media/2006/feb/06/pressandpublishing.politics (accessed June 10, 2009).

24. See the embarrassingly gushing interview between Flemming Rose and Daniel Pipes, the noted Islamophobe, "The Threat of Islam," October 29, 2004, available at Daniel Pipes's website: http://www.danielpipes.org/article/3362 (accessed June 10, 2009).

25. Daniel Pipes and Lars Hedegaard, "Something Rotten in Denmark?" *New York Post*, August 27, 2002, available at: http:// www.meforum.org/article/pipes/450 (accessed June 10, 2009).

26. For a brilliant analysis of the Danish cartoon controversy that makes the obvious though often neglected point that this controversy should be situated in its immediate Danish context, see the insightful essay by the Danish American Muslim intellectual Svend White, "*Jyllands-Posten* and the Otherization of Europe's Muslims," in *The Cartoon Debate and the Freedom of the Press: Conflicting Norms and Values in the Global Media Culture*.

27. Al-Qa'ida is often estimated at 8,000 to 10,000 members, which is of course a significant membership—until we recall that the worldwide Muslim population is 1.5 billion. In an admittedly anachronistic comparison, in the 1920s around 15 percent of eligible voters in the United States belonged to the Ku Klux Klan, whose membership numbered over 5 million among adult white men.

28. For the story of how the first volume was reconstructed, see Gordon Darnell Newby, *The Making of the Last Prophet*.

29. Brannon Wheeler, *Prophets of the Quran: An Introduction to the Quran and Muslim Exegesis.* For more online images, see: http://www.usna.edu/Users/humss/bwheeler/prophets/abraham.html (accessed June 10, 2009).

30. Sarah Henrich and James L. Boyce, "Martin Luther—Translations of Two Prefaces on Islam," *Word and World* 16, no. 2 (Spring 1996): 263, available at: http://www.luthersem.edu/word&world/Archives/16-2_Islam/16-2_Boyce-Henrich.pdf (accessed June 10, 2009).

31. See Center for Muslim-Jewish Engagement, "Fighting for the Cause of Allah," available at: http://www.usc.edu/dept/MSA/fundamentals/hadithsunnah/bukhari/052.sbt.html#004.052.177 (accessed June 10,2009). The statements of hadith are not from the text of the Qur'an, which is attributed directly to God, but statements, sometimes contested, traced back to the Prophet Muhammad.

32. In the 1960s, the policy of mutual assured destruction (MAD) was advocated by U.S. Secretary of Defense Robert McNamara. The acronym betrays its own irony.

33. Martin Luther King Jr., "Beyond Vietnam," speech at Riverside Church, New York, April 4, 1967, full text available at: http://www.stanford.edu/group/King/liberation_curriculum/speeches/beyondvietnam.htm (accessed June 10, 2009).

34. Ibn Kathir, *The Life of the Prophet Muhammad: A Translation of al-Sia al-Nabawiyya*, translated by Trever Le Gassick, 4 vols, 1:151.

35. Kathir, *The Life of the Prophet Muhammad*, 1:147.

36. Kathir, *The Life of the Prophet Muhammad*, 1:151.

37. Kathir, *The Life of the Prophet Muhammad*, 1:153.

38. For confrontations on the radical right between Michael Hart and David Duke, the former Ku Klux Klan leader, see Heidi Beirich and Mark Potok, "Intelligence Report: Irreconcilable Differences," Southern Poverty Law Center (Summer 2006),

available at: http://www.splcenter.org/intel/intelreport/article.jsp?aid=644.

39. See Michael H. Hart, "Racial Partition of the United States" (1996), available at the Stalking the Wild Taboo website: http://www.lrainc.com/swtaboo/taboos/mhhart01.html#MHHart.

40. Aflaki, *Manaqeb al-'arefin*, 1:226, 366.

41. Rumi, *Masnavi* (Este'lami edition), 3:145, lines 3112–20.

Chapter One: The World Before Muhammad

1. Lings, *Muhammad*, 83. Ja'far's presentation also appears in Ibn Ishaq, *The Life of Muhammad: A Translation of Ibn Ishaq's Sirat Rasul Allah*, translated by A. Guillaume (Oxford: Oxford University Press, 1955), 151–52.

2. Even if we exercise extreme caution about the historicity of Ja'far's speech in Abyssinia, it still remains the case that Muslims by the time of Ibn Ishaq (the source of Ja'far's speech as quoted here) characterized the pre-Islamic period in such a way. In other words, less than 150 years after the time of the Prophet they were already viewing the time before Muhammad as a time of *Jahiliyya* (ignorance).

3. One important exception, naturally, is language, which Muslim scholars understood as essential for a proper understanding of the Qur'anic.

4. Gordon Newby, *A History of the Jews of Arabia*, 10.

5. Poetry of Labid, from A. J. Arberry, *Seven Odes*, 143, cited in Frederick M. Denny, *An Introduction to Islam*, 50.

6. Cited in Toshihiko Izutsu, *Ethico-Religious Concepts in the Qur'an*, 55.

7. See Wellhausen, *Reste arabischen Heidentums*, 186ff.; and "K is ás" in *Encyclopedia of Islam*, 2nd ed.

8. From Arberry, *Seven Odes*, 62; cited in Denny, *An Introduction to Islam*, 49.

9. Cited in Izutsu, *Ethico-Religious Concepts in the Qur'an*, 64 (slightly modified).

10. Michael Sells, *Desert Tracings*, 14.

11. Michael Sells, *Early Islamic Mysticism*, 58.

12. Translated by Michael Sells (*Early Islamic Mysticism*, 44). See also Sells, *Approaching the Qur'an*.

13. In modern Islamic circles some fundamentalists characterize twentieth-century times as a period of Jahiliyya, but that is a separate story that we will get to later.

14. The translation is slightly modified from Muhammad Asad.

15. The phrase "engaged surrender" is one that Amina Wadud, the noted Muslim scholar of the Qur'an, has beautifully and fully articulated in her many writings.

16. Abid b. al-Abras, in Izutsu, *God and Man in the Koran*, 124.

17. Denny, *An Introduction to Islam*, 52.

18. For this section, I am indebted to Toshihiko Izutsu, *God and Man in the Koran*, which remains one of the classic studies of the Qur'anic worldview.

19. See Richard Bulliet, *Conversion to Islam in the Medieval Period: An Essay in Quantitative History*.

20. Ibn Ishaq, *The Life of Muhammad*, 79–81.

21. Newby, *History of the Jews of Arabia*, 38.

22. Translation slightly modified from Muhammad Asad, *Message of the Qur'an*.

Chapter Two: The Muhammadi Revolution

1. Richard Hooker, *Eccl. Pol.* V. lxx. §9, cited in *Oxford English Dictionary* (accessed online September 22, 2007).

2. Quoted in Nasr, *Muhammad Man of God*, 22.

3. Lings, *Muhammad*, 43.

4. Ibn Ishaq, *The Life of Muhammad*, 105.

5. Lings, *Muhammad*, 43.

6. Ibn Ishaq, *The Life of Muhammad*, 106.

7. Ibn Ishaq, *The Life of Muhammad*.

8. For one example of these narratives, see the twentieth-century Shi'i biography of the Prophet by Ja'far Subhani, *Furuq-i abadiyat* (The Flame of Eternity), which protests that, if Moses and Jesus are depicted as perfectly calm and serene in their encounters with the Divine, why would one expect Muhammad to have been terrified? This source dismisses the narratives that record Muhammad's anxiety as being to the result of later accretions.

9. Ibn Ishaq, *The Life of Muhammad*, 106–7.

10. Ibn Ishaq, *The Life of Muhammad*, 107.

11. The translation is from both Lings, *Muhammad*, 44, and Ibn Ishaq, *The Life of Muhammad*, 107.

12. See the Arabic original of Ibn Ishaq, *Sirat Rasul Allah*, 1:243.

13. Ibn Ishaq, *The Life of Muhammad*, 107.

14. Ibn Ishaq, *The Life of Muhammad*, 111 (translation slightly modified).

15. One of the classical commentaries on this hadith is from Ibn 'Arabi, in *Fusus al-Hikam*. This hadith is reported in the collection of Ibn Hanbal.

16. Ibn Ishaq, *The Life of Muhammad*, 115.

17. Lings, *Muhammad*, 51. The narrative is cited by Tabari.

18. Ibn Ishaq, *The Life of Muhammad*, 119.

19. Lings, *Muhammad*, 53. Cf. Ibn Ishaq, *The Life of Muhammad*, 119.

20. Lings, *Muhammad*, 53.

21. Lings, *Muhammad*, 79.

22. Lings, *Muhammad*, 98–99 (slightly modified).

23. Ibn Ishaq, *The Life of Muhammad*, 183.

24. See Ibn Ishaq, *The Life of Muhammad*, 222.

25. Lings, *Muhammad*, 118.

26. Lings, *Muhammad*, 121.

27. Lings, *Muhammad*, 125, Ibn Ishaq, *The Life of Muhammad*, 229.

28. Ibn Ishaq, *The Life of Muhammad*, 231.

29. See Moshe Gil, "The Constitution of Medina: A Reconsideration"; see also Gordon Newby, *A History of the Jews of Arabia*, 80–82.

30. Ibn Ishaq, *The Life of Muhammad*, 231–32.

31. Ibn Ishaq, *The Life of Muhammad*.

32. Ibn Ishaq, *The Life of Muhammad*, 233.

33. Ibn Ishaq, *The Life of Muhammad*.

34. The prohibition against killing women, children, and the elderly is traced to a hadith narrated through Anas, the son of Malik. It can be found in the hadith collection of Abu Dawud.

35. This tradition is narrated through Rabah, the son of Rabi'a. For a discussion, see Rudolph Peters, *Jihad in Classical and Modern Islam*, 29–37.

36. In the premodern world, the modern distinctions between civilian and military did not exist as firm boundaries, yet the statements cited here continue to serve as important reference points for Muslims.

37. This observation is not meant to downplay the atrocities and bloodshed committed during the Crusades, but to state that in terms of numbers we are still dealing with the difference of tens of thousands of casualties during one period of conflict (the Crusades) and tens of millions during the other (twentieth-century warfare). Also, for all of the bloodshed, some sense of nobility was brought to bear on the medieval Crusades, as the Muslim diaries from that period indicate.

38. Lings, *Muhammad*, 143.

39. See Ibn Ishaq, *The Life of Muhammad*, 241, n. 1.

40. Ibn Ishaq, *The Life of Muhammad*, 239.

41. Lings, *Muhammad*, 161.

42. Ibn Ishaq, *The Life of Muhammad*, 260.

43. Newby, *A History of the Jews of Arabia*, 87.

44. See Barakat Ahmad, *Muhammad and the Jews: A Reexamination*, 55–62. See also Newby, *A History of the Jews of Arabia*, 87–88.

Ahmad contends that these accounts should be traced to the later source al-Waqidi.

45. This point deserves to be kept in mind in light of the atrocities committed by some Muslim extremist groups in Iraq after the U.S. occupation of that country in 2003.

46. Wael N. Arafat, "New Light on the Story of Banu Qurayza and the Jews of Medina," *Journal of the Royal Asiatic Society of Great Britain and Ireland* (1976): 100–107. See also Newby, *A History of the Jews of Arabia*, 92–93. Newby ultimately defers to the authority of M. J. Kister, "The Massacre of Banu Qurayza."

47. Newby, *A History of the Jews of Arabia*, 93.

48. Lings, *Muhammad*, 278–79.

49. This hadith is found in book 23, number 5112, of the Muslims' *Sahih* collection, which is available at: http://www.usc.edu/dept/MSA/fundamentals/hadithsunnah/muslim/023.smt.html#023.5109.

50. Lings, *Muhammad*, 168.

51. Lings, *Muhammad*, 273.

52. Lings, *Muhammad*, 211.

53. Lings, *Muhammad*, 273.

54. Lings, *Muhammad*, 270–71.

55. Lings, *Muhammad*, 206.

56. Lings, *Muhammad*, 268–69.

57. There is a great deal of ambiguity about Mariya's exact status. She may have been a concubine, and though some sources include her as one of Muhammad's wives, that status seems dubious.

58. Ibn Ishaq, *The Life of Muhammad*, 793 (from notes of Ibn Hisham).

59. For discussions of A'isha's age at marriage, see Kecia Ali, *Sexual Ethics in Islam*. See also Denise Spellberg, *Politics, Gender, and the Islamic Past*.

60. Lings, *Muhammad*, 294.

61. Ibn Ishaq, *The Life of Muhammad*, 549.

62. Lings, *Muhammad*, 298.

63. Ibn Ishaq, *The Life of Muhammad*, 550. This was 'Abd Allah, the son of Sa'd, who was the half-brother of Uthman, the third Sunni Caliph. Later on, Muslim jurists would declare apostasy a crime punishable by death.

64. Ibn Ishaq, *The Life of Muhammad*, 552.

65. Ibn Ishaq, *The Life of Muhammad*.

66. Lings, *Muhammad*, 303.

67. Ibn Ishaq, *The Life of Muhammad*, 552.

68. Lings, *Muhammad*, 300; cf. Ibn Ishaq, *The Life of Muhammad*, 552.

69. Ibn Ishaq, *The Life of Muhammad*, 552–53.

70. Ibn Ishaq, *The Life of Muhammad*, 555.

71. Lings, *Muhammad*, 330–31. See also the first hadith in the first chapter of Muslims' *Sahih* collection. An English translation is available at: http://www.usc.edu/dept/MSA/fundamentals/hadithsunnah/muslim/001.smt.html.

72. Refer to the chapter on Dhu 'l-Nun Misri in Farid al-Din 'Attar, *Tadhkirat al-Awliya*, which is available through the English translation of A. J. Arberry as *Muslim Saints and Mystics*.

73. See the chapter on Rabi'a in 'Attar, *Tadhkirat al-Awliya*.

74. This account appears in the sixty-first chapter of Bukhari's *Sahih* collection. An English translation is available at: http://www.usc.edu/dept/MSA/fundamentals/hadithsunnah/bukhari/061.sbt.html.

75. Ibn Ishaq, *The Life of Muhammad*, 651.

76. Ibn Ishaq, *The Life of Muhammad*.

77. Cited in Nasr, *Muhammad Man of God*, 37.

78. Lings, *Muhammad*, 334.

79. My translation here closely follows Lings, *Muhammad*.

80. Recorded in the sixty-second chapter of Bukhari's *Sahih* collection.

81. From Lings, *Muhammad*, 341.

82. Lings, *Muhammad*, 345.

Chapter Three: The Ascension of Muhammad:
Face-to-Face with God

1. Ibn Ishaq, *The Life of Muhammad*, 186.

2. Ibn Ishaq, *The Life of Muhammad*, 182; Lings, *Muhammad*, 101.

3. 'Attar, *Manteq al-Tayr*.

4. See "Examples of Islamic Depictions of Muhammad," available at: http://www.religionfacts.com/islam/things/depictions-of-muhammad-examples.htm.

5. This statement is found in the Bukhari hadith collection, volume 8, book 76, number 572, available at: http://www.usc.edu/schools/college/crcc/engagement/resources/texts/muslim/hadith/bukhari/076.sbt.html#008.076.572; cited in Lings, *Muhammad*, 102.

6. Translation by Michael Sells, *Early Islamic Mysticism*, 35.

7. Translation by Sells, *Early Islamic Mysticism*, 36.

8. Al-Suyuti, *al-La'ali al-masnu'ah*, in Jeffrey, *Islam: Muhammad and His Religion*, 43.

9. Al-Suyuti, *al-La'ali al-masnu'ah*, in Jeffrey, *Islam: Muhammad and His Religion*, 43.

10. Al-Suyuti, *al-La'ali al-masnu'ah*, in Jeffrey, *Islam: Muhammad and His Religion*, 43.

11. Michael Sells, "On the Vision of Abu Yazid in Quest for Allah Most High," in *Early Islamic Mysticism*, 248–49.

12. Sells, "On the Vision of Abu Yazid."

13. Al-Suyuti, *al-La'ali al-masnu'ah*, in Jeffrey, *Islam: Muhammad and His Religion*, 44–45 (translation slightly updated).

14. Cited in Muhammad Iqbal, *Reconstruction of Religious Thought in Islam*, 99. My gratitude to Omer Mozaffer for his generous assistance in locating this citation.

Chapter Four: Islam as an Abrahamic Tradition

1. Ibn Ishaq, *The Life of Muhammad*, 104.
2. This figure comes from a hadith of the Prophet recorded by Ibn Hanbal. The number of messengers—prophets with a scripture—is put at 315.
3. In April 2006, there was in fact such a historic meeting between His Holiness the Dalai Lama and many Muslim leaders in San Francisco.
4. Translation from Muhammad Asad, *Message of the Qur'an*. The word *din* is used twice in this verse, yet Asad translates the first occasion as "religious law" to narrow its scope. Many other translations simply translate the first part of the verse as "Today I have perfected your religion for you."
5. See Neal Robinson, *Christ in Islam and Christianity*, as well as Jane D. McAuliffe, *Qur'anic Christians*, for a survey of these debates.
6. See Rumi, *Mathnawi*, II:450: "The Jesus of your spirit is present with you; beg aid from him." See also John Renard, *All the King's Falcons*.
7. Kabalah has always been an esoteric and elite practice within the larger Jewish community. Sufism, on the other hand, is intellectually pervasive, politically patronized, and popular among Muslims. In some societies, such as Egypt and Senegal, it has been estimated that the majority of people are initiated into Sufi orders.
8. Jane S. Gerber, "Judaism in the Middle East and North Africa Since 1492," *Encyclopedia of Religion*, 8:158, cited in Steven Wasserstrom, *Between Muslim and Jew: The Problem of Symbiosis Under Early Islam*, 18.
9. Martin Luther King Jr., "I've Been to the Mountaintop," speech delivered in Memphis, Tennessee, April 3, 1968.

Chapter Five: Life After the Prophet, Death After Hossein

1. The quotes are from the historians Tabari and Dinawari, cited by S. H. M. Jafri, *The Origins and Early Development of Shi'a Islam*, 193.

2. The quote is from Ali Shari'ati. The term "Ashura" refers to the tenth day in the month of Muharram. Shi'i Muslims mourn and commemorate Hossein's sacrifice during the whole month, but particularly during the first ten days, and most intensively on the ninth (Tasu'a) and tenth (Ashura) days.

3. Ibn Ishaq, *The Life of Muhammad*, 682–83 (slightly updated).

4. Lings, *Muhammad*, 345.

5. That phrase, as well as "Companion of the Cave," became two of Abu Bakr's honorifics in the Sunni tradition.

6. Wilferd Madelung, *The Succession to Muhammad: A Study of the Early Caliphate*, 53.

7. Ibn Ishaq, *The Life of Muhammad*, 689.

8. In fact, Ali Shari'ati, a leading Iranian Shi'i thinker of the twentieth century, identifies Abu Dharr as the example of social justice in Islam par excellence.

9. I am here indebted to Madelung, *The Succession to Muhammad*, 84, n. 22.

10. Mahmoud Ayoub, *The Crisis of Muslim History*, 92–93.

11. Madelung, *The Succession to Muhammad*, 309.

12. Jafri, *The Origins and Early Development of Shi'a Islam*, 84.

13. Ali ibn Abi Talib, *Nahj al-Balagha* (1358), translated and with notes by Daryush Shahin (Tehran: Intisharat-e Javidan, 1979), 1428–29, 1468.

14. Talib, *Nahj al-Balagha*, 1427.

15. Talib, *Nahj al-Balagha*, 1447.

16. *Living and Dying with Grace: Counsels of Hadrat 'Ali*, translated by Thomas Cleary (Boston: Shambhala, 1995), 1.

17. The only exception is the Naqshbandi order, who set themselves apart by tracing themselves to Abu Bakr instead.

18. Ibn Ishaq, *The Life of Muhammad*, 455–57.

19. The quotes from the *Masnavi* are all from the masterful translation by Jawid Mojadeddi, *Rumi, The Masnavi: Book One* (Oxford:
Oxford University Press, 2004), 227–34.

20. Cited in Jafri, *The Origins and Early Development of Shi'a Islam*,
135.

21. Jafri, *The Origins and Early Development of Shi'a Islam*, 136.

22. This letter, quoted by sources like Tabari and Shaykh Mufid, is
cited in Jafri, *The Origins and Early Development of Shi'a Islam*,
179.

23. Jafri, *The Origins and Early Development of Shi'a Islam*, 188–92.

24. Jafri, *The Origins and Early Development of Shi'a Islam*.

25. *A Shi'ite Anthology*, edited and translated by William C. Chit-
tick, 94.

26. The quote is from the famed commemoration of Hossein's
martyrdom, *Rawdat al-shuhada* (The Garden of Martyrs), written by Hossein Va'ez Kashefi. The translation is by Kamran
Scot Aghaie, "The Gender Dynamics of Moharram Rituals" in
Kamran Scot Aghaie, ed., *The Women of Karbala*, 53.

27. Aghaie, "The Gender Dynamics of Moharram Rituals."

28. Tayba Hassan al-Khalifa Sharif, "Sacred Narratives Linking
Iraqi Shiite Women," in *Muslim Networks: From Hajj to Hip-
Hop*, 139.

29. Sharif, "Sacred Narratives Linking Iraqi Shiite Women," 136
(spelling modified).

30. See, for example, Martin Luther King Jr.'s eulogy for the three
girls killed in the church bombing in Birmingham, Alabama,
in 1963, "Eulogy for the Martyred Children," September 18,
1963, available at: http://mlk-kpp01.stanford.edu/index.php/
kingpapers/article/eulogy_for_the_martyred_children/.

31. *A Shi'ite Creed*, 35 (spelling modified).

Chapter Six: Echoes of Muhammadi Grace

1. See the record by Derek and the Dominos, *Layla and Other Assorted Love Songs* (1973). On the LP jacket, Clapton credits the Persian poet Nezami. The tale of how Clapton came to hear about Nezami is itself a fascinating story of spiritual seeking, drugs, and loss in the 1960s. A friend of Clapton's, Ian Dallas, presented him with the translation of the love story (for information on Dallas, see http://www.imdb.com/name/nm0198036/bio). Dallas went on to become a Sufi teacher, under the name Abdalqadir as-Sufi. He is a charismatic, though controversial, figure in Western Sufism.

2. Rumi, *Fihi Ma Fihi*, Thackston translation as *Signs of the Unseen*, 110.

3. Performed by Pakistani Na't-reciter Qari Wahid Zaffar Qasim from the CD recording *Guldasta-e-Aqidat*. Translation is mine.

4. Tirmidhi, *Shama'-il Tirmidhi with Commentary Khasaa-il Nabawi Sallahu' Alayahi Wasallam.*

5. ESPN rated this commercial as one of the top seven sports commercials of all time. For the background story of how Gatorade and corporate culture use the power of suggestion, see Darren Rovell, *First in Thirst: How Gatorade Turned the Science of Sweat into a Cultural Phenomenon.*

6. Tirmidhi, *Shama'il*, 368.

7. This analogy comes courtesy of Martin Lings, who passed away in 2005.

8. Carl Ernst, "The Hilya, or the Adornment of the Prophet: A Calligraphic Icon," available at: http://www.rasheedbutt.com/about_hilya.htm.

9. Ernst, "The Hilya, or the Adornment of the Prophet."

10. There was a clear demarcation between the Qur'an (which was both memorized and written down) and the hadith (which in general were not written down).

11. Titus Burckhardt, "The Prayer of Ibn Mashish," *Islamic Quarterly* (1977): 68–69.

12. See BBC, "Religion and Ethics—Islam: al-Burda," available at: http://www.bbc.co.uk/religion/religions/islam/art/alburda.shtml.

13. Schimmel, *And Muhammad Is His Messenger*, 181–83.

14. Schimmel, *And Muhammad Is His Messenger*, 186.

15. Necipolğlu, *Architecture, Ceremonial, and Power: The Topkapi Palace in the Fifteenth and Sixteenth Centuries*, 150.

16. Necipolğlu, *Architecture, Ceremonial, and Power*, 151.

17. For a detailed presentation of the *Burda*, see Hamza Yusuf's commentary at: http://www.youtube.com/watch?v=mLnHZgsh0Ik. For what is essentially a Muslim music video, see http://www.youtube.com/watch?v=yJQgVYG7ELE. For recitations by both men and women, see: http://www.youtube.com/watch?v=UwRhLkmoa1Q. And for a children's recitation of the *Burda*, see: http://www.youtube.com/watch?v=jqBKPImNIso.

18. The quotes are from Schimmel, *And Muhammad Is His Messenger*, 236–37.

19. See BBC, "Religion and Ethics—Islam: al-Burda," available at: http://www.bbc.co.uk/religion/religions/islam/art/alburda.shtml.

20. Algar, *Wahhabism*, 27.

21. Sheikh Nuh Ha Mim Keller, "The Story of Dala'il al-Khayrat," available at: http://www.dalail.co.uk/dalail.htm.

22. Iqbal, *Rumuz-e BeKhudi*, cited in Schimmel, *And Muhammad Is His Messenger*, 256.

Conclusion

1. Muhammad Iqbal, *Javid-nama*, cited in Schimmel, *And Muhammad Is His Messenger*, 239.

2. Schimmel, *And Muhammad Is His Messenger*, 239.

3. Originally quoted in Ibn Ata Allah, *Lata'if al-Minan*, edited by Abdel Halim Mahmoud (1974), 169, cited in Jonathan Katz, *Dreams, Sufism, and Sainthood: The Visionary Career of Muhammad al-Zawawi*, 212. I am grateful to my graduate student Rose Aslan of the University of North Carolina for this citation.

4. The anecdote from Anas and this translation are from Imam Zaid Shakir, "The Blessed Mawlid," available at: http://www.zaytuna.org/seasonsjournal/seasons6/2-4Final_Mawlid.pdf.

SCRIPTURE INDEX

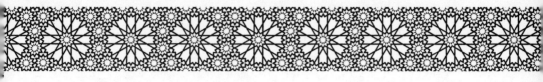

SUBJECT INDEX